Prince
Edward

Other books by Paul James include:

Princess Alexandra
Margaret: A Woman of Conflict
Diana: One of the Family?
Anne: The Working Princess
At Her Majesty's Service
At Home with the Royal Family
The Royal Almanac
The Secret Journals of Queen Elizabeth II
The Secret Royal Love Letters
Prince Philip's 101 Great Games
Excuses, Excuses . . .
It's A Weird World
Sleep at Last
The V.V.I.P. Diaries

Prince Edward

A Life in the Spotlight

PAUL JAMES

PIATKUS

© 1992 Paul James

First published in 1992 by
Judy Piatkus (Publishers) Limited
5, Windmill Street, London, W1P 1HF

The moral right of the author has been asserted

A catalogue record for this
book is available from the British Library
ISBN 0-7499-1186-7

Edited by Kelly Davis
Designed by Sue Ryall

Set in Linotype Baskerville by
Computerset, Harmondsworth
Printed and bound in Great Britain by
Mackays of Chatham PLC

CONTENTS

Acknowledgements

It started with a telephone call.

Having broadcast regularly about the Royal Family for more than a decade, I find that the 'phone-in' has become an increasingly popular format for programmes on both radio and television. For the broadcaster it is an exciting challenge. On a live programme there is never any room for the evasions beloved of politicians. The callers want definite answers. Inevitably over the years certain questions become commonplace. What does the Queen do with her old clothes? How do the Royals do their Christmas shopping? I've even been asked how our monarch eats a banana!

On a programme for BBC Radio Sussex in July 1991 I was asked something different.

'Why has there never been a biography of Prince Edward?' asked Tony Cable of Eastbourne. 'To me he's one of the most interesting of all the Royal Family.'

Considering the apparently insatiable appetite for information about members of the House of Windsor, it certainly seemed strange that one of Queen Elizabeth II's children should remain such an unknown quantity. Whilst the lives of

ix

the Prince of Wales, Princess Royal and Duke of York had been well documented, Prince Edward has deliberately kept a low profile in order to maintain his privacy. In many ways this has been counter-productive, for much of his public work has remained a mystery, and most of his achievements throughout three decades have passed unrecorded.

In the months after that radio programme I met many people who echoed Tony Cable's sentiments and expressed their admiration for Prince Edward. A few cynics only wanted to know whether he was gay and why he had resigned from the Royal Marines; the majority could see in him a strong, determined character and were keen to discover more about the least known of the Queen's four children.

I approached Buckingham Palace with some trepidation, knowing that they had already refused to co-operate with some authors in the past who had wanted to delve deeply into Prince Edward's life. My proposal for this book was put to the Prince who, although keen to point out that he considered himself 'still too young to have a book written', did not raise any objections. His Private Secretary informed me that they would be delighted to answer my questions.

This book is not, however, an official biography. These are commissioned only after a royal personage's death. Neither can it be considered a definitive work, bearing in mind the Prince's age. This will be left to a future biographer. As one of the first books ever written about him, it is more of an interim report and exploration of the Prince's life, character and achievements to date. In looking at the influences that have shaped his life so far, I have also tried to ascertain what his future might hold.

Writing about all the Queen's children back in 1978, when Prince Edward was still only fourteen, journalist Donald Edgar made a very astute remark: 'As for Edward it would be splendid if he developed an interest in the arts. They are no longer the preserve of a small minority . . . The opportunities for Edward would be boundless'. Considering the Prince's choice of career a decade later, this was an almost prophetic statement.

Although Prince Edward may feel that he is still too young for a biography, the first book about his mother was written in 1930 when she was only four years old (authoress Anne Ring somehow managed to fill 126 pages!). The lives of his brothers and sister have been chronicled since their teenage years; and even his sisters-in-law inspired numerous volumes when they were much younger than he is now. By the time she had reached the age of twenty-five, for instance, some 116 books had been published about the Princess of Wales.

I make no apology for believing that, as he approaches his thirtieth birthday, Prince Edward's achievements are worthy of wider recognition. I have tried to steer clear of sensationalism but neither I, nor, I suspect, Prince Edward, would want this to be a hagiography. I have gone in search of the truth, attempting to discover his strengths and weaknesses, likes and dislikes, failures and triumphs. I hope the Prince will seem less remote and more easily understood as a result.

Many people have given me help, advice and information, for which I am immensely grateful. Some, for various reasons, wish to retain their anonymity, which I respect. I would particularly like to thank Geoffrey Crawford, Assistant Press Secretary to the Queen, who has dealt patiently and courteously with all my enquiries; Lieutenant Colonel Sean O'Dwyer, Private Secretary and Equerry to The Prince Edward; Miss Sophie Tyler, Secretary to Lieutenant Colonel O'Dwyer; Lady Susan Hussey for confirming details about the Prince's education; Sasa Assari, Press Officer for Madame Tussaud's, where Prince Edward became the first member of the Royal Family to attend the unveiling of his figure; BBC News Services for background information; Liza Wong for telling me of her meeting with Prince Edward; Ed Riseman for talking to me about the Prince's visit to the World Airline Entertainment Conference; Shirley Price, South East Regional Officer of the Duke of Edinburgh's Award; the actor and theatre director David Horne; Terry Johnson of the market research company Framework; Sarah Greene and Julian Clegg for unearthing many invaluable details about the Prince's life; the staff and listeners to BBC Radio Sussex and BBC Radio Surrey who over the years have offered many new insights into the Royal Family; J.M. and E.M. for their support and encouragement; my agent Andrew Lownie for his enthusiasm; my publisher Judy Piatkus, for her continued confidence in my work; editorial director Gill Cormode for her astute judgement; not forgetting Jana Sommerlad and Heather Rocklin, or Tony Cable who set the ball rolling.

In many ways Prince Edward has been misunderstood, and his actions too often misinterpreted. I hope this book will go some way towards setting the record straight. Any opinions expressed are my own, as are any unwitting errors or omissions. As the Queen's youngest son, Prince Edward has been forced to live his life in the full glare of the spotlight. Invariably the focus has been too narrow, the angle way off centre. I hope this book will succeed in showing him in a clearer, more truthful light.

Paul James
Brighton

OVERTURE

Strongest minds
Are often those of whom the noisy world
Hears least.

WILLIAM WORDSWORTH,

The Excursion

It was difficult to believe that this was Buckingham Palace. As midnight approached on a cold November night in 1988, police marksmen patrolling in the stark artificial light made no attempt to conceal their lethal weapons. In the shadows it felt like the Kremlin. Gone were the hundreds of tourists who earlier that day had photographed the Queen's official residence in the bright winter sun. Gone too the cosy picture postcard image of the Palace. The guns were a harsh reality of late twentieth-century security. Quite suddenly the traffic stopped as two police motorcycle outriders emerged from a small side street, followed a few seconds later by a maroon Rolls Royce. In the back seat could clearly be seen the lonely figure of Prince Edward. He looked across and half-smiled at us as the royal car silently glided into the heavily guarded fortress that is his home.

Only hours before we had watched a performance of Andrew Lloyd Webber's *Phantom of the Opera* at Her Majesty's Theatre. In the programme, almost hidden amongst the backstage credits, was the name of the Production Assistant, Edward Windsor.

In that one evening the Queen's youngest son had presented two contrasting personae. The first Edward was working in the profession of his choice, seeking some sort of anonymity, the other, more dominant, vision was of a Prince of the royal blood, heavily guarded. The two aspects of his life seemed incongruous.

It was in January 1988 that Prince Edward accepted Andrew Lloyd Webber's offer of employment on condition that he received no privileges. He wanted to learn the theatrical profession from the bottom. Yet the very fact that he was the Queen's son meant that he could never be treated as 'ordinary'. Conscious of the 'tea boy' image created for him by the media, he jokingly arrived at the theatre on his first day carrying a box of PG Tips tea bags. But he still travelled to work in a chauffeur-driven limousine and had a personal detective permanently in tow. His arrival was heralded by police sniffer dogs searching for IRA bombs. Clearly this was no ordinary employee.

Coming from the richest family in Britain, there is a certain irony in the fact that Prince Edward opted for what is generally considered to be the poorest paid and most over-populated profession. From day one it was clear that any attempt at a normal working life was doomed. Although his official working hours were originally 9 a.m. to 6 p.m., Edward frequently had to take time off to attend to more princely matters. In his first twelve months with the Really Useful Group he attended twenty-seven ceremonies, thirty-eight gala/charity shows, seven receptions, six official lunches, ten official dinners (including state banquets), one Privy Council meeting, and three audiences with Ambassadors. He also spent seventeen days overseas on official royal tours undertaking sixty-seven different engagements. With a total of 156 engagements in that year, he undertook more duties than the Duke and Duchess of York, the Queen Mother and Princess Margaret. To the general public, however, he seemed little more than a glorified tea boy. Torn between Queen and Lloyd Webber, there must have been times when the young Prince hardly knew where his allegiance lay. Ultimately it was Buckingham Palace that won hands down over the Palace Theatre.

This dichotomy in Prince Edward's life is a problem that only time will solve. As the Queen's third son and youngest child, currently seventh in line of succession and due to be pushed even further down the line by any subsequent child of his elder brothers, Edward is sufficiently removed from the throne to live the most normal life of any of the monarch's children. In many ways this would seem like an advantage – to have the privileges of position without the heavy duty of responsibility – yet in reality it is a double-edged sword. In an interview with writer Douglas Keay, Prince Philip once explained that there were very few career options open to his children: 'They could go into the Church but any commercial or competitive activity is always criticised.' The only safe choice, he felt, was the services. Prince Edward's experience of the services is well known.

Any difficulties that Prince Edward has encountered in his short life seem to stem from his royal birth. Seemingly trivial incidents are often given far more weight because of his title. At Cambridge, for instance, he was forced to give up playing rugby for the college 2nd XV. The official reason given by Buckingham Palace was that he retired 'through injury', but Prince Edward himself revealed that it was really because 'I became a sort of target, and I got fed up with being beaten up all the time.' The implication was that he suffered because of *who* he was. Not surprisingly, he now prefers individual sports to team games.

Much has been made of the problems that commoners experience when marrying into the Royal Family – Antony Armstrong-Jones, Mark Phillips, Diana Spencer and Sarah Ferguson all took a long time to adjust, and ultimately only one of them stayed the course – yet few appreciate the other side of the coin. In the months leading up to her separation from Prince Andrew, the Duchess of York found herself the target of severe press censure after holiday photographs were found of her with Texan oil tycoon Steve Wyatt. At the time a member of the Queen's Household blamed 'Fergie's' undignified behaviour on the fact that she was not born royal. Certainly there is something which appears to set those born into the Royal Family apart, but this is of little consolation to a Prince intent on making his own way in the outside world. Edward's situation is a complete reversal of the commoner adjusting to being a royal. He is a royal wanting to live an ordinary life.

The dilemma Edward faces is that he is a Prince too many. Prince Charles's future, whether he likes it or not, is assured; Princess Anne has created her own individual royal niche; Prince Andrew has had the temperament to follow the tried and trusted path of a career in the services combined with various royal duties, but Prince Edward has found himself surplus to requirements. Duties can always be found for any number of Royals, but Edward knows only too well that there would be no gaping hole without him. In this sense there is a distinct parallel between Prince Edward and his own great-uncle George, the late Duke of Kent (father of the present Duke of Kent), Princess Alexandra and Prince Michael of Kent).

As the younger son of King George V and Queen Mary, George had three elder brothers and a sister to fulfil royal duties. His elder brother David had a role to play first as Prince of Wales and later as King Edward VIII. After the abdication in 1936 the next brother 'Bertie' became King George VI, which still left Henry (the Duke of Gloucester) and Mary (the Princess Royal) to carry out official engagements. George felt superfluous. Although he once expressed a desire to be a doctor, at that time only the services were considered suitable for a Prince.

When the Second World War broke out George continually complained that he was never allowed to see any action and lamented the fact that, as a member of the Royal Family, he was 'too protected'. He felt that his war work visiting factories lacked any real purpose. Ironically he was on a safe tour of inspection to Iceland when he was killed in a plane crash in August 1942. It was intended to be his last such visit. Had he lived, one wonders how the restless Duke's career would have developed. Certainly Prince Edward can sympathise with his great-uncle's frustration.

Meeting Neil Armstrong, the first man to walk on the moon, during a visit to London while he was still a child, Prince Edward revealed that he would like to be an astronaut. Whether this was a genuine desire or an early sign of royal diplomacy, there is little doubt that Prince Edward would now be a professional actor if the choice were his. Whilst professional parts have been offered to him, including a chance to appear in the BBC series *Dr Who* in 1989, he knows that it is not a realistic option. Many might say that being a member of the Royal Family *is* an acting job anyway.

At the age of twenty-two, Prince Charles complained, 'There is no set role for me. It depends entirely on what I make of it. I'm really rather an awkward problem.' Even more than his elder brother, Prince Edward now faces the challenge of weaving a satisfactory private career with royal duty and obligation, while ultimately achieving fulfilment in his life. At the same time his royal position always takes precedence. When he joined the Royal Marines full-time in 1986 a spokesman said, 'Prince Edward will be treated as any other Royal Marine Officer. But, of course, you always have to remember who his mother is!' Meant as a joke, this has nevertheless been the crux of Prince Edward's problems. While working with both the Really Useful Group and Theatre Division, he was never allowed to forget his parentage. If any of his colleagues did forget, the presence of the personal detective acted as a very quick reminder. Throughout his life, if anything he does fails, it is a higher-profile failure simply because his mother is Queen.

Prince Edward's life to date has been one of considerable contrasts. He lives in a 600-room palace with seventy-eight bathrooms, yet his own apartment on the second floor of the north-west wing is modest and unostentatious. He hates caviar, seldom drinks alcohol, and drives (in private) a 3.5 litre V8 Rover Vitesse built for durability rather than sporty style. Described by a senior member of the Royal Household as 'the best of the Queen's children', Edward has known a freedom not experienced by his brothers or sister. While working for the Really Useful Group he was able to walk through the streets of Soho, eat in restaurants or go shopping, usually unnoticed. One mild winter day he chose to walk from Buckingham Palace into the West End and was spotted by a wide-eyed female who shouted, 'Ooh look! There's Prince *Andrew.*'

This encounter illustrates the relatively low public profile that Prince Edward has been able to maintain, in contrast to his brothers and sister who have been kept relentlessly under the media spotlight from earliest childhood. In 1958, when he was just ten years old, one newspaper drew up a list of potential brides for Prince Charles. Neither Charles, Anne nor Andrew could walk through the streets of London unrecognised, yet at the opening night party for the musical *Aspects of Love* photographer Richard Young captured Prince Edward on film being asked to show his invitation at the door before he was allowed in. He has been described as the member of the immediate Royal Family most in touch with the realities of everyday life. While a student at Jesus College, Cambridge, he cooked his own meals, did his own laundry and surprised fellow students by his unaffected manner. One contemporary described his voice as 'strangely devoid of all royal intonation'.

Yet no matter how ordinary Prince Edward has tried to be he has always been set slightly apart, for royal training begins early. At the age of four he was sitting for his first royal portrait by the highly acclaimed artist June Mendoza; at five he presented a cup at a Windsor polo match; his bedtime story was sometimes read by his mother in full-length evening gown, tiara and decorations, dressed for that evening's state banquet. Like thousands of other youngsters he later achieved a Duke of Edinburgh's Award Gold Medal through his own efforts, but his skills test and residential project included learning to sail a hydrofoil and gaining his private pilot's licence (not exactly run-of-the-mill activities).

Prince Edward has the confidence of his sister, the Princess Royal, and the dry humour of his brother, the Prince of Wales, but he is reserved with strangers, and is often seen standing alone at parties. When his cousin, Viscount Linley, organised a Raj Ball at the London Lyceum in December 1984, Prince Edward joined in with the spirit of the event by dressing in costume with a metal helmet and gold-braided uniform; yet he entered quietly through the back door for fear of an IRA attack and was protected by police dogs. While his cousins, including Lady Helen Windsor and Lady Sarah Armstrong-Jones, danced the night away, Prince Edward arrived without a partner and left early. At social events, he is always conscious that any stranger who talks to him may have an ulterior purpose, taking an interest not in him as a person, but in what he represents as a member of the Royal Family. Equally he says, 'The nice people hold back,' not wishing to be seen as social climbers. It is at family parties that Edward really sparkles, when he can relax and be himself.

Just as his aunt, Princess Margaret, has always fought an inner battle between the public duty expected of her as the Queen's sister and her private desires as a woman, so the private world of Edward Windsor will always be at odds with the public life of Prince Edward. Both Prince Edward and Princess Margaret have a strength of character that can be misinterpreted by those who do not know them. The first glimpse of Edward's strength was shown publicly in January 1987 when he chose to resign his commission from the Royal Marines. He was still only twenty-two years old, had undertaken training courses with the Marines for four years, and could easily have finished the twelve-month training programme at Lympstone and quietly moved on. 'It was nothing to do with the physical side,' he said. He knew he did not have the 100 per cent dedication that being in the services requires.

It took guts for the young Prince to go against royal tradition and assert his own wishes in the face of what could have been public humiliation, coupled with personal embarrassment at the fact that his father happened to be Captain General of the Marines. Public opinion, however, turned out to be on Edward's side. 'The country is solidly behind Prince Edward,' the *Sunday Express* declared after conducting a poll throughout Britain which showed that 80 per cent were in favour of Edward's decision. In the 55 to 64 age group, an overwhelming 99 per cent supported the Prince. 'This endearing young man,' wrote Prince Charles's biographer, Anthony Holden, in the *Daily Mail* of 10 January 1987, 'has a chance to build a bridge not across some icy stream on Dartmoor, but between the monarchy and the 21st century. This week we have seen him display the courage and maturity to seize that chance, rather than a rifle, with both hands.'

Time and again when the subject of Prince Edward has arisen on radio phone-ins, I have heard callers express their admiration for him *because* he had the courage to resign. From a family who continually have to disguise their emotions, Edward's was an open statement of unhappiness and the nation saw it as a refreshing change. Never frightened of setting himself up as a target, Prince Edward is the first member of the Royal Family ever to discuss his sexuality in public. He is also the only one of the Queen's children to have earned a living in the outside world (outside the services, that is), and in his quiet, determined way he will continue to follow his own heart rather than kow-tow to convention. As he matures it is noticeable that he is finding ways of shaping his royal duties to fit in with his own interests, turning what could be drudgery into opportunity.

Prince Edward's character, as he approaches his thirtieth birthday, has been forged and strengthened by his royal training and by the events of the last decade. He survived the extremely tough regime of Gordonstoun school, spent almost a year away from his family and friends in New Zealand, combined the academic requirements of studying for a degree at Cambridge with the severe physical demands of training courses for the Royal Marines, and has battled to build a career of his own choosing while fulfilling a total of more than 1,500 official duties. At times his frustration has been misinterpreted as arrogance, and lack of public awareness of his many duties has seen him unfairly accused of idleness. That he has emerged from all this relatively unscathed says much for his underlying resilience. As the youngest son, Prince Edward does have the advantage of two elder brothers to use as role models. At the very least he has been able to learn from their mistakes. With the hindsight of their courtships he has, for example, learnt to play his romantic cards very close to his chest. Born at a time of change within the Royal Family, he has greater freedom of choice in his marriage partner. Having completed his apprenticeship, he has laid firm foundations for a successful career in the arts.

Today Prince Edward is at a crossroads: behind him the position of world's most eligible bachelor; ahead the path of matrimony. Around him there are signs pointing towards career satisfaction and also towards royal duty. One thing is certain, whichever road Prince Edward follows in the future, the decision will be his and his alone.

Chapter 1

FIRST ENTRANCE

His will is not his own,

For he himself is subject to his birth.

WILLIAM SHAKESPEARE,

Hamlet (Act 1, Scene III)

With the Queen already in bed, Prince Edward is invariably the last person to return to Buckingham Palace at night. After an official engagement, his chauffeur drives the car under a stone portico on the north side of the Palace and deposits him quietly at the Garden Entrance. Crossing the stone floor interlaced with small black squares of Belgian marble, past the honeysuckle frieze adorning the walls, the Prince makes his way along the red-carpeted corridor to the nursery lift where a footman escorts him to the second floor. Here, in Prince Edward's apartment overlooking Constitution Hill, his valet will have left a cold supper (in the refrigerator, a plentiful supply of carbonated mineral water and soft drinks). Earlier in the evening the housekeeper, Miss Colebrook, will have arranged for the curtains to be drawn, the bedcovers folded back.

Off the silent corridor, between the present nursery and the rooms housing the Queen's considerable wardrobe, Prince Edward closes his door to the world. These unpretentious rooms contain a lifetime of recollections: framed posters of theatrical shows with which he has been associated; photograph albums filled with pictures of himself on stage – as Lord

9

Fancourt Babberley in the farce *Charley's Aunt* in New Zealand, as Deputy-Governor Danforth in *The Crucible* at Cambridge, and as the wrestler known as the 'Sandringham Slammer' in *Trafford Tanzi* for the National Youth Theatre. In his own capacious wardrobes, beside the numerous ready-made and off-the-peg suits that have become his trademark, hang the ceremonial Royal Marines uniform that he wore at the Duke of York's wedding and a blue silk blouson jacket with the words 'Starlight Express' in sequins on the back – reminders of two contrasting experiences.

As the Queen and the Duke of Edinburgh rest soundly in their rooms directly beneath him, Edward will watch a video or listen to some music and unwind before retiring to bed himself. Confident of being undisturbed, he will occasionally practise his secret hobby: performing magic tricks. Fascinated by the art of illusion, not only does Edward aim to become a member of the prestigious Magic Circle, he also uses his considerable skills to entertain younger members of the Royal Family. Uncle Edward is particularly popular with Princesses Beatrice and Eugenie for this reason, and he has always been close to his sister's children, Zara and Peter Phillips.

Prince Edward's apartments are situated off the Nursery Corridor where, twenty-five years ago, he rode a tricycle up and down. His rooms are those which, as a child, he once shared with Prince Andrew. Although the Queen has many residences it is Buckingham Palace that Edward considers to be his home. Here he feels the most secure and when the rest of his family have eagerly escaped to Balmoral or Sandringham, he has frequently remained alone at the Palace with only a small retinue of staff. He can swim in the Palace pool, play squash in basement courts, or entertain friends – such as broadcaster Richard Baker's son James – in his own private sitting room.

Whilst the Queen and many members of her family look upon Buckingham Palace more as a place of work, an administrative centre for royal duties and a central London venue to entertain officially, Prince Edward has a greater affection for the building. He was born on the ground floor of the Palace, overlooking the 40-acre garden, on Tuesday 10 March 1964, the fourth and last of Queen Elizabeth II's children.

The first inkling of the monarch's pregnancy came in the summer of 1963 when the Queen missed the opening day of the Goodwood races because of a private appointment. When she eventually arrived it was noticeable that she was in high spirits. Only much later was it revealed that the mystery meeting had been with Sir Wilfred Sheldon, Physician-Paediatrician to the Queen, who had confirmed her condition. Other than members of her immediate family, the first person to be told the good news was the then Prime Minister, Harold Macmillan, on a weekend visit to Balmoral. On 16 September an official statement was made: 'It is announced from Buckingham Palace that the Queen will undertake no further engagements after Her Majesty leaves Balmoral in October.' To the public it could only mean one thing.

Scarcely a month short of her thirty-eighth birthday when the baby was due, many wondered whether the pregnancy had been planned. Speculation was fuelled years later when Prince Philip spoke of 'procreation' in a speech:

People want their first child very much when they marry. They want the second child almost as much. If a third comes along they accept it as natural – but they haven't gone out of their way to get it. When the fourth child comes along, in most cases it's unintentional.

Inevitably his words were assumed to be based on personal experience, but the Queen confided in a close friend that she very much wanted a fourth child to complete her family and had known that time was running out. Indeed, in her teenage years she told her then governess, Marion Crawford, that she hoped one day to have 'Four children. Two girls and two boys.' Finishing up with three boys and a girl is proof that even the Royals have no control over Mother Nature, but Elizabeth had the family she hoped for.

Throughout her four pregnancies the Queen never once expressed any fear – 'It's what we're made for,' she told a friend – and she seemed to enjoy her final confinement more than the others. By this time she had been on the throne for almost twelve years. Not only had she relaxed into the role of Sovereign, but changes had been made at Court which made life less formal than in her predecessors' reigns, and advances in transport and technology had made travel easier. Prince Edward was part of what the Queen referred to as her 'second family', with some sixteen years separating the births of her first and last sons.

When Prince Charles and Princess Anne were young, the recently crowned Elizabeth II missed much of her son and daughter's upbringing because the demands on her time were so great. When she embarked on a tour of the Commonwealth in November 1953 she and Prince Philip did not see their children for six months. Although she spoke to them frequently on the telephone she missed the pleasure of watching Prince Charles learning to read and could not be with them for Christmas. When they were finally reunited in Gibraltar the Queen later revealed in a rare television interview that 'They were terribly polite. I don't think they really knew who we were', a sad admission about her own children. As Queen she placed duty before her family. If the children were ill, and there was any risk that she might catch something, she was kept isolated from them. This is a far cry from the present Princess of Wales who fought to take Prince William on her first tour of Australia so that she would not miss his first steps, and when one of her sons is ill she is first at his bedside, regardless of the risk to her own health.

By the time the Queen had her 'second family', Princes Andrew and Edward, improvements in transport had reduced overseas tours from six months' duration to a couple of weeks. The Queen was also acutely aware that she had missed much of Charles's and Anne's childhood. On occasions her elder son appeared quiet and withdrawn, confused and daunted by the gradual realisation of his royal destiny. Princess Anne, conscious that her brother was treated differently because he was a future king, became rebellious and unruly. When the Queen once asked her daughter to fetch one of their dogs the temperamental Princess snapped defiantly, 'Fetch it yourself!' Perhaps mindful of all this, when given a second chance at motherhood the Queen, within the confines of her public role, gave her younger sons priority. As a result, a far happier childhood lay in store for Prince Edward than his eldest brother.

Determined to enjoy what she knew was almost certainly her last pregnancy, the Queen stayed longer than usual in the peaceful atmosphere of Balmoral. Although the infamous red boxes containing state papers continued to arrive daily, the Queen ordered a large supply of 5,000-piece jigsaw puzzles. She took long walks through the heather-clad hills with her dogs, went for gentle rides each day on her beloved horses, and tasted a freedom from duty that she would not experience again. The general public scarcely saw their monarch until the annual televised broadcast that Christmas. The Queen Mother, Princess Margaret, the then Princess Royal (Princess Mary, King George VI's sister) and Princess Alice (Duchess of Gloucester) deputised for her at engagements, investitures and the wreath-laying ceremony on Remembrance Sunday.

The enjoyment of her pregnancy was further enhanced by the news that Princess Margaret, Princess Alexandra (who had married in April 1963), and the Duchess of Kent were all expecting babies the following spring. This quirk of fate was to have a significant effect on Prince Edward's life. That Christmas there was much giggling in the corridors of Sandringham House when the four pregnant women met, and Prince Philip was heard to complain that it was like living in an ante-natal clinic. His toast after their Christmas dinner was 'To the four little strangers whom we know are present!'

Little could dampen the Queen's spirits, although the assassination of President Kennedy in November emphasised for her the vulnerability of world leaders. In early February 1964, a month before Prince Edward was born, the Queen Mother was suddenly rushed to hospital suffering from appendicitis. This meant an early return from Sandringham for the anxious, now heavily pregnant monarch. Although all photographs of the Queen's 'condition' were banned by Buckingham Palace (unlike present-day royal mothers who find themselves the subject of photographers' attention throughout pregnancy), while in London the Queen did agree to a few private audiences, meeting for example Mrs Nikolayeva-Tereshkova, Russian cosmonaut and first woman in space.

Princess Alexandra became the first royal mother of 1964, a leap year, giving birth to a son – James Robert Bruce Ogilvy – on 29 February. 'It's bad enough having my own birthday on

Christmas Day,' the Princess joked when the Queen visited her at Thatched House Lodge, 'I didn't want my son to only have a birthday once every four years!'

Prince Edward made his entry into the world a week earlier than anticipated, on Tuesday 10 March. Like Prince Andrew, four years earlier, he was born in the Belgian Suite of Buckingham Palace, where the large bathroom (still containing an enormous ornate bath designed for George IV) had been turned into a comfortable delivery room. The labour was the easiest the Queen had experienced, the 5lb 7oz baby weighing in at almost 2lb lighter than either Prince Charles (7lb 6oz) or Prince Andrew (7lb 3oz). 'The Queen was safely delivered of a son at 8.20 this evening,' announced the official bulletin from Buckingham Palace. 'Her Majesty and the infant Prince are both well.'

The Queen was visited the next day in what is now a guest bedroom for official visitors in the four-roomed Belgian Suite (named in honour of Queen Victoria's uncle, Leopold I of the Belgians) by the convalescing Queen Mother and the still pregnant Princess Margaret. The latter gave birth to Prince Edward's cousin, Lady Sarah Armstrong-Jones on 1 May, just two days after the Duchess of Kent had brought a daughter into the world, Lady Helen Windsor.

Born within weeks of each other, Edward, James, Sarah and Helen were destined to form a close-knit branch of the family. Each year one large family party is held at Windsor to mark the royal quartet's birthdays. From childhood playmates to fellow scholars, the four have grown up as close confidantes and mix more easily with their contemporaries than some members of the Royal Family. Having spent a great deal of his early childhood with his grandmother, the Queen Mother, Prince Charles for example has always felt more comfortable with people much older than himself.

Less well known is the fact that a fifth baby was born into the Royal Family at the same time, but this child was excluded from all the celebrations. The Queen's cousin George, the 7th Earl of Harewood (elder son of George VI's sister, Mary, the Princess Royal), had a son in 1964 by his secretary Patricia 'Bambi' Tuckwell whom he married three years later. The baby, Prince Edward's second cousin, was legitimised and given a title as the

Honourable Mark Lascelles, but – being born out of wedlock – has been excluded from the line of succession which currently includes twelve members of the Lascelles family. Had the circumstances of his birth been different, Mark Lascelles could well have been part of this young royal group.

On Saturday 2 May the six-week-old Prince was christened in the private chapel at Windsor Castle by the Dean of Windsor, Robert Woods, and was given the names Edward Antony Richard Louis. His middle names are those of his three god-fathers, Antony Armstrong-Jones (then married to Princess Margaret), Prince Richard (now Duke of Gloucester), and Prince Louis of Hesse. Louis was also a tribute to his uncle, Earl Mountbatten of Burma. Edward was chosen as a universally popular royal name, that of eight Kings of England and also of the Queen's cousin, the present Duke of Kent. Prince Edward also had two godmothers, Princess George of Hanover (Prince Philip's sister Sophie) and the present Duchess of Kent. Having given birth to Lady Helen Windsor only three days earlier, the Duchess was absent from the christening ceremony itself and was represented by her mother-in-law, Princess Marina.

So convinced was the Queen that her last child would be a daughter, only girls' names had been chosen. Legally Prince Philip was obliged to register the baby's birth within forty-two days, but the deadline drew dangerously close and Prince Edward still had no birth certificate. Forty-one days after his birth, the Prince's names were officially announced, to the relief of Caxton Hall, who would have been obliged to impose a fine for non-registration.

During the period leading up to Prince Andrew's birth in February 1960, the question of the Royal Family's surname had come to the fore. The Queen was born a Windsor and was a monarch of the House of Windsor, her grandfather George V having adopted the name during the First World War to replace the German surname Saxe-Coburg-Gotha. Yet surely, people enquired, as the Queen had married Philip Mountbatten, *that* must be the surname of their children. On 8 February 1960, just eleven days before Prince Andrew's birth, the Queen issued the following statement:

. . . while I and my children will continue to be styled and known as the House and Family of Windsor my descendants, other than descendants enjoying the style, title or attributes of Royal Highness and the titular dignity of Prince or Princess, and female descendants who marry and their descendants, shall bear the name Mountbatten-Windsor.

The statement concluded by saying that the Queen had always wanted to keep the name of the Royal House established by her grandfather yet also to associate the name of her husband with her own and his descendants. When Princess Anne married in 1973 she was registered as Mountbatten-Windsor, the first time that this surname had been used on any official document. Andrew and Edward, however, seem to prefer to be called Windsor, adhering to the Queen's 1960 statement.

Having established the baby's names, the newest addition to the Royal Family became officially His Royal Highness *The* Prince Edward, the definite article being reserved only for the children of the Sovereign. Wearing the traditional Honiton lace christening gown made originally for Queen Victoria's eldest daughter in 1841 and worn by all subsequent royal children, Edward was baptised with holy water from the River Jordan, held in a Victorian silver gilt font. Screaming loudly throughout, the baby was later laid in a crib once used by the infant Princess Elizabeth. Already the tiny Prince was being surrounded by history and royal tradition.

Taking photographs three weeks after the christening, Cecil Beaton noticed the Queen's attitude towards Prince Edward. She was in 'a happy, contented and calm mood,' he noted in his diary, 'and not only smiled to my instructions but with amusement at the activities and fast-developing character of the newborn.' The sitting took place at Buckingham Palace in the magnificent Blue Drawing Room, the Queen appearing more relaxed than he had ever seen her. Even though the sitting overran, making her late for an appointment with her dressmaker, the monarch smiled and cooed over the baby like a young mother with her firstborn. 'Look, his eyelashes are all tangled!' she laughed, 'It's most unfortunate that all my sons have long eyelashes while my daughter hasn't any at all.' The session resulted in some of the most natural pictures ever taken of the

Queen with her children. That night Cecil Beaton wrote in his diary that Prince Edward was 'alert, curious and already a character'.

Unusually, the Queen decided to postpone a previously planned state visit to Federal Germany until May 1965 so that she could spend more time with her son. Possibly in her mind was the memory of 1951 when, as heir presumptive, she had begun to undertake an increased number of duties owing to her father's poor health. That summer she had set out for a lengthy tour of America and Canada and, as she waved good-bye to two-and-a-half-year-old Prince Charles and one-year-old Princess Anne, she was visibly fighting back the tears at yet another separation. Now, in 1964, she did not intend to miss any of her youngest son's development.

Despite the close bond between Edward and his mother, the Queen could not neglect her royal duties for long. The Prince was placed in the care of a nanny, Mabel Anderson, who had originally been employed as nurserymaid to Prince Charles in 1948. Miss Anderson remained at the Palace until November 1977 when she moved to Gatcombe Park to look after Princess Anne's son, Peter Phillips. She retired in 1981 after more than thirty years' royal service. Inevitably Prince Edward grew up seeing more of Mabel Anderson than he did of his own mother, but the Queen put on a rubber apron to bath her son each night, and if any friends or family happened to be visiting the Palace they too were dragged to the nursery. On one occasion a king and three queens were present at bathtime!

Whenever possible the Queen had her baby with her. After Trooping the Colour on 13 June 1964 she rushed in to see Edward as soon as she returned to the Palace and, to the delight of the crowds thronging the Mall, she proudly carried the baby on to the balcony for his first public appearance. When she sat in her study working on state papers, she had the Prince with her, a privilege she had denied her eldest children. Public engagements permitting, the Queen and Prince Philip visited the baby after breakfast for half an hour's play, returning again at mid-morning and lunchtime, and wheeled him out in his pram during the afternoon around the Palace gardens. Another hour's play would ensue before bath and bedtime. On Wednesday evening, which became known as 'Mabel's night off', the Queen would take over the running of the nursery completely, looking after Andrew and Edward.

The second-floor nursery consisted of a day room, two bedrooms, a bathroom and kitchen, which now make up the adult Prince Edward's own self-contained apartment. Originally the rooms had belonged to Prince Charles but, with the arrival of Prince Andrew, the twelve-year-old Prince was moved to new rooms at the front of the Palace. Prince Edward slept in the same cream-painted cot that his brothers and sister had used, purchased in 1948. As the fourth child, Edward was to receive many hand-me-down toys from the thrifty monarch. At night, Mabel Anderson slept in the nursery with the Princes. Nicknamed 'Mamba' by Prince Andrew, Mabel was assisted by a nurserymaid, June Waller, who undertook the less pleasant chores such as washing baby clothes, and a nursery footman, Michael Perry. As the young Princes grew up, it was Michael Perry who taught them basic personal training when more intimate matters could be better dealt with by a fellow male. Nowadays, thirty years on, Michael Perry is Prince Andrew's valet, still laying out his clothes, running his bath and attending to personal matters.

When Prince Charles and Princess Anne were young, their nanny, Helen Lightbody, had very strict control of the nursery. This was her domain and the children were in her charge. At this stage the Queen had neither the time, nor the experience as a mother, to interfere. A product of the old school, Nanny Lightbody's earliest lessons included teaching her young charges to bow and curtsey to their parents. Prince Charles obeyed; Princess Anne rebelled. Helen Lightbody retired in 1956, once Princess Anne had begun her education, and with her 'second family' the Queen decided that she wanted a less formal approach. Firmness tempered with love was the order of the day, and this time the Queen wanted to keep overall control.

Mabel Anderson, already a long-time employee, was happy to go along with this. She was almost the same age as the Queen, and was half Scottish, half Liverpudlian, which met with royal approval. The Queen's own nursemaid and lifelong confidante Margaret 'Bobo' MacDonald came from Scotland, as did her governess, Marion Crawford. The nanny, Helen Lightbody, and the governess employed to teach Charles and Anne,

Catherine Peebles, were both Scottish. Clearly, Mabel Anderson's Scottish background was a point in her favour. So devoted was 'Mamba' to Andrew and Edward that the Queen sometimes had difficulty persuading her to take any time off at all. This deep affection and sense of security could only have a beneficial effect on the young Princes.

Kept out of the public eye, apart from the release of Beaton's official photographs and a brief glimpse of him on the balcony, there was inevitable press speculation that something was wrong with Edward's health. The Royal Family ignored the rumours and the young Prince remained oblivious of the gossip. The Queen had Prince Edward vaccinated against polio, whooping cough, smallpox, diphtheria and tetanus, thereby encouraging other mothers to follow suit, and has always put the Prince's robust good health down to the fact that he was born in the spring. The Queen is also a great believer in 'plenty of fresh air' and ordered that Prince Edward's pram be placed outside every afternoon, regardless of the weather.

From an early age the Queen insisted that her son be referred to as 'Edward' by the staff. The title 'Prince' was not to be used until he reached the age of eighteen. It is valets who frequently have the privilege of making the change, greeting their Prince with 'Good morning, Sir' each day and then delighting them on their eighteenth birthday by amending this to 'Good morning, Your Royal Highness'. The Queen wanted to shield Edward from his royal position for as long as possible, realising that the pressures would come all too soon. Edward's upbringing was made easier because he was never alone. Prince Andrew was always there in the nursery and, as they grew older, they could share experiences and problems. There was always someone who understood. Whereas Prince Charles has been called one of the loneliest men in the world, isolated by his position, and much older in years and attitude than his younger brothers, Andrew and Edward – with just four years separating them – have developed a close bond. Edward also had the distinct advantage of having three cousins, James, Sarah and Helen, who played together in the nursery and grew up as part of a close-knit family. The fact that Edward grew up to be so well adjusted, with a greater acceptance and tolerance of his royal position, almost certainly stems from the security of the nursery.

Although Prince Edward's formal education did not begin until 1968, by the time he was two the Queen started to teach her son simple lessons herself. With a child-size blackboard in her sitting room she began by teaching the alphabet, followed by numbers and, with the help of a clock face, taught her son to tell the time. Prince Philip taught Andrew and Edward to swim and the Queen indulged her own passion by giving her sons riding lessons. When the Princes reached their teenage years it was Prince Philip who gave them their first driving lessons along private roads on the Windsor estate. They were taken to a skating rink (before it was opened to the public), were taught tennis by Dan Maskell, and even had dancing lessons. Unlike the more outgoing Andrew, however, Edward did not join the boy scouts.

It was a cosy, privileged world in which to grow up. At Balmoral, Prince Philip would take Edward rowing on their own private loch, having first travelled to Scotland on board the luxurious *Britannia*. The Queen drove him in a Land Rover through the hills for picnics beside the River Dee. Yet, despite his apparently idyllic childhood, Edward was never allowed to have things all his own way, and strict attention was paid to his manners. Visitors to the Palace commented on the Prince's politeness and quiet nature. Less boisterous than Andrew, he was happy to sit placidly for hours with a book. When out in public the smartly dressed boy always held his mother's hand extremely tightly. 'He's certainly the quietest of all my children,' the Queen commented.

In the 1960s a change occurred which was to affect the rest of Prince Edward's life. As the end of the decade approached, there was a feeling that the Royal Family were in danger of becoming an anachronism unless they became less remote. Until this time only formal events had been filmed; it was believed that anything too intimate might destroy the essential mystery of the monarchy. Already the media were making clumsy and irresponsible attempts to get closer to royalty. A few months after Prince Edward's birth the Queen complained to the Press Council when pictures were taken of her by two photographers hidden in undergrowth. She and Princess Margaret had been picnicking and waterskiing at Sunninghill Park, near Windsor, unaware that zoom lenses were trained on them. The Queen was said to be livid when the pictures subsequently appeared in the press.

In October 1968 Prince Edward was unknowingly at the centre of a public scandal caused by photographs. His birth had coincided almost to the day with the death of Prince Philip's cousin, King Paul I of Greece (father of the now ex-King Constantine, Edward's 'Uncle Tino'). Prince Philip flew out of the country for the state funeral in Athens just as Prince Charles and Princess Anne were being brought home from their respective boarding schools to see their newborn brother. Returning home straight after the funeral, with death very much on his mind and the life of his young son just beginning at home, Prince Philip took the very first photographs of the baby as soon as he arrived at the Palace. The Queen sat in a negligée, propped up in bed, with Edward in her arms. These innocent, private photographs were to become the subject of great controversy four years later.

The Queen was travelling home from Balmoral by train when news reached her that photographs of the baby Prince Edward had been published in the French magazine *Paris Match*. The same photographs were offered to the British press and appeared in early editions of the *Daily Express*. As Prince Philip still had the negatives, the obvious question was how this breach of privacy could have occurred. Suspicion fell on close family friends and members of the Royal Household who were the only people who knew that the photographs existed. Pictures of the Queen in bed were thought to lessen the monarch's dignity, but the Queen was more horrified by the thought that someone close to the Royal Family had betrayed them. Buckingham Palace issued an indignant statement to all British newspapers saying: 'Since the pictures are of such a personal kind, the Queen would naturally prefer that they had not been published. For that reason, we are unable to approve their future publication.' However the Palace had no such control over European newspapers and magazines who, believing them to be stolen anyway, blatantly reproduced them directly from

Paris Match without paying a copyright fee. During investigations *Paris Match* would only admit that an 'unknown gentleman' had offered them the photographs.

The perpetrator of what the British newspapers termed the 'Prince Edward photograph scandal' was never identified, although the mystery of how these and other private royal photographs came into the hands of European magazines was eventually solved a year later. After Prince Philip had taken his photographs, a detective delivered the finished roll of film to a well-known developer's in London. The detective then remained outside the darkroom throughout the processing and was finally handed a sealed packet containing the finished photographs *and* the negatives. Unfortunately the elaborate procedure intended to prevent private royal photographs from falling into the wrong hands was not foolproof. It had never been considered that whoever developed the film could easily make a set of copies. When the scheme was discovered, so too was a stack of photographs over three inches thick that had been taken by the Queen and her family over the years. The best had been sold to European publications.

The mystery solved, the Queen did not on this occasion complain to the Press Council for it might be considered that she was partly to blame for not taking even stricter precautions over the method by which her snapshots were developed. Today zoom lenses surreptitiously trained on the Royal Family in private situations are so prevalent that action is only taken in similar cases to that of the 'Prince Edward scandal'. When, in 1988, the *Sun* newspaper in Britain published private family photographs taken of Princess Beatrice, they were fined £1 million as a future deterrent. Prince Edward had been born at a time when the Royal Family ceased to be revered and the appetite of the press became voracious enough to go to almost any lengths to unearth a scandal. It was only a matter of time before he would find himself a target.

Although the publication of the photographs had no immediate effect on the four-year-old Prince, another major media intrusion in 1968 did. For a whole year, between July 1968 and April 1969, the Royal Family were trailed by an eight-man camera crew who were making a documentary about their public and private life. This film – revolutionary at the time –

was the brainchild of William Heseltine (then Press Secretary to the Queen) who, sensing a decline of public interest in the Royal Family, thought such a documentary might bring the monarch closer to the people. He contacted Richard Cawston, Head of Documentary Programmes at the BBC, to discuss his plans.

Having been granted unprecedented access to the Royal Family, Cawston spent twelve months filming the Windsors in all sorts of situations, from decorating the Christmas tree at Windsor Castle to hosting a diplomatic reception at Buckingham Palace. The finished film, called simply *Royal Family,* was a joint project between ITV and the BBC and was eventually shown in 141 countries, raising more than £120,000 in profits for charity. It was the first time the general public had heard the Queen speak informally, rather than reading from a prepared speech, and it was the first glimpse they had had of Prince Edward as a young boy.

For the Prince himself, being trailed by a camera crew must have been a novel experience. Perhaps the memory of it planted in his subconscious the seeds that would one day germinate into a future career. Prince Edward's appearances in the film were numerous and proved that he was not banished to the nursery like many an aristocratic child, but was very much part of the family. What came across very strongly was Prince Edward's maturity for one so young. In one scene he was shown sitting on a sofa with Prince Andrew while the Queen showed them a photograph album.

'Who's that?' the Queen asked.

'Queen Victoria?' Edward suggested.

'No, Queen Mary. That's Gan-Gan,' said the Queen.

For a four-year-old his conversations on film were intelligent and displayed a remarkable knowledge and interest. He was filmed helping to decorate the Christmas tree at Windsor, throwing snowballs, playing with puppies at Sandringham, and driving with the Queen to a village shop where he paid for an ice-cream from a small bag of pocket money. For those who saw the film, the scene of Prince Edward with the cello is probably the most memorable. For New Year 1969 the Royal Family moved from Windsor to Sandringham. During their stay Prince Charles was filmed tuning a cello which he was learning to play while a student at Cambridge. Prince Edward leant over to inspect the instrument when a string unexpectedly snapped and stung him on the neck. Knowing that the cameras were still rolling, his early royal training had taught him not to cry, but Edward was clearly on the verge of tears. It was the one scene that Richard Cawston had misgivings about including in the final documentary. Filming had ceased the moment Prince Edward had been hurt, but he was unsure of the Queen's reaction. In the end it was included, but Cawston later received many letters of complaint from viewers who thought that the cello string had been broken deliberately for the benefit of the cameras.

Some twenty-seven million viewers watched the first showing of *Royal Family* and it had its intended effect. Milton Shulman wrote in the London *Evening Standard:*

> *What has actually happened is that an old image has been replaced by a fresh one. The emphasis on authority and remoteness which was the essence of the previous image has, ever since George VI, been giving way to a friendlier image of homeliness, industry and relaxation. But just as it was untrue that the Royal Family sat down to breakfast wearing coronets as they munched their corn flakes, so it is untrue that they now behave in their private moments like a middle-class family in Surbiton or Croydon.*

Twenty-two years were to pass before the exercise was to be repeated, when the Queen once again agreed to be trailed by a camera crew for a whole year. This time the filming took place from September 1990 to October 1991 to make a documentary marking the fortieth anniversary of her accession on 6 February 1992.

By the end of filming in 1969 the absence of a film crew left a strange gap in the Royal Family's lives. When a lightbulb exploded just as the Queen was entering an official function, she automatically walked out and entered again for another 'take'. On a state visit to Brazil, when a power cut blocked out all the lights, the Queen joked to Prince Philip, 'Where's Cawston?' By Prince Edward's fifth birthday in March 1969, 20 per cent of his life had been spent with a film crew dogging his family's every footstep. For someone who would one day be in the full glare of the spotlight, it was perfect training.

Prince Edward's official education had originally been planned to start in the Buckingham Palace schoolroom under the tutelage of Catherine Peebles. 'Mispy', as she was known, had already taught Prince William and Prince Richard of Gloucester, as well as Prince Michael of Kent, before being employed by the Queen in 1953 to teach Prince Charles. By the time he went on to Hill House School in 1957 she was already educating Princess Anne. In 1963 the Princess went to Benenden but Miss Peebles had a new pupil in Prince Andrew and it was assumed that Prince Edward would eventually join the class. It came as a shock to the Queen and her family when in September 1968 'Mispy' was found dead in her room at Buckingham Palace, the month before Prince Edward was due to start his formal education.

Finding a replacement governess at short notice was no easy task. The Dumbartonshire-born Miss Peebles had spent over twenty years teaching royal children. Discreet and efficient, she was skilled at handling the temperament of Princes; knew how to take her pupils out to museums and art galleries without being recognised and, more importantly, had the Queen's trust. It was the Queen's lady-in-waiting, Lady Susan Hussey, who came to the rescue, suggesting her own governess, Miss Adele Grigg, as a temporary replacement until the position could be filled. From October to December 1968 Prince Edward was driven each day to Chelsea to attend Miss Grigg's class. As a result Edward became the first member of the Royal Family not to begin his formal education at home.

By Christmas the Queen had engaged a new governess, Miss Lavinia Keppel. Having first taught at Lady Eden's School, she had gone on to teach private pupils before applying for the job. By a strange twist of fate Miss Keppel was from the same family as Alice Keppel, the mistress of King Edward VII. In January 1969 Prince Edward began lessons in the Palace schoolroom. Talking on a television chat show, Princess Anne once expressed her relief at going to boarding school. Being in the Palace schoolroom with just a governess, she explained, 'required an awful lot of concentration'. Edward, however, was not alone. He was joined in his studies by Lady Sarah Armstrong-Jones, James Ogilvy, Princess Tanya of Hanover (grand-daughter of Prince Philip's sister), and occasionally the off-spring of family friends and senior members of the Royal Household.

In the bright airy schoolroom, situated directly above the famous Buckingham Palace balcony and looking directly down the Mall, the day usually began with a Bible story, followed by a morning of formal lessons: learning to read and write, basic arithmetic, and geography using a large globe to plot the countries of the Commonwealth. There was a mid-morning break for orange juice and biscuits, and the afternoons were occupied with painting, drawing, sports and occasional outside visits to galleries and exhibitions.

Although still sheltered from the outside world and mixing only with children of a particular social standing, Prince Edward was nevertheless learning to communicate with his contemporaries which saved him from the culture shock Prince Charles had suffered. Charles had been almost eight years old before he mixed with children of his own age. Until that time his companions had been his baby sister Anne, his nanny and Miss Peebles. So terrified was he of being sent to school that when he started at Hill House he began by going only in the afternoons. Intended to introduce him gently, this only served to alienate him from the other children. Throughout his schooldays Charles had few friends, was often bullied, and has described the experience as 'miserable'. When Edward began his education Charles was twenty and on the verge of completing his. Only too aware of Prince Charles's experiences, the Queen was able to ensure that Andrew and Edward did not suffer in the same way. The early signs were that she had succeeded. Although Edward was more cautious and reserved than Andrew, they both had confidence with strangers. However age and experience were gradually to erode their trust as the years progressed.

Already Prince Edward's character was beginning to assert itself. As his features started to look more Windsor than Mountbatten, Edward's nature was said to be that of the young Princess Elizabeth. Restrained rather than shy, both occasionally seemed to be overshadowed by their more ebullient siblings. Both Princess Margaret and Prince Andrew won people over quickly with their wit and lively personalities, while Princess Elizabeth and Prince Edward took their time to weigh people up. Most of their friendships have been both lasting and rewarding as a result. While Prince Andrew was content to kick a football around, Prince Edward would be making a model aeroplane. A favourite game, as he grew older, was to listen to classical music on the radio and identify the pieces before their titles were announced. Edward was quite jealous when the Queen of Denmark gave Andrew a gift of a stereo system and some classical music records.

Like the Queen, Prince Edward also enjoyed watching *Coronation Street* on television, displaying an essential ambivalence to his character. Amid the grandeur of their surroundings and the great antiquities that are so much part of their home life, both he and the Queen will often prize their simplest possessions, perhaps of least monetary value, most. A soft toy will stand beside a Meissen figurine. Able to eat lavishly whenever he wishes, Prince Edward's favourite food today is said to be a bread roll filled with barbecued fish or meat because the taste reminds him of picnics at Balmoral.

In July 1969 Prince Edward experienced his first major royal ceremony, the Investiture of his brother as Prince of Wales. Although Edward had been present regularly at Church services, watched his mother Trooping the Colour and on Remembrance Sunday laying a wreath at the Cenotaph on television, the Investiture – hailed as the most spectacular pageant since the Coronation – was the first royal ritual the five-year-old had actually attended. The young Prince looked forward to the event, which necessitated sleeping on the royal train, oblivious of the Queen's greatest worry, security. In Wales there was a great deal of ill-feeling that an Englishman was being created their Prince and a survey revealed that 44 per cent of Welsh people considered the £500,000 ceremony a waste of money. Twelve serious bomb attacks were made in the months leading up to the event. Two men were blown to pieces as they attempted to plant an explosive device on the night before the ceremony itself, and the Royal Family's overnight train from London was delayed several times en route by a series of bomb hoaxes. Even as Prince Charles was driven to Caernarvon Castle on the day, a bomb exploded within earshot.

Returning to London after the event the Queen uncharacteristically cancelled her engagements and took to her bed for
four days.

For Prince Edward there were mixed feelings. Yes, he had
enjoyed the spectacle of his brother's crowning but as an astute
child he must also have sensed danger for the first time in his
life. He knew nothing of bomb threats or elaborate security
arrangements. He could have no conception of the depth of
feeling that might actually lead people to kill his mother or
brother, not out of hatred for them personally but purely
because of what they represented. Nevertheless he could see for
himself that his family needed protection. He must have been
aware of his mother's anxiety, his brother's tension. This was the
moment when Prince Edward's sense of security began to be
eroded.

Shortly afterwards Edward made his first overseas visit. It
had been a stressful year for the Windsors, with the strain of the
Investiture following hot on the heels of making the *Royal
Family* documentary. For a family who experience so little
privacy at the best of times, it was if they had been unable to
relax at all. Even Scottish holidays, Christmas at Windsor and
New Year at Sandringham had been dogged by a film crew.
Eschewing tradition for once, instead of going straight to
Balmoral that August, the Queen took her family on a leisurely
cruise in the royal yacht *Britannia* to Norway. Here they joined
King Olav on his own yacht *Norge* and sailed along the Norwegian coast to Andalsnes, Molde and into Trondheim Fjord.
Although basically a family holiday, and classed as an 'unofficial
visit', King Olav met them in full admiral's uniform. A guard of
honour from the Army, Navy and Air Force lined up to meet
them and a band played the two countries' national anthems.
When Edward walked the short distance to change yachts it was
inevitably along *red* carpet, blinded by camera flashes. The next
day they lunched with the Norwegian Prime Minister, Per
Borten. Even in private, on his first foreign holiday, it seemed
there was to be no escape from duty, no relaxation of protocol,
for the young Prince.

When Edward was next seen by the British public at the
Braemar Highland Games on 6 September he seemed to have
matured beyond his years. Photographs show him wearing a kilt

in the traditional Balmoral tartan and, as he walked, his hands were clasped behind his back in perfect imitation of the Duke of Edinburgh and Prince of Wales.

Returning to Buckingham Palace to continue his studies that autumn, it was a more serious, less carefree Prince Edward who entered Lavinia Keppel's schoolroom. It was as if the gradual realisation of his royal position had suddenly taken hold.

Chapter 2

LEARNING
THE ROLE

The childhood shows the man,

As morning shows the day.

JOHN MILTON,

Paradise Regained

'Everybody thinks I was a proper little goody-goody, but they don't really know, do they?' Prince Edward once said of his schooldays. Although he was clearly never an undisciplined child, the implications of his remark are significant. Basic royal training involves learning to disguise one's emotions in public and Edward's quiet exterior often belies his true character. When asked if he got into any scrapes at school, he replied, 'Not many, but that's always the sign of a good criminal, isn't it? Just because I wasn't on punishment doesn't mean I was on the straight and narrow.'

When he reached the age of seven, the Queen decided that Prince Edward was sufficiently well advanced in his studies at Buckingham Palace to begin attending a day school, which would provide a wider curriculum. He was sent to Gibbs Pre-Preparatory School and arrived on his first day in uniform looking confident and smiling (a far cry from Prince Charles's reaction on being taken to Hill House School as a child). Once again, Prince Edward benefited from being joined in the class-room by his cousin, James Ogilvy, who was a friend and ally. Attendance at the small select school in Kensington, a short drive from the Palace, served as a gentle introduction to the education system before he went on to boarding school.

Prince Andrew had not been allowed this period of adjustment. He went straight from the Palace schoolroom to Heatherdown Preparatory School near Ascot as a boarder. Was this because Prince Andrew's ebullient personality made an induction period seem unnecessary, or could it have been the Queen's reluctance to see her youngest son leave the nest? At Gibbs, Edward had the benefit of an outside education, learned to socialise with his contemporaries, but still came home to the palace each evening. While Andrew joined the cubs and later became a boy scout, and was allowed to stay with friends at weekends, (as when he visited Katie Seymour, a classmate in the Palace schoolroom, at her home on the Isle of Wight), Edward was the one who always seemed to stay at home with mother.

Despite his quiet confidence in public, Edward was an energetic child. Sharing the nursery with his mischievous brother Andrew meant that there were frequent fights and outbursts of youthful rivalry. Andrew occasionally taunted and teased his younger brother. He would summon footmen on wild goose chases to empty rooms and then blame Edward. Eventually Edward began to stand up for himself and would wrestle his bigger brother to the ground. Andrew's practical jokes were legendary, and even in adulthood his antics have not always found favour, most notably when he sprayed press photographers in Los Angeles with white paint, causing hundreds of pounds worth of damage to their equipment, which the Queen had to pay for. Many hoped that Andrew would calm down and learn some discipline when he went to boarding school. Edward's pranks were less outrageous, but he shared his family's love of practical jokes. Although his teachers were given instructions that he was to be treated in exactly the same way as other children, Edward realised that the staff would not dare to be too strict with the monarch's son.

Even from his earliest schooldays Prince Edward was treated differently. If the children's names ever appeared on a list for any reason, his was always the only one not to include a surname. The ever-present personal detective standing guard over the playground or watching from the sidelines during sport was to be a permanent feature of the Prince's life, as was

the small contingent of press photographers that waited outside the school to photograph the royal pupil. However much
Edward tried to behave like the other children his royal upbringing always set him apart. 'You can't have it both ways,' said
the Duke of Edinburgh in a television interview. 'We try to keep
the children out of the public eye so that they can grow up as
normal as possible, but if you are going to have a monarchy you
have got to have a family and the family's got to be in the public
eye.'

Unlike someone who joins the Royal Family through marriage, Edward has never known anything other than the royal
way of life. To him it is normality. When he was at Gibbs the
children were asked to draw a house. While everyone else drew
a normal-size, instantly recognisable house, Edward drew a
palace, yet he did not realise what was different about his
picture. Even today he still calls Buckingham Palace 'the
House', and could not understand why, when he worked at the
Palace Theatre in London and made telephone calls, his colleagues would smile when he said, 'It's Edward here from the
Palace.'

At the age of six Prince Edward's finances were already the
subject of public debate. Shortly after the *Royal Family* documentary had been screened Prince Philip had surprised Americans by claiming publicly that the Windsors were 'going into the
red'. Traditionally the Royal Family's Civil List Allowance was
established on the monarch's accession and remained un-
changed for the entire reign. In 1936 when Edward's grandfather, George VI, came to the throne his Civil List annuity
amounted to £410,000 a year and remained the same until his
death; in 1952 Queen Elizabeth II's was set at £475,000 and it
was assumed that no increase would be necessary. However
inflation in the late 1960s meant that the allowance was no
longer sufficient to cover the expenses of royal duty, so a Select
Committee was established in 1970 to look into the Royal
Family's finances. The Committee's findings in 1971 were that
the Civil List Allowance should be doubled and reviewed as and
when necessary. The Queen's allocation was increased to
£980,000; and, although seven-year-old Prince Edward was
unaware of it, the allowance he was due to receive at the age of
eighteen doubled overnight to £20,000 a year. Already it was

being taken for granted that he would undertake royal duties, and his future continued to be mapped out for him by tradition.

After a year at Gibbs, Prince Edward and James Ogilvy both followed Prince Andrew to Heatherdown Preparatory School near Ascot. Yet another royal cousin, George, Earl of St. Andrews, the eldest son of Edward's godmother, the Duchess of Kent, was also a pupil there. Heatherdown had originally been selected for Prince Andrew because of its proximity to Windsor Castle, and with so many royal pupils under one roof appropriate security arrangements were already in place. However this did not prevent the IRA threatening on more than one occasion to kidnap one of the prestigious pupils. The threats meant that by the time Prince Edward arrived as a boarder, on 15 September 1972, even greater security precautions had to be taken.

Prince Edward arrived at the school with his parents on a Friday afternoon, which gave him the weekend to settle in before classes started on Monday. Whereas Princess Anne had been late on her first day at boarding school because the royal car had been forced to stop so that she could be sick, Prince Edward showed no outward signs of nerves as he was greeted by the headmaster, James Edwards. Nevertheless this must have been a difficult period for him. After a summer in the tranquil atmosphere of Balmoral, having only ever shared an apartment (never even the same room) with his brother, suddenly having to sleep in a boys' dormitory must have been an alarming prospect. Not only did the Prince lose his privacy for the first time, he also faced a completely new regime.

At Heatherdown there was a strict timetable. Sharing a small room with six other pupils, Edward was woken each day at 7.15 a.m. The boys dressed in identical grey suits with white shirts and red school ties. After breakfast there were lessons until 12.30 p.m. The Prince studied mathematics, geometry, English, history, geography, physics, biology, and scripture, subjects chosen to provide a good general education in addition to preparing him for the 'O' and 'A' level courses that he would eventually take. In the Palace schoolroom he had studied basic French grammar at the Queen's insistence and this was continued at Heatherdown. As a result the Prince now speaks the language fluently. He also studied Latin and took lessons in music and woodwork. Although his academic record at Heatherdown was unremarkable, he was conscientious, and had clearly benefited from the discipline of his first small class with a governess. His general aptitude was for English and history rather than mathematics or the sciences.

Most afternoons at Heatherdown there were various sports, according to the season. It was here that Prince Edward started to play rugby for the first time and before long he was playing as wing three-quarter for his house. He has never enjoyed football and does not share his family's love of polo, but at Heatherdown he proved to be surprisingly good at cricket. He and Prince Andrew had both played with friends at Burton Court in Chelsea on the Brigade of Guards' ground and later had private coaching with Len Muncer, the former Glamorgan county player, at Lords. Again, because they were royal, the boys received the best training available. When members of the Royal Family wanted to learn tennis they turned to Dan Maskell for coaching, and champion motor racer Graham Hill taught Prince Andrew to drive. Heatherdown was set in 30 acres of grounds and had its own football, rugby and cricket pitches, but Edward most enjoyed the fact that the Victorian building also had its own swimming pool. In the evenings, supper was at 6 p.m., followed by a period of private study, before bedtime at 8 p.m. Evening activities were occasionally arranged, but television was allowed only on a 'controlled basis'. Edward quickly fitted into the strict regime. Only the presence of his personal detective singled him out.

According to the rule, Edward was only allowed home for one weekend each term, but as the Royal Family were usually at Windsor Castle, only 7 miles away, Andrew and Edward would frequently be collected by car and taken to have tea with the Queen on a Saturday or Sunday afternoon, on condition that they returned to the school by 6.30 p.m. Invariably Edward would also be required at family gathering, a royal wedding or ceremony, and would be granted special leave of absence. On 20 November 1972, for example, he was included in the Queen and Prince Philip's Silver Wedding celebrations. No other boys were afforded such treatment. On his birthday in March the Queen's chef always prepared a large cake for Edward to take back to school which added to his popularity. Occasionally a friend would be taken to have tea at Windsor, but never with 'mother'.

It was at Heatherdown that Prince Edward, nicknamed 'Earl' because of his initials (**E**dward **A**ntony **R**ichard **L**ouis), first displayed a real interest in the theatre. After taking part in a school concert he received a certificate for giving the best performance. James Edwards, the headmaster, insisted that the Prince had not been honoured because of his family but in recognition of his genuine acting abilities. Certainly if Edward had given an appalling performance the award would have been difficult to justify. His talents remained unknown to the public, with Prince Charles being considered the actor of the family at that time after his well-publicised comedy performances while at Trinity College, Cambridge. On stage Prince Edward felt that people were watching him as a character, not as royalty, and he enjoyed the sensation.

Going to Heatherdown was the greatest challenge he had faced as yet. He was young enough not to be self-conscious and in many ways coped with the experience better than the other boys. Edward was used to never being alone, having always been in the company of Mabel Anderson, a nurserymaid or a footman when not with his family. He also found it quite easy to fit in with the school timetable because so much of royal life has to comply with a tight schedule. The greatest adjustment he had to make was to the noise. The corridors of Buckingham Palace have the hushed and tranquil atmosphere of a museum, with even the nursery lift slowed down to a genteel pace. Staff walk silently, although they no longer have to remain 'out of sight' as they did in previous reigns. (In the old days they even had to hide behind pillars if there was any danger of encountering a member of the Royal Family in the corridor!) Royalty themselves speak quietly in case their private conversations should be overheard by the staff.

At Heatherdown Prince Edward was initially very consscious of the constant clamour of boys' voices and the clanging of bells. He was also embarrassed about having to undress in front of others in the dormitory. In addition, as his brothers and sister had discovered before him, having to talk innocuously about his family was very hard. He could never let slip any intimate details about his homelife, or even discuss future family plans.

At times when this necessary reticence meant that he could not join in with certain conversations, his silence was thought to be due to sullenness. It was in fact almost certainly due to frustration.

Schooldays for Princes can be very lonely. Although rarely alone in a physical sense they can feel mentally isolated by their position. Consequently their circle of close friends tends to remain small, with no room for misjudgment. Young boys have a habit of repeating to their parents conversations that they have had at school, and not all parents can be relied upon to be discreet. In the spring of 1973 Prince Edward was privy to a royal secret. His sister Princess Anne was to marry, but even if other boys quizzed him over the rumours of romance Edward had to deny all knowledge. That January the then Lieutenant Mark Phillips had been a guest at Sandringham over New Year, which had prompted press speculation. This was fuelled when the Princess later drove him to Harwich where he was joining his regiment for the journey to Germany and kissed him goodbye on the dockside. The Buckingham Palace press office issued a formal denial, and even when the couple were quizzed at the Badminton Horse Trials that April they shrugged off all rumours.

This was to be one of Anne's lowest points in media relations, especially when she shouted at reporters while on a visit to Cirencester, 'I don't know why I am being subjected to this nonsensical treatment. This is what raises my blood pressure. I'm just sitting here doing nothing.' Despite all Princess Anne's denials, Buckingham Palace announced a month later than she and Mark Phillips were engaged and would be married in Westminster Abbey on 14 November, Prince Charles's twenty-fifth birthday. Throughout the episode Prince Edward had to maintain a discreet silence. Even as the wedding approached and he learned more of the plans he had to keep the information to himself.

At the ceremony Edward made his major public debut. He was by now attending the Trooping the Colour ceremony each June, and had already presented trophies at a Windsor polo match, but this was the first ceremony in which he played a significant part. Preferring simplicity, Princess Anne had dismissed the idea of a string of bridesmaids, and chose to have

Prince Edward and Lady Sarah Armstrong-Jones as her only two attendants. Looking the part of a traditional pageboy, Edward was kitted out with full Highland Dress, including a kilt in the Royal Stewart Tartan, and even a miniature dirk tucked into his right sock. Lady Sarah wore a white pinafore dress and a jewelled Juliet cap, to match Princess Anne's Tudor-style wedding dress. Arriving in a carriage behind the bride and her father, Prince Edward and Lady Sarah joined the procession at the West Door of the Abbey. On reaching the Sacrarium the press noted that Edward and Sarah 'stood like statues throughout the wedding service', adding that it was only something that children with 'their background and training could manage'. At the wedding of the Duke and Duchess of York in 1986, at which Edward was best man, the press equally noted how badly behaved Prince William was, while Princess Anne's own children acted impeccably.

Only once at Princess Anne's wedding did Edward display any sign of uncertainty. Immediately after the couple had been pronounced man and wife by the then Archbishop of Canterbury, Dr Michael Ramsey, they progressed into the Chapel of Edward the Confessor for the signing of the register. As Anne and Mark moved off, Edward looked at Sarah, not knowing whether or not they should follow, then glanced at his mother for guidance. A nod from the Queen indicated that they too should follow, and the two attendants signed their names on the documents for posterity before returning to Buckingham Palace for the traditional appearance on the balcony, and the wedding breakfast of lobster and partridge. That evening, once the happy couple had departed for their honeymoon – spending the first night at Thatched House Lodge, the home of Princess Alexandra – Prince Edward joined his family at a party to celebrate Prince Charles's birthday. The return to Heatherdown that weekend was an anti-climax.

Edward has always been closer to his sister than to his brothers. With an age gap of some sixteen years, Edward felt, as a schoolboy, that Prince Charles was more like an uncle than an elder brother. When Edward was born Charles was a boarder at Gordonstoun School in Scotland. Then, in 1966, Charles spent six months in Australia, before going to Cambridge the following autumn for three years, after which he went into the services for five years. By the time Charles left the Navy in 1977, Prince Edward was himself a boarder at Gordonstoun. Consequently, to Edward, Charles seemed of a different generation. Although he is closer to Prince Andrew the two have very different characters.

Princess Anne is more of a kindred spirit. When Edward was a child Anne spent a great deal of time with him during her school holidays from Benenden, becoming almost a surrogate mother when the Queen was away. The two are very alike in temperament. Neither will suffer fools gladly, and each has a fiery temper when aroused. Both have a stern exterior that can mask their deep compassion and caring nature. They also share a love of horses and a preference for competitive individual sports rather than team games.

Not surprisingly, when Princess Anne married, Edward became a frequent visitor during school holidays to their first home, Oak Grove House at Sandhurst, and later to Gatcombe Park which is still the Princess's home today even though her marriage has ended. In Anne's house Edward could relax. He enjoyed the lack of formality and the peace of the Gloucestershire countryside. When the Queen was presented with an Arab mare while on a Middle East tour she passed it on to Edward, who kept it stabled at Gatcombe Park so that he would always have a horse to ride when visiting his sister. It was at Gatcombe that Edward had his first taste of romance. During his school holidays one of his riding companions was Princess Anne's stable girl, Shelley Whitborn. For a while the two youngsters were said to be 'dating', but whether it was puppy love or just a teenage friendship there was never any serious future for the Prince and the stable girl.

Throughout his life, if there has been a problem Princess Anne is the one Edward has turned to. She now has an office (and keeps much of her official wardrobe) on the same floor as Prince Edward's suite at Buckingham Palace. When time allows in her busy schedule she will visit her younger brother for a chat, and since the breakdown of her marriage she will often stay the night at the Palace (rather than drive home to Gatcombe) if she has several days of engagements in London. It is significant that when Edward left the Royal Marines and needed time to gather his thoughts he went, not to Sandringham with the Queen, but to Gatcombe Park with Princess Anne.

In the year of Princess Anne's marriage Edward was taken to Cowes for the first time to take part in the annual yachting regatta off the north coast of the Isle of Wight. Prince Philip had borrowed a racing yacht for the event and this was the beginning of Edward's love affair with the sea. Not only does he enjoy yachting, but he now goes water-skiing and windsurfing whenever possible. Cowes Week has had royal patronage almost since its inception. In 1817 King George IV (then Prince Regent) and his brother the Duke of Clarence (later William IV) joined the Yacht Club, which in 1820 duly became the Royal Yacht Club. Today yachtsmen compete for the Britannia Cup, first presented in 1951 by Edward's grandfather King George VI, and the America's Cup. Prince Edward now attends each year and stays on the Royal Yacht *Britannia* with members of the Royal Family, the event marking the start of their annual summer holiday.

Bachelor Princes' choice of female guests for Cowes Week can often prove to be significant. In August 1980 Lady Diana Spencer was Prince Charles's guest for the regatta, although the press took little heed of her at the time. A former Prince of Wales, King Edward VII, owned a number of racing yachts and used the regatta to indulge in more than one sport. His mistress, Lillie Langtry, rented a small cottage opposite West Cowes Castle for the event. Prince Edward has been much more discreet over his choice of guests.

That same year another person became a dominant feature in Prince Edward's life. Police Constable Andrew Merrylees, then aged thirty-three, was appointed bodyguard to the nine-year-old Prince. He remained Edward's personal protection officer for the next eighteen years until November 1991 and when the time of parting came it proved distressing for both. The two had built up a great rapport and Edward had learned to trust the tall, gentle bodyguard implicitly. One of Andrew Merrylees' first jobs was to teach Edward to ski and from then onwards he remained a constant companion throughout the Prince's schooldays, college years and working life. As a result he became friend and confidant as much as bodyguard. If Edward went mountain climbing, Merrylees climbed too; if he flew abroad, the bodyguard was a few paces behind him throughout; even when Prince Edward joined the Royal Marines, Andrew Merrylees inevitably went too. Because he needed security protection throughout his life, Edward was to see more of his bodyguard than anyone in his own family. When Edward passed an examination at school, it is said that Andrew Merrylees was even more excited and proud of the achievement than Prince Philip. After Heatherdown Prince Edward went through the remainder of his education without any royal relatives in the classroom and it was Andrew Merrylees who provided continuity and stability.

Prince Edward's final year at Heatherdown coincided with the Queen's Silver Jubilee of 1977, marking her twenty-five years on the throne. It was by far the most eventful year he had yet experienced, starting with a two-week skiing holiday in the Italian Alps, a package tour organised by his school. The kidnapping of children with wealthy parents was commonplace in Italy and as the Prince was an obvious target he was forced to travel incognito. Details of their private visit were not released to the press and he travelled under the name of 'Edward Bishop'. On the ski slopes Edward stood out from the other boys as the only one to have a burly bodyguard always skiing behind him. Andrew Merrylees was not prepared to take any risks.

It was a year of street parties and celebrations as the nation expressed their loyalty and affection for their monarch. Even though Edward had by now accepted the constant interest in his family, he was still over-awed by the reception they received throughout Jubilee Year. On Monday 6 June, the eve of Jubilee Day, he stood wide-eyed in the back of an open-topped car behind the Queen as they drove down the Long Walk in Windsor Great Park, escorted by thirty-six young people carrying flaming torches. At 10 p.m. he watched as his mother lit a bonfire, just as Queen Elizabeth I had done in 1588 to warn her subjects of the approaching Spanish Armada, and heard an hour later that 102 beacons had been lit across the country as far as Saxavord in the Shetlands to mark the official commencement of Jubilee celebrations. Bonfires continued to be lit throughout the Commonwealth as the Royal Family sat at the foot of a statue of George III to watch a spectacular firework display. Unknown to them, five million visitors had arrived in London that day for the Jubilee. London had seen nothing like it since the Coronation.

That year Queen Elizabeth II was to have little time for her family. In February and March she visited Tonga, Fiji, New Zealand and Australia; in October she toured Canada, the Bahamas, the Virgin Islands, Antigua and Barbados. In the months between she travelled the length and breadth of Britain at an unrelenting pace, from Portsmouth to Strathclyde, from Norwich to Newcastle. She reviewed the Army in Germany, attended a musical pageant performed by 17,000 school-children in Liverpool, met the cast of *Coronation Street* in Manchester and went on a walkabout in Dyfed. On one Thursday in June, for example, a series of festivities began for her in Greenwich at 10.30 a.m. and she did not return to Buckingham Palace until 11 p.m., after more than twelve hours of non-stop handshaking, small talk, receiving bouquets and meeting dignitaries, ending with yet another firework display in the presence of 750,000 onlookers. During this time Prince Edward saw more of his mother in the newspapers and on television than in the flesh. For this reason he was present at more public engagements than ever before.

Amid the year-long celebrations, Tuesday 7 June was designated 'Jubilee Day' and Prince Edward joined the entire Royal Family at a Thanksgiving Service in St Paul's Cathedral. Seven carriages left Buckingham Palace at 10.25 a.m., the Prince travelling in the seventh with the Queen Mother and his two brothers, theirs reputedly receiving the loudest cheers recorded by a decibel counter. Finally the Queen emerged in the Golden Coach, built in 1762 and last seen at her Coronation, to the most enthusiastic welcome of the day. After the pomp, the pageantry, and a lunch with the Lord Mayor of London at the Guildhall, came the sight that was to leave a lasting impression. As Edward walked out on to the balcony of Buckingham Palace with his family, more than one million people thronged into the Mall outside. There were crowds as far as the eye could see, and all there for the love of one woman: his mother.

Two months later, on 10 August, Prince Edward was present when the Queen went on a Jubilee visit to Northern Ireland. Eighty people had already been killed in Ulster that year and the planned two-day trip was threatened with cancellation several times. In the end it was one of the biggest security operations ever mounted, with nearly 32,500 soldiers and policemen protecting the royal visitors. For the first time in her life the Queen had to be transported by helicopter rather than car for reasons of safety. In the event of trouble she could be quickly airlifted away from the scene. Again, for security reasons, the Queen was not allowed to sleep on Irish soil and used the royal yacht *Britannia* as a floating base. The Queen and Prince Philip visited Londonderry, Belfast and Coleraine, and while Prince Andrew was allowed to join them on the afternoon of the second day (attending a Youth Festival of 1,800 people), Prince Edward was confined to the royal yacht. Due to an IRA bomb threat at the University of Ulster the Queen was not prepared to put her youngest son at risk. Once again, Edward could not be shielded from the tension his family suffered or ignore the intense security that surrounded their floating base. It was with a sense of relief that they finally arrived in the Western Isles for a brief respite in Scotland. The next day most of the front page of the *Daily Express* was taken up with a cartoon of Queen Victoria giving Queen Elizabeth II a medal 'For courage beyond the call of duty'.

If the Queen was able to relax at Balmoral that August, the same cannot be said of Edward. Earlier in the summer he had spent his final term at Heatherdown and was now destined to follow his father and elder brothers to Gordonstoun, a school renowned for its tough character-building regime. Before he could be accepted, Edward had to pass a common entrance examination, for which royal status was not taken into consideration. From Prince Charles had come stories of physical torture at Gordonstoun, early morning runs before breakfast wearing just shorts whatever the weather, followed by ice-cold showers. Although Prince Andrew had been a pupil since 1973 and enthused about the school, he had a greater resilience and aptitude for physical activity.

As he grew older Prince Edward appeared to become more introverted. The once happy-go-lucky blond-haired boy gradually developed into a lanky, thoughtful teenager, his hair darkening to mid-brown almost symbolically. While Andrew was being tagged the 'Clown Prince', Edward already appeared much more mature in his behaviour. At a party to celebrate the Queen's Silver Jubilee Edward watched his brother become slowly inebriated and noted the hangover Andrew suffered the following day. As a direct result Edward has only ever consumed alcohol in moderation. Edward was also aware of the reputation his brother was gaining, as reports were leaked to the press of Andrew kicking a football through the greenhouse at Windsor and putting detergent in the swimming pool. At Gordonstoun he was nicknamed 'The Sniggerer' because he constantly told jokes. Spending two terms at Lakefield College in Canada, he became known as 'Randy Andy' after going out in a small boat with a girl and a bowl of cherries. Although Edward teased his brother about the incidents, he was subconsciously learning how not to behave. Those close to the Royal Family felt that, when the Queen had Prince Andrew, the novelty of having another child after ten years meant that he was occasionally spoiled, and developed a defiant streak as a result. By the time Edward was born more attention was paid to discipline.

As if to mark Prince Edward's departure from prep school and childhood, Mabel Anderson left the Queen's employ in September 1977. She had been a part of Edward's life since his birth, but at the age of thirteen he had no need of a nanny. With Princess Anne's first child due in November, Mabel moved to Gatcombe Park to establish the nursery there, and her presence was another reason why Edward so enjoyed his holiday retreats to Gloucestershire. Prince Edward's first nephew, Peter Phillips, was born on 15 November. By this time Edward had been at Gordonstoun for two months and was allowed no leave of absence to celebrate the birth.

It was with a certain amount of trepidation that Edward went to Gordonstoun that September. At Heatherdown he had been just 7 miles from Windsor, but at Gordonstoun he would be 595 miles from his family. In the past it had been described as 'the toughest school on earth' and 'a gymnasium of muscles and morals', and although the cold showers Prince Charles had endured were now warm, the emphasis on physical fitness remained. The prospect seemed daunting at the time, but the passing of the years had mellowed the school's regimes and the

philosophy of self-improvement suited Edward's temperament. Although traditional team sports were played at the
school, Dr Kurt Hahn, the original founder, believed that
competition brought out the worst in boys. They were therefore
encouraged to compete against themselves, for example, in
athletics. They threw the javelin, discus and shot, and they did
long jump, high jump and the triple jump, but to improve their
own individual performance rather than compete with others.
If they cheated then they cheated themselves. Discipline, too,
was based on trust. If any boy broke a school rule then he had to
walk around the school grounds for anything up to three hours,
supposedly thinking pure thoughts. No pressure was put on the
boys to carry out this punishment – it was entirely a matter for
their own conscience – but it says much for the system that
pupils did do the required walk. There is no record of Prince
Edward being punished in this way.

Dr Kurt Hahn had established the school in 1934 with just a
handful of students, one of whom was Prince Philip. Hahn was
originally born in Berlin in 1886 and was himself educated at
Christ Church, Oxford, and the University of Heidelberg.
During the First World War he worked for the German Foreign
Office, before becoming Private Secretary to Prince Max of
Baden (Prince Philip's brother-in-law), the last Imperial Chancellor of Germany. After the war, Hahn and Prince Max
established a co-educational boarding school at Salem, near
Lake Constance, based on Hahn's theory that pupils had the
ability to realise their own potential. Salem eventually became
known as one of the best private schools in Europe and Prince
Philip's education would have continued there when he
reached the age of thirteen. However Dr Hahn was strongly
opposed to the Nazi regime in Germany, and in 1933 he was
arrested and imprisoned for 'the decadent corruption of German youth', only being released after intervention from the
then British Prime Minister, Ramsay MacDonald. He fled to
Britain and decided to found a new public school based on the
same principles as Salem, a school that would 'train men for
leadership'.

The 300-acre estate at Gordonstoun near Elgin was once
known as 'the Bog of Plewlands' and stands in the biting winds
of Morayshire. There was a towerhouse dating from the fif-

teenth century, a dilapidated manorhouse, the Do'ecotes, which had originally been built in 1616 for George Gordon, 1st Marquis of Huntley, and the remains of earlier buildings dating from the mid-thirteenth century. The house was substantially extended in 1638 by George Gordon's cousin, Sir Robert Gordon. Having changed the name to Gordonstoun, Sir Robert became the 1st Baron. His son, also called Sir Robert Gordon and known as 'the Warlock Laird', built the Round Square which now houses dormitories, classrooms and a library. Legend has it that Sir Robert, while a student in Padua, struck a bargain with the Devil. In return for 'the hidden secrets of the universe that the King of Heaven has denied to men' the Devil was promised Sir Robert's soul. Sir Robert therefore constructed a round building, instead of the traditional square, as a 'mathematical sanctuary' in which the devil would be unable to catch him. However the Devil won in the end by capturing him outside the Round Square, supposedly in 1704.

When Kurt Hahn took over the estate in 1934 it needed a great deal of money spent on it. There were few facilities and few pupils. Some came on the strength of Dr Hahn's reputation at Salem; others were boys who had simply failed to get into any other public school. The previous owner, Sir William Gordon Cumming, had been publicly disgraced in the 'Royal Baccarat Scandal' after allegedly cheating during a game of cards with Edward VII. As a result the house had fallen into disrepair, and part of the boys' physical training was the actual reconstruction of the building.

Hahn's approach to education was revolutionary at the time. Self-discipline and a healthy outdoor life were his basic tenets, drawn from the philosophy of Plato:

> *Our youth should dwell in the land of health, amid fair sights and sounds; and beauty, the effluence of fair works, will meet the sense like a breeze, and insensibly draw the soul even in childhood into harmony with the beauty of reason.*

Initially the school was spartan out of necessity, yet even when its finances became healthier, its reputation established, the austere surroundings remained. Hahn felt that physical hardship gave the boys genuine values. 'Some people look for faults,' he would say of his pupils, 'I look for pure gold and I usually find it.' He encouraged boys to discover their own strengths and talents, an emphasis expressed in the school motto *Plus est en vous* – 'There is more in you'. In Prince Charles's days at Gordonstoun (May 1962 to July 1967) the headmaster was Robert Chew, who simply continued the regime that Hahn had established. Boys were woken at 7 a.m. and immediately went on a brief morning run, wearing nothing but shorts and running shoes. This was followed by a cold shower before breakfast. After morning prayers there were five 45-minute lessons and a 'training break' for exercise before lunch. In the afternoon there was sport and manual work on the buildings or grounds. This was followed by two more 45-minute lessons before the evening meal, private study, and then bed at 9.30 p.m. The dormitories were cold and austere, without carpets. The chairman of the Board of Governors once expressed his amazement at the strange sense of values at the school: 'The search for a missing sixpence was carried out as if it were a murder hunt; the careless disposal of a biscuit wrapping treated as if it were the placing of a pound of gelignite.'

By the time Prince Edward arrived at the school in 1977 John Kempe was headmaster, carpets and central heating had been installed, and there was even a heated swimming pool. It was now also co-educational, with sixty girl pupils, including one of Edward's Mountbatten cousins, Amanda Knatchbull. An extensive rebuilding programme in the 1960s had created new houses, laboratories and classrooms. Although the emphasis on sport and physical activity predominated, seamanship was included in the curriculum and the school now had its own yacht, *Sea Spirit*, which Edward (already an experienced sailor) was able to use. There were expeditions and the pupils took part in local sea rescues. In March 1978 it was announced that John Kempe would retire at Christmas and he was replaced by Michael Mavor who, at thirty-one, was the youngest headmaster ever to take charge of a leading public school. With him, yet more of Hahn's tough measures were removed. The emphasis on self-improvement remained, however. Boys continued to be awarded colours for being 'good' and 'honest' and could even be awarded colours by their fellow pupils. In most schools colours were given for sporting achievements but, with his hatred of competitiveness, Hahn had seen that they were only given for personal qualities.

The famous early morning run still existed at Gordonstoun, but Edward was relieved to discover that it was now only expected in fine weather. Unlike Prince Philip's time at the school, when there were less than twenty-five pupils, Gordonstoun now had 400 boys and girls, many from overseas. Through one of the frequent overseas exchanges Prince Andrew was able to spend two terms at Lakefield College in Canada. Many more sporting options were open to Prince Edward too. He learned how to play golf, and as a member of the Air Cadet Corps took an Air Cadet Proficiency Gliding Course in the summer of 1980, when he made his first solo flight and earned his glider wings. The headmaster, John Kempe, said, 'Every child can excel at something. It is our job to find out what and bring it out.' Having had a taste of flying at Gordonstoun, Prince Edward went on to take an intensive flying training course at the Basic Flying Training School at Cranwell. Here, at eighteen, he was taught in a Bulldog two-seater piston-engined trainer, and in July 1982 gained his private pilot's licence. During the spring and summer of 1984 he continued his flying training at university to the Air Squadron's Preliminary Flying Badge standard, with a sense of personal achievement and satisfaction that Kurt Hahn would have been proud of.

While Prince Edward quietly adapted to life at Gordonstoun, Prince Andrew was gaining a 'Casanova' reputation and becoming known as 'the one with the Robert Redford looks'. When Edward returned home to London for the Christmas holidays in the first year, during which he was also present at Peter Phillips's christening in the Music Room at Buckingham Palace, his brother was dating a fellow pupil, Kirsty Richmond, who spent a few days with them at Sandringham over New Year. By the time Easter came, and Edward returned to Windsor to be confirmed on 5 April in St George's Chapel by the then Archbishop of Canterbury, Donald Coggan, his brother had another female guest. Cleo Nathaniels, again a fellow pupil at Gordonstoun, joined Andrew and Edward at a cross-country riding event organised by the North Warwickshire Hunt in which Prince Charles was competing. Five days later Prince

Edward was at the Badminton Horse Trials wearing a tweed cap and watching Princess Anne compete. The press noted how Edward had grown up during his time at Gordonstoun and revealed that he was already being taught to drive by Prince Philip. At the same time royal 'expert' Michèle Brown noted that he enjoyed 'bird-watching and skateboarding'. It was still hard to believe how quickly the baby of the family was maturing.

Although Gordonstoun was far enough from London to escape day-to-day media reporting, the school was to find itself at the centre of a scandal in the autumn of 1978 when five boys and one girl were expelled for possessing cannabis. Although neither Edward nor Andrew were implicated, the fact that they were pupils at the school led to wider media coverage than the incident might otherwise have received. One of the boys was the son of Stavros Niarchos, the Greek shipping tycoon and friend of the Royal Family. Although expulsion was humiliating, especially from a school where so much emphasis was placed on personal pride, 15-year-old Constantine Niarchos was flown away from the school in his father's private jet. Edward and Andrew speculated that they would not have been honoured with such a luxurious departure under similar circumstances, royal or not.

That summer the two Princes did, however, travel with the Queen and Prince Philip to Canada for the Edmonton Commonwealth Games. It was Edward's second visit to the country, having previously visited in July 1976 with the Prince of Wales to watch their sister compete in the Montreal Olympic Games. Never having travelled further than Germany and Lichtenstein (a private visit with Prince Philip in April 1978) it was the longest trip he had ever made. Initially there were no plans to take Edward. The Queen had considered that a major world event such as the Olympic Games was too public an occasion to expose her young son to. He was to remain behind at Buckingham Palace, but Edward had other ideas. He spoke to Prince Charles about it.

'Why can't I go to the Olympics too? Why should I be left out?'

Prince Charles sympathised with his young brother and telephoned the Queen, who was already in Canada. The conversation is unrecorded, but when the Prince of Wales stepped off the plane in Montreal Prince Edward was by his side.

By the time of the Commonwealth Games of 1978 there was no question of Edward remaining behind. This time the Canadian press also noted his increased maturity. He had no need to impress people as Charles did; he made no attempt to win them over with his personality like Andrew. Instead he displayed a quiet confidence which caused one Canadian journalist to describe Edward as 'more Princely' than his brothers. Those who knew him attributed his manner to personal strength and determination. When Prince Charles celebrated his thirtieth birthday in November 1978 Edward again resolved not to be left out and travelled 600 miles just to be at the party, having obtained special leave of absence from Gordonstoun. Three hundred and fifty guests were serenaded by two bands and the Three Degrees.

Increasingly Edward's strong will would assert itself. Once, after a school holiday when he had not wanted to return to Heatherdown, he had simply refused to go. Neither Mabel Anderson nor Michael Perry, the nursery footman, could persuade him. He held tightly to his bed and had to be physically dragged away. Once inside the nursery lift he clung tightly to a rail and refused to come out. Eventually the Queen had to be summoned and after a few quiet words together Edward finally agreed to go. 'That was very painful indeed,' said the Queen as she waved goodbye to her son. Although he was less dramatic about returning to Gordonstoun after the holidays he was still reluctant to leave his family. Staff noted how he would suddenly develop a cold or stomach upset as the day of departure approached. In a television interview Edward very pointedly said, 'A school is a school. I don't agree with the statement that schooldays are the happiest days of your life.'

Nicknamed 'Educated Eddie' by the media and 'Jaws' by his friends at school because of the brace he was forced to wear to straighten his teeth, Edward was a conscientious pupil. He was also considered to be popular, due to lack of affectation (in marked contrast to Prince Andrew who many thought arrogant). Edward was not brilliant academically, but he was at least able to narrow his curriculum down to subjects that he enjoyed. After obtaining nine 'O' levels in 1980 he concentrated

49

on English literature, history, politics and economics for 'A' level. As at Heatherdown, Prince Edward took an active part in drama while at Gordonstoun, playing the lead in both Peter Shaffer's *Black Comedy* and the Feydeau face *Hotel Paradiso*. He was already gaining experience for a theatrical career, but in the immediate future he had to achieve good enough 'A' level grades to get into university. In November 1978 it had been announced that Prince Andrew hoped for a career in the Royal Navy, but Prince Edward preferred to follow the path taken by his elder brother and gain a degree at Cambridge first. Although it seemed unlikely that members of the Royal Family would ever require academic qualifications to gain employment, three years at university delayed the moment when a career decision would have to be made and, more importantly, provided an opportunity to broaden their experience of life. For as long as Prince Edward could continue in education lost amid a crowd of students, he also had a certain amount of freedom that would be denied him later on.

At the beginning of 1981 a major revolution took place within the Royal Family when Prince Charles became engaged to Lady Diana Spencer. No one at the time could have foreseen how a girl, not yet twenty-one, would take the world by storm. Interest in her was to be expected during the months preceding the wedding, but more than ten years on the public fascination with the girl who will one day be Queen has not abated.

Prince Edward first met Lady Diana Spencer during Cowes Week in August 1980, when she was the Prince of Wales's guest, and a few weeks later she joined the Royal Family on holiday at Balmoral. It was a particularly poignant time for the family, for 27 August marked the first anniversary of Lord Louis Mountbatten's assassination by the IRA, a tragedy which had affected them all very deeply. No one had been more saddened than Prince Charles who had called Lord Louis his 'Honorary Grandfather'. The horrors of that day twelve months earlier were foremost in all their minds and Diana's presence at the Castle did much to ease the suffering. It also marked the beginning of her romance with Prince Charles.

With an age difference of barely two and a half years, Diana and Edward had an instant rapport. In many ways she was far more in tune with Edward's generation than that of the man

who would one day be her husband. Diana liked Edward's dry
sense of humour and his ability to send himself up. She was
amused by the way he teased his elder brother, and Royal-
watchers later noted that Prince Edward's girlfriends tended to
be Diana lookalikes. At the wedding itself in St Paul's Cathedral
on 29 July 1981 Prince Edward acted as a supporter to Prince
Charles, a royal best man, a role he shared with Prince Andrew.
The two stood just behind Prince Charles throughout the
ceremony and it was the first time many of the 500 million
people around the world who watched the ceremony on television had really seen Edward since Princess Anne's wedding
eight years earlier. Now seventeen, with thick dark blond hair,
vivid blue eyes and already a fraction taller than Prince Andrew,
journalists began to declare him 'the most handsome of the
Queen's children' – hardly a flattering remark on Prince
Charles's wedding day but certainly a boost to Edward's ego.

At the wedding breakfast afterwards at Buckingham Palace,
Edward and Andrew stood at the door with football rattles and
took it in turns to announce the guests. 'One King in Exile,'
shouted Edward as Uncle 'Tino', King Constantine of Greece,
entered. 'One King of Norway. One Queen of Denmark . . .'
Later they teased Diana for calling Prince Charles 'Philip'
during the wedding ceremony. 'You've just married my father,'
Prince Andrew joked. When the new Prince and Princess of
Wales departed in a carriage for the first stage of their honeymoon, Edward and Andrew decorated it with silver gas-filled
balloons. On the back of the carriage they had hung a 'Just
Married' sign, written hastily in red lipstick. Was it Princess
Anne's colour, some wondered.

That autumn Edward returned to Gordonstoun for his final
year, unaware that as a direct result of his new sister-in-law the
probing media spotlight would turn away from the Queen and
focus mercilessly on the younger generation of the Royal Family. Although the residents of Buckingham Palace had been
likened to a 'soap opera' by Malcolm Muggeridge as far back as
1956, twenty-five years later his assessment had a certain ring of
truth. Until Diana's arrival, royal wardrobes had been merely
functional. Yes, we vaguely knew that the Queen was dressed by
Hardy Amies or Norman Hartnell, she chose bright colours
that would make her stand out in a crowd and selected designs

that might photograph well in black and white but no one genuinely believed that one of the monarch's roles was to be a leader of fashion. Occasionally people copied Princess Anne's hats or dressed their babies in yellow if royal mothers did, but it did not reach cult proportions until the advent of a glamorous Princess of Wales.

From 1981 no newspaper report of a royal event omitted to mention what Diana was wearing and who had designed it. Until that time scarcely a word was said about the attire of Princes. They generally wore suits in public and there was no interest in who the tailor was, but in the years A.D. (After Diana) if Prince Edward was seen wearing a ready-made suit from Burtons, or was spotted going into the prestigious London tailors Hawes and Curtis in Burlington Gardens, it was considered newsworthy. Fashion experts dipped their pens in vitriol when he committed the unforgivable sin of wearing brown shoes with black trousers. It was an aspect of life he had not previously considered.

In his final year at Gordonstoun Prince Edward was appointed head boy, or 'guardian' in the language of the school. It was an honour both Prince Philip and Prince Charles had received before him, although not Prince Andrew. The first half of 1982 was intended to be a period of intense study for Edward so that he would obtain respectable grades in his 'A' level examinations that June. Without them there would be little hope of getting a place at Cambridge, royal or not. Contrary to popular belief, there was never any question of false marking or leniency with his work. The Prince's examination papers were always submitted anonymously with the other boys' so that no preferential treatment could be given.

Although Edward spent much of his time studying in the Round Square library, unexpected events at home were to dominate his thoughts. On 2 April Argentina invaded the Falkland Islands, precipitating a conflict over sovereignty. The invasion caused humiliation for the British Foreign Office and led to the resignation of Foreign Secretary, Lord Carrington. Within three days a task force of thirty ships containing 6,000 troops set off on the 8,000-mile journey to defend British territory. One of those men was Edward's brother, Prince Andrew.

A photograph of the Queen, Prince Andrew and Prince Edward taken by Cecil Beaton to commemorate Edward's christening in 1964. Cecil Beaton noted that Prince Edward was 'alert, curious and already a character'.
(Camera Press, London)

*Prince Edward's official 18th birthday photographs were taken by Tim Graham.
Here he is in the grounds of Buckingham Palace with his labrador Frances.
Much comment was aroused in the press by the fact that his trouser hems
had very clearly been let down!* (Tim Graham, London)

*Prince Edward with his waxwork dummy at Madame Tussaud's in 1988. He was
the first member of the Royal Family to donate his own clothes and to be
photographed with his dummy.* (Photographers International)

For two months the conflict raged. On 2 May British aircraft bombed Port Stanley and a British submarine sank the Argentine cruiser *General Belgrano*. In retaliation the British destroyer *HMS Sheffield* was attacked by an Exocet missile two days later. Throughout May the *Ardent, Antelope, Coventry, Atlantic Conveyor, Tristram* and *Sir Galahad* were all attacked by the Argentinians, causing heavy casualties. The *Queen Elizabeth II* was called into service as a hospital ship to convey the wounded home to England. Daily Prince Edward listened for news of *HMS Invincible*, the aircraft carrier his brother was on, which had travelled out with the Atlantic convoy. Buckingham Palace were quick to point out the danger that Andrew was in. He could not be singled out for special protection and at the same time he faced the extra risk of being considered a prime target. It would have been a great coup for the Argentinians to have shot down the Queen's son.

In the Falklands Prince Andrew was involved in rescue operations, such as the one when a Sea King helicopter from *HMS Hermes* ditched into the sea in bad weather. Not only did he ferry supplies between ships but, more dangerously, he had to hover his helicopter close to *Invincible* as a decoy for Exocet missiles. As Andrew explained later:

> *The helicopter is supposed to hover near the rear of the carrier, presenting a large radar target to attract the missile. The idea is that the Exocet comes in low over the waves and is not supposed to go above a height of 27 feet. So when the missile is coming at you, you rise quickly above 27 feet and it flies harmlessly underneath. In theory! On the day* Sheffield *was hit, one Exocet was seen to fly over the mast of the ship and that's well over 27 feet.*

In constant contact by telephone with the Queen in London, Prince Edward knew of his mother's deep concern for Andrew's safety. Practised at disguising her emotions, even she could not hide the fear she felt. Like thousands of other families in Britain who had sons, husbands and brothers fighting in the conflict, Prince Edward knew the feeling of helplessness suffered by those at home. As daily reports came of deaths and casualties Edward had to put these concerns to the back of his mind and concentrate on his studies. While he was completing his exams, paratroopers captured Darwin and Goose Green and on 6 June took Bluff Cove and Fitzroy. On 14 June the British took Port Stanley and the Argentinians agreed to a ceasefire. Nearly 1,000 servicemen and civilians (255 British and 720 Argentinian) had lost their lives in the conflict. On 16 June Britain celebrated VF Day and Prince Edward saw his mother's face alongside that of Prime Minister Margaret Thatcher on the front page of every national newspaper – hailed as the two most relieved women in the world. In those few months the Queen had visibly aged, and when Prince Andrew finally returned home in September he had matured and a stronger bond had been forged between him and Edward.

'Danger is part of the job,' the Queen once said to Harold Macmillan, but the early 1980s were unexpectedly fraught. In June 1981 blank shots had been fired at the Queen as she rode on horseback to the Trooping the Colour ceremony on Horse Guards Parade. 'Life must go on,' she said, but she knew only too well that if the bullets had been real she would have died. Later that year she walked within yards of 7 lb of gelignite, which exploded soon afterwards at Sullum Voe oil terminal. If the gelignite had gone off as planned the Queen would have been blown to pieces. Incidents such as these affected Prince Edward more deeply than he showed. In many ways closer to the Queen than any of her other children, the very idea of her assassination horrified him. With age he became more withdrawn and fearful of the risks and responsibilities his family faced. Even at Gordonstoun, Andrew Merrylees had carried a gun for Edward's protection. As a child the idea of having an armed guard is exciting and strangely comforting; in adulthood the implications are at times too much to live with.

On Friday 9 July what could have been an implausible plot for a work of fiction became stark reality when the unthinkable occurred. At 7.17 a.m. the Queen was woken by the sound of movement at her window to find thirty-one-year-old unemployed labourer Michael Fagan in her bedroom. He had already been in the Palace for half an hour and had not only penetrated security to get into the building but, incredibly, had discovered the Queen's bedroom. By sheer misfortune and ill-timing, the room was unguarded. Having smashed a glass ashtray, possibly with the intention of committing suicide, Fagan sat on the Queen's bed. The Queen pressed the panic button beside her bed, but it went unanswered. Contrary to stories of the Queen having a conversation with the intruder, Fagan has since revealed that she screamed at him to get out and ran from the room. Fagan was detained by a footman until the police arrived, but the Queen was justifiably angered that she should have been subjected to such as ordeal.

Fagan was harmless enough and the Queen reassured Prince Edward that she was all right, but they both knew that, had he been a terrorist, the Queen could have been quite literally murdered in her own bed. A week later she was admitted to hospital for the first time in her life to have a wisdom tooth removed, and two days after that faced the resignation of her personal bodyguard, Commander Trestrail, after a homosexual prostitute had attempted to blackmail him. That summer the Royal Family needed their summer holiday at Balmoral more than ever.

Prince Edward had his eighteenth birthday that year, a milestone which brought its own responsibilities. After the Fagan incident he knew that security within his own home would now be even tighter. Although he joked that if a member of the Royal Family was seen anywhere alone outside the Palace the cry would go up 'One of them has got away!', the remark was a bit too close to the truth. At the age of eighteen the Prince automatically qualified for a Civil List allowance to undertake royal duties, although the £20,000 a year he received was not his to spend. Instead it was invested for him, to be used in the future when he needed an office and staff of his own. From the date of his birthday members of the Royal Household began to refer to him as 'Your Royal Highness' instead of simply 'Edward'. He was given his own crested monogram of the letter 'E' with a crown above it, designed by the College of Arms, and had to pose for his first solo official photograph.

Having deliberately avoided photographers for most of his life, Prince Edward was nervous and uncertain about posing on his own. He was even more unhappy when the shoot was organised in London for what should have been the last day of his school holidays at Sandringham. A young freelance photographer called Tim Graham had been selected by the Queen's then Press Secretary, Michael Shea, to take the photographs. Nicknamed 'The Squirrel' by his colleagues, Graham was noted for his royal pictures but had never before been commissioned to take an official portrait. His youth and informal approach made him an ideal candidate to put the Prince at ease. Knowing that Edward had a black labrador dog called Frances, he asked if she could also be brought to London for the session. Again Edward was not happy with the idea, as he was going directly to Gordonstoun and would have to leave his dog behind for someone else to return to Sandringham.

Tim Graham was shown various rooms at Buckingham Palace beforehand and selected both the Chinese Room and Edward's own sitting room where he would ask the Prince to pose at his large desk. The day of the shoot was bitterly cold. It had snowed the day before, and after three hours of picture-taking in the Palace itself, Edward agreed to have a few pictures taken in the garden. In between shots he ran around in circles to keep warm and remained smiling even when asked to sit in a pile of damp leaves. These last few informal shots were the ones eventually released for publication. 'I was delighted with the coverage that the pictures were given in hundreds of news-papers and magazines in this country and overseas,' said Tim Graham, 'and knew that the pictures had been a real success when one of them was chosen for the cover of *Dog World*!' Certainly he felt that the presence of Frances had made Edward relax, although he was well aware that Edward looked upon being photographed as a necessary evil. With no experience of such a situation, the Prince was uncertain as to how informal he should be and so confined his conversation to the dog.

One concern of Graham's was that Edward's black shoes did not match his brown corduroy trousers or brown jacket, and as the rest of the Prince's clothes were packed ready for Gordonstoun his feet had to be kept out of shot. Outside Graham hid them with leaves. Although the released pictures proved popular, eagle-eyed picture editors noted that the hems of Prince Edward's trousers had quite clearly been let down, but as their release on Edward's birthday coincided with Budget Day the Queen was praised for making sensible economies. As a direct result of the success of these portraits of Edward, Tim Graham was invited to photograph the Prince and Princess of Wales and was to become a royal favourite. When Edward needed official twenty-first birthday portraits three years later, Graham was selected again.

Prince Edward's eighteenth year coincided with the birth of Prince William of Wales. Having been third in line to the throne for his entire life, Edward was suddenly pushed down to fourth place. In the years that followed, the children of his brothers would continue to supersede him. As he left Gordonstoun for the last time that summer he must have pondered on his future. With the size of the Royal Family increasing he knew he need not be condemned to a life of duty like his mother and eldest brother, but could have a career of his own choosing. Significantly, when asked in a television interview about the highlights of his years at Gordonstoun he answered, 'As far as the good times are concerned, I think I'll remember the theatre.' Of equal consequence that summer was Prince Edward's decision to take a potential officers' course with the Royal Marines. Both experiences were to have a dramatic effect on him.

Chapter 3

THE STUDENT PRINCE

*He was sent, as usual, to a Public School where
a little learning was painfully beaten into him,
and from thence to University, where it was
carefully taken out of him.*

T.L. PEACOCK,

'Nightmare Abbey'

The scheduled flight left Gatwick Airport as planned on Sunday 5 September with 308 passengers bound for New Zealand. Amongst them, almost unnoticed, sat Prince Edward, embarking on the longest journey of his life to face yet another character-building test. Still wholly subject to royal tradition, the eighteen-year-old Prince was forced to follow in the footsteps of his brothers and diplomatically spend a period of time in one of the Commonwealth countries. Prince Charles had been sent to Timbertop in Australia, Prince Andrew to Lakefield in Canada, and now it was Prince Edward's turn to spend two terms at Collegiate School in Wanganui, New Zealand. He would not be a pupil, however, but a house tutor and junior master teaching English and History.

Barely more than a schoolboy himself, it was a daunting prospect. In the preceding months he had matured noticeably. He had survived a gruelling training course with the Royal Marines (a taste of things to come), and just four weeks before landing in New Zealand he had gained his private pilot's licence, but he was not a trained teacher and within two months of his arrival he was describing the experience as 'sheer hell' at

58

times. The initial months were not made any easier by the knowledge that he was the cause of controversy back home.

In August it had been revealed that Prince Edward had passed his three 'A' levels and at first the newspapers had hailed him as the most 'academically accomplished' of the Queen's children. He had even passed an 'S' level paper in history, reviving his 'Educated Eddie' nickname. Shortly before he flew to New Zealand, however, his actual grades were leaked to the press: grade 'C' in English, grade 'D' in history and grade 'D' in economics and politics. This was far from outstanding and well below what would generally be required to go to Cambridge, most students being expected to achieve all 'A' grades. If the Prince was accepted at Cambridge an outcry was inevitable; if he was rejected he would be deemed a failure. He could not win.

As the Prince left Gatwick Airport there were rumours that he had been offered a place at Jesus College, Cambridge, and speculation was fuelled by the news that he would not be asked to sit an entrance examination like the other prospective students. The National Union of Students were up in arms and nearly 200 graduates signed a petition objecting to his admission to one of the most élite colleges, arguing that his academic qualifications were insufficient to warrant a place that might otherwise be taken by a more deserving student who would ultimately benefit from a Cambridge education. 'Most students here have "A" grades at "A" level,' said one of the protesters, 'and those who haven't are usually admitted on the grounds of underprivilege. You can hardly say this of Prince Edward. We are simply objecting to the principle that privilege can get you into university.' It was argued that if Prince Edward could get to Cambridge on those grades then about 10,000 other students in the United Kingdom would qualify too.

Buckingham Palace declined to comment, but it was eventually decided that the Prince would definitely be going to Jesus College and would become an undergraduate through the Royal Marines University Cadets Scheme, thus satisfying entry requirements. As he had so far only undertaken one short training course with the marines this news did little to placate the students who began painting 'Go Home, Edward' signs in preparation for his arrival. Later allegations that Prince Edward had a special advantage because his father happens to be

Chancellor of Cambridge University were hard to refute, and the implication that he had got his place 'through the back door' ensured that he would receive a less than warm welcome.

Whilst the debate over his eligibility raged in England, Prince Edward was adjusting to life in New Zealand which he described as 'Not quite the same as Britain, where everything is go, go, go. You can actually stop to think for a while.' Although far from the mêlée at home the news of his 'A' level results inevitably reached the New Zealand newspapers. He refused to comment but his low grades did nothing to enhance his standing with the pupils he was assigned to teach and led to a certain amount of mockery.

The Collegiate of Wanganui has been described as 'the Eton of New Zealand' and is one of a number of schools which offered exchanges with Gordonstoun. Prince Edward wanted to arrive in a low-key manner so that he could easily integrate into school life. In theory this may have seemed possible. In practice he arrived with three bodyguards and an equerry and was met formally by Sir David Beattie, the Governor-General of New Zealand. This was rather like someone coming to England to teach anonymously but being greeted on the tarmac by the Queen. As usual, Edward's royal position could not be ignored. The British press followed this now newsworthy young man to New Zealand and met with a frosty response from him. At the time both Prince Philip and Princess Anne were giving journalists short shrift and the inexperienced Edward was also in no mood to co-operate. In return, reporters delighted in giving him his first bad press, describing the Prince as 'moody and arrogant'. Newspapers had been writing false stories about his aunt, Princess Margaret, since she was seven years old, so Edward had perhaps got off relatively lightly so far. 'I just want to live as normal a life as possible,' he insisted. 'It's not difficult, if only people will allow me to.' That simple statement was to become a refrain that echoed throughout his life.

Once the novelty of his presence in New Zealand had worn off, the Prince was allowed some measure of privacy to enjoy the country. Unlike England with its long history (ruled by Edward's ancestors for more than a thousand years, with his own descent being traced back directly to William the Conqueror and beyond), New Zealand was the last major land area in the world to be claimed by man. It is said that if the estimated time of the human race on earth were reduced to twenty-four hours, then man would have arrived in New Zealand only eight seconds ago.

The town of Wanganui – the Maori name means 'big stretch of water' – is on the west coast of the North Island and is dominated by the Wanganui River which meanders through it as the River Thames divides London. Not known as a tourist area, it gets the full force of the winds blowing through the Cook Strait and gales are quite common. Rainfall is heavy and summers are warm but temperatures rarely higher than 30°C. In the winter there are frequent frosts and occasionally snow, so Prince Edward did not find it difficult to adjust to the climate. Apart from the transposed seasons – he left England in the autumn and arrived in New Zealand in the spring – it was not unlike England. The terrain consists of sandy coasts, rolling grassland, and mountain ranges forming a spine up the centre of the island. With a population of around 40,000, and a port, the city of Wanganui is a trading centre for wool, grain, meat and dairy produce. It is also known for its iron ore deposits and steel processing. Much of its charm stems from the broad river mouth which is the starting point for jet-boats and cruisers embarking on journeys along its 165 mile length. Locally it is known as 'the garden city' because of the wooded area around St John's Hill and the landscaped waterfowl sanctuary at Virginia Lake. The city has many open spaces, a deer park and a scenic reserve at Bushy Park, plus four good beaches. Prince Edward enjoyed the slow pace of life in New Zealand and particularly appreciated the elegant old opera house at Wanganui.

At the school he had his own self-contained flat on the campus and was able to cook for himself if he wished. He also became adept at doing his own laundry. At the Palace his clothes had gone into a laundry bag which could be identified only by a number, but at the school he could not risk any of his clothes being stolen and sold as royal mementos. In an interview Prince Charles once refused to reveal the colour of his underpants or say whether or not he wore anything in bed; by doing his own washing in New Zealand, and later at Cambridge, Prince

Edward could also prevent any similar potentially embarrassing revelations.

'He has successfully begun teaching English grammar and literature to a third form class,' said headmaster, Ian McKinnon, after Prince Edward had been at the school for three weeks, keen to point out that 'the boys think very highly of him'. As a housemaster in a boarding school the Prince had many other duties besides teaching. He was expected to supervise his class from the time they got up in the morning to the time they went to bed. As at Gordonstoun there was a strong emphasis on sport and physical exercise, and the Prince had to take a team of boys out cross-country running four times a week over a 4-mile endurance course, whatever the weather. In his second term, which was summer in New Zealand, he took parties out on hiking expeditions into the mountains and organised entertainments around the camp fire. He also introduced the boys to the game of charades, a firm favourite with the Royal Family.

One of the Prince's pupils was thirteen-year-old John Tanner who had started at the school that September. Ten years later Prince Edward was horrified when he heard that John Tanner had confessed to the murder of his girlfriend Rachel McLean in April 1991. When Rachel first went missing, Tanner had calmly carried out a charade of reconstructing for the police what he claimed had been the last time he had seen Rachel alive at Oxford Station. Her body was subsequently discovered under the floorboards of her lodgings and Tanner confessed to killing her. At the time the public were shocked by the way in which he had carried out the reconstruction, knowing full well that she was dead, but Prince Edward knew how keen John was on acting. He had told the Prince that one day he hoped to go on the stage. When he finally achieved notoriety it was not the kind of fame Edward had expected for his former pupil.

A month after Prince Edward's arrival in New Zealand an earth tremor, registering five on the Richter Scale, shook the North Island and the whole of Wanganui. The alarmed Prince found himself carrying out emergency procedures and civil defence exercises. There were concerns that a full-scale earthquake might occur. Whilst his bodyguards were prepared to protect Edward against any kind of attack, they had not bargained on natural disasters.

Despite his responsibilities at the school Prince Edward did find time for relaxation, and part of the attraction of travelling to the other side of the world was the opportunity it offered for exploration. Having obtained his pilot's licence just before leaving England, he was able to undertake some training exercises with the Royal New Zealand Air Force's 42 Squadron who were stationed just 30 miles from Wanganui. His first Christmas away from Windsor Castle was spent in Auckland with the family of Sir David Beattie, the Governor-General, at Government House. Despite the sun, sea, and the freshly picked strawberries, this was the time when Prince Edward felt most homesick. Notwithstanding the time difference, he was able to speak to his family on the telephone, and listened to his mother's traditional Christmas Day speech to the Commonwealth privately on the radio, but it was still a lonely holiday. Shortly afterwards he flew to Australia where James Graham, one of his former teachers at Gordonstoun, was now teaching at Armidale Private School near Sydney. It was a tenuous but comforting link with home. Away from the press and the school Edward went water-skiing at Nambucca Heads on the coast of New South Wales.

When the Prince and Princess of Wales visited New Zealand officially from 17 to 30 April 1983 he flew to Wellington to see them and invited them to the school at Wanganui. They visited him two days later and the Prince seemed at his most relaxed. Having been made an honorary chieftain of the Ngati Awa tribe during his stay, Prince Edward greeted his brother and sister-in-law wearing a cloak of kiwi feathers.

'Good Lord!' Prince Charles teased, 'It must be a fancy dress party. What have you come as?' Then, examining his baby brother's outfit more closely, he exclaimed, 'It looks like a blanket.' This was exactly the kind of family rapport he had missed.

Whilst the kiwi cloak may have appeared outrageous to Prince Charles, he would have been even more amused if he had been able to see his brother later in the month. At Heatherdown and Gordonstoun Prince Edward had already proved that he had a talent for acting, but at the end of April he displayed his comic gifts dressed as a woman! For the school drama society's production of *Charley's Aunt*, the Brandon

Thomas farce, the Prince played the leading role of Lord Fancourt Babberley who is required to dress up as his aunt 'from Brazil, where the nuts come from'. By coincidence the title of the play was the nickname Edward's aunt, Princess Margaret, had given herself when Prince Charles was born.

After nine months in New Zealand Prince Edward knew in his own mind that his interests were veering more towards the theatre than teaching. 'I am not cut out to be a teacher,' he had said after just three months at the school. 'There are times when it's been sheer hell.' This was a point he reiterated in March when he again said, 'I don't agree that schooldays are the happiest days of your life.' He had now experienced both sides of the teacher's desk and had not really enjoyed either. He had no regrets, however, about the time he had spent in New Zealand. When Prince Charles had completed his time in Australia as a student, his equerry David Checketts said after those seven months, 'I went out there with a boy and returned with a man,' (quoted in *Charles* by Anthony Holden). Much the same could be said for Prince Edward.

For one so interested in travel, being based in New Zealand offered the Prince excellent opportunities to explore that area of the globe during the school holidays. In December 1982 he made a week-long visit to the Antarctic region, travelling in a New Zealand Air Force Hercules from Christchurch airport, accompanied by an official of the Science and Industrial Research Department. In 1956 the Duke of Edinburgh had toured scientific posts and ice stations in the Antarctic region. Prince Edward was now able to follow in his father's footsteps, but went one better by actually reaching the South Pole and walking around it. The only member of the Royal Family to have done this, he saw huts that had been used by explorer Robert Falcon Scott on his last fatal expedition in 1912. On a stop at Scott Base on Ross Island he drank water which had allegedly fallen as snow seventy years earlier. He followed routes taken by explorers Sir Ernest Shackleton and Roald Amundsen, explored Mount Erebus in Victoria Land, and slept in an igloo. As an accomplished skier, Edward took advantage of the snowy mountains and was made an honorary member of the world's southernmost skiing club. When back in New Zealand he was able to ski down the spectacular Mount Ruapehu on

North Island, a 9,157-foot volcanic peak. Later Prince Edward undertook a short tour of the South Pacific, visiting Rarotonga and Aitutaki in the Cook Islands, and Niue (also known as Savage Island), Tonga, Western Samoa and Fiji.

Having gained his pilot's 'wings' in 1982, Prince Edward was offered membership of the Wanganui Aero Club during his stay, but as they only had single-engined planes he was forced to decline. No other pilot would have thought twice about it, but as a member of the Royal Family Edward was only allowed to fly a twin-engined aircraft which had been thoroughly checked beforehand. As an heir to the throne his personal safety is always taken into consideration, just as it was forbidden for him to travel in any aircraft with Charles, Anne and Andrew all at the same time. Today Prince Charles cannot fly in the same plane as his two sons, William and Harry, for fear that the first three heirs to the throne could be wiped out in one fatal crash. Even on holiday the business of being royal can never be forgotten.

During his final term at Collegiate School Prince Edward made his first foray into the world of publishing. Together with two members of staff and two pupils he co-wrote a spoof on public schools called *Full Marks for Trying* which was published in the United Kingdom in 1983 under the pseudonym Fenton Ryder. Until the true identity of the author was revealed the book presented a guessing game for many a reviewer. This game became even more tantalising with increasing speculation as to which of Prince Edward's experiences of public school had been included.

Prince Edward left New Zealand in May 1983 and a month later it was announced that he would be joining the Royal Marines in September as a second lieutenant on probation. Many had hoped that he might in fact serve full-time with the Royal Air Force as his great-uncle the late Duke of Kent had done. The announcement had been timed deliberately because the Prince would be going to Jesus College, Cambridge, as a 'fresher' that October and was doing so under the Royal Marine University Cadets entry scheme. Even though he had been out of the country for nine months the controversy about his place at Cambridge had continued to simmer slowly.

As the Michaelmas term and his first day at university approached, the issue came to a head. The press discovered that out of 126 students who had been accepted at Jesus College, only nine had been offered places with low grades; 'a clear indication that the class system is flourishing,' according to the *Eton College Chronicle* where future Cambridge students were nurtured. The man who was to be Edward's senior tutor, Dr Gavin MacKenzie, stipulated that 'He was evaluated and went through the normal admission process.' When a Mrs Sheila Clements of South Shields wrote a letter of complaint to Buckingham Palace, they replied as follows (quoted in *Royal Family Yearbook* by Trevor Hall):

> *No doubt there are others who achieved better "A" level results and did not gain admission. It is, however, perhaps fair to point out that his admission to Jesus College was a matter entirely for college authorities, and there was no question of any pressure being brought to bear on them to ensure his admission.*

The then Master of Jesus College, 64-year-old Sir Alan Cottrell, insisted that when students were offered a place it was based not solely on examination results; there had also been a report from the Headmaster of Gordonstoun and Prince Edward's interview was taken into consideration. 'He's just an ordinary young man at an ordinary college,' said Sir Alan later. Few believed him on either count. On arrival Prince Edward was invited to take lunch with Sir Alan, a privilege not granted to all students.

Prince Edward became a student in October 1983, and the other students, although wary of him at first, quickly accepted him. Indeed he received a large number of invitations from female students wanting to make him welcome. Most realised that the furore had not been caused by Edward himself and appreciated the pressures on him to study at Cambridge. There was also, it seemed, a certain amount of pride in being able to say that they had 'been at college with Prince Edward'.

For reasons of security the Prince was accompanied throughout his years at Cambridge by two personal detectives, Andrew Merrylees and Derek Griffin, who were allocated rooms next to him. Edward was given a balconied room in the modern Chapel Court – known as 'Millionaire's Row' – and the landing that would normally have accommodated four students became his own private floor. He had one room to himself with standard furniture: a single divan bed, wardrobe, a large desk, bookshelves and armchairs. Like any other student he quickly covered the walls with posters and photographs. He also had to share a bathroom, lavatory and kitchenette with three other students, but certain concessions were made to protect the royal 'guest'. The windows that had originally been fitted in 1965 were replaced with bulletproof glass and a private telephone was installed in his room. From the outside his block was only recognisable by the fact that his name was painted on a varnished wooden board along with those of his fellow residents, but if anyone visited his room they had to be discreetly vetted by one of the detectives. When Prince Edward went from his room to a tutorial, the bodyguard trailed behind. When the Prince was seen riding through the streets of Cambridge on a bicycle (once illegally on the pavement) so was his bodyguard, both on brand new five-speed Raleigh Falcon Londoner bicycles. 'Security must be very tight,' said his senior tutor Gavin MacKenzie. 'We do not want anything to happen to him while he's in our care.' Just as there had been kidnap threats at Heatherdown and Gordonstoun, Prince Edward was clearly vulnerable on a university campus.

Cambridge, like Wanganui, originally grew up around a river which provided a ready transport system, and the River Cam is still an important feature of the town today. One advantage of Jesus College is that it is set back from the main road and has larger grounds than any other college in Cambridge. The site of the college is that of St Radegund's Priory, founded in 1130. Some thirty years later King Malcolm IV of Scotland, who was also Earl of Huntingdon, gave the nuns 10 acres of land around the priory on which they were able to build a church and additional buildings. In 1496 the dissolution of the monasteries saw the buildings converted into an academic establishment from which Jesus College developed. The original Benedictine priory was cased with brick and the church became the college chapel. Initially there was a Master, William Chubbes, six Fellows and six boy scholars. An early Fellow was Thomas Cranmer, later Archbishop of Canterbury, who was burned at the stake under the orders of one of Prince Edward's ancestors.

By 1880 there were 200 undergraduates at the college and many new buildings were erected, including the present court-yards where students can be fined for walking on the grass, a privilege reserved for dons. At the same time the sport of rowing, now synonymous with Oxford and Cambridge, was introduced. A century later rowing still remained popular, but the number of undergraduates had more than doubled. Jesus College is renowned for its teaching of history and for high-quality drama, both of which were important factors to Prince Edward.

At Jesus College the Prince fitted into the routine quickly, just as he had at school. In Wanganui he had been set apart both through being royal and as a temporary teacher, but at Cambridge he could return to being just a face in a crowd of students his own age and enjoy the experience of university life. He was present for the freshers' dinner of prawn cocktail, lamb chops, carrots, peas and potatoes, followed by apple pie and cream, and posed for a group photograph with his fellow students. It made a refreshing change to be photographed legitimately in a group instead of being singled out by a prying lens. Each morning he could be seen going off to lectures wearing a tweed jacket, flannel trousers and a black under-graduate gown, looking like any other male student . . . apart from the detective shadowing him. 'I try to have a normal day like everybody else,' he insisted, although he carefully chose the times when the college launderette was quiet to do his washing.

As expected, Edward's first weeks at Cambridge were dogged by reporters, and they were to become almost a permanent feature of his university life. If he visited a local pub with friends there were always people present who wanted to catch him with a girlfriend. Unscrupulous journalists attempted to bribe students for intimate stories and a few even more un-scrupulous students, who had not even met the Prince, in-vented stories to earn themselves a little extra income. During his first year at Cambridge Edward's relationship with the press was to turn distinctly sour. At the end of March, for example, Edward went on a private skiing holiday to the Austrian Tyrol and was constantly pestered by journalists. Eventually he snapped that he was not there 'for other people's entertainment. If I have to cancel this holiday because of you people, I will make sure that you never forget it.' How remarkably like his father's and sister's admonishments to the press.

Two weeks after arriving at Jesus College Prince Edward joined the Very Nice Society, which appealed to his sense of humour. The group had no specific aims other than to be nice to each other, but it was what the Prince needed at the time, for not all his contemporaries were entirely happy about having a Prince in their midst. Once when a gang of rowdy youths was ejected from a local hostelry they caused embarrassment by claiming that Prince Edward had been amongst them. When the Graduate Randomly Organised Theatrical Society – GROTS – put on a show, again Edward was the butt of much of their humour.

On a more serious level the Prince joined the university's Light Entertainment Society and in October auditioned for a part in Arthur Miller's *The Crucible*. He was cast as Deputy Governor Danforth in the drama about a seventeenth-century witch hunt in Salem, Massachusetts. Although not appearing until Act Three, Danforth as a judge is a crucial character in the play and is described by Miller as 'a grave man in his sixties, of some humour and sophistication'. One criticism by reviewers was that Prince Edward's make-up did not age him sufficiently, but his performance was generally well received. 'He never needs to raise his voice to shout to make his passion felt,' said one critic, a comment which is also true of the Prince in real life.

When Prince Charles was at Trinity College, Cambridge, Lord Butler, the Master of Trinity, once said, 'He should be encouraged to act. He will have to spend much of his life as an actor.' Certainly much of royal life involves playing a part, rarely showing true emotion, continually saying the right lines so as not to cause controversy, and always dressing the part. The Queen Mother once described her familiar upturned-brim hat and matching coat dress as 'her props', and when the Queen gets ready for a state banquet or opens Parliament she puts on the tiara or crown, dressing the part of monarch. One disadvantage of being royal, however, is that it is a lifelong vocation that cannot be surrendered. For this very reason, being able to act the part of another character has many attractions.

Much has been made of Prince Edward's love of acting, as if this were somehow a unique characteristic, yet the theatre has played a significant role in the lives of many of his relatives. Few, for example, have not heard of the Windsor Castle pantomimes that the young Princess Elizabeth and Princess Margaret used to put on in the Waterloo Chamber during the war years. In 1954 Princess Margaret once almost appeared in an Edgar Wallace thriller called *The Frog*, which was put on at the Scala Theatre in the West End to raise money for the Invalid Children's Aid Association. The Princess originally intended to play one of the parts. However in the end she took on the role of Associate Director, while understudying the character of a nightclub hostess. The part was played by Raine Legge who later became the present Princess of Wales's stepmother, Countess Spencer. She did not miss a performance so Princess Margaret did not get a chance to appear. Noël Coward slated the show, writing in his diary that the actors were incompetent, conceited and impertinent, with no talent whatsoever. Princess Margaret was probably relieved that she had not taken part.

While at Cheam School, Prince Charles played the Duke of Gloucester in a compilation of Shakespeare plays and took the title role in *Macbeth*. He also sang the part of the Pirate King in *The Pirates of Penzance* at Gordonstoun, and acted in many revues at Cambridge. Prince Andrew's acting roles have included Mr Brownlow in *Oliver* and Adolphus Bastable in *Passion, Poison and Putrefaction* at Lakefield, and even Princess Anne acted while at Benenden. She played Alfred Fipps in Christopher Fry's play *The Boy with a Cart* and a drunken sailor in *Dido and Aeneas*. While at school in Canada Prince Andrew had said he wanted to study drama because 'I became bored with being myself and like taking other roles. My brother [Charles] is far better at dramatics; I make a comedian myself.' So Prince Edward's stage appearances were merely following the family tradition. His great-grandmother Queen Mary had once played Wall in *A Midsummer Night's Dream*, and his great-great-great grandmother Queen Victoria even sang the part of Buttercup in *HMS Pinafore*.

All the Royal Family today support the arts. Princess Margaret shares with Prince Charles a love of opera, and, like the Princess of Wales, adores ballet. Every member of the family attends a theatrical gala or charity première at least once a year. Many of the day-to-day trappings of monarchy are pure theatre. For ceremonial pageantry, such as the annual Garter Ceremony each June, they don Tudor robes. From medals and decorations to hats and white gloves, there is a continual need to present a regal image. When the Queen enters the House of Lords to open Parliament, wearing the Imperial State Crown and a 24-foot long ermine-trimmed velvet robe, the lights are brightened as she enters to heighten the spectacle. In a piece of pure theatre, before a state banquet, when guests are gathered in the White Drawing Room at Buckingham Palace, at a certain moment a cabinet swings back at the touch of a button and the Royal Family mysteriously appear from behind a hidden panel. Some, like Princess Anne, scorn the glamour and pretence. Prince Edward has always been drawn to it.

While at Jesus College, Prince Edward found many opportunities to involve himself in theatrical productions. After *The Crucible*, which was performed in the College Chapel in December 1983, he had his first taste of directing when he produced *The Tale of Toothache City*, a show specifically designed to entertain mentally handicapped children. The Prince selected the actors, helped paint the scenery and set up the stage, he got together the props and drove the minibus to the venues. 'He could not have got more involved if he'd tried,' said one of the cast. 'He really got the theatrical bug in a big way,' revealed another.

In 1984, he was chosen to organise the University Rag Week Revue and for once used his royal status to his own advantage. He walked unannounced into the offices of the local newspaper, the *Cambridge Evening News*, and offered them a deal. To advertise the revue, called *Glitter Ball Prizes*, he wanted to drive a taxi through the streets of Cambridge with two students dancing on the roof. If the newspaper agreed to provide a taxi with a platform on the roof, they could have exclusive photographs. Naturally the paper seized the opportunity and during the Rag procession the Prince drove the taxi himself while two of his fellow actors danced energetically on the roof.

Like all members of the Royal Family, Edward has fought to enforce a distinction between what he considers to be a public appearance, during which he accepts that photographs will be taken, and a private appearance when he considers the camera to be intrusive. As he left a Light Entertainment Society party late one night he was annoyed to find photographers waiting for him. 'You are the most boring people in the world,' he scowled, and was inevitably quoted in national newspapers the following day. 'He should know,' complained the *Daily Star*, 'that it certainly is boring, waiting all night for royals like himself to finish their champagne revels, and then be greeted with pompous remarks.' This comment merely served to anger Prince Edward even more. Leaving the stage door after a matinée of the *Glitter Ball Prizes* he was furious to find some fifteen press photographers waiting for him. 'If you don't lose yourselves before long, I shall lose my temper,' he said. Still only nineteen, Edward was inexperienced at dealing with such situations. His reactions were partly due to fear: he had not yet come to terms with the fact that, as the Queen's son, he was never off duty and always newsworthy. In a documentary to mark the fortieth anniversary of her accession to the throne in 1992 the Queen spoke about being royal as 'a way of life' and it is a fact of life that Edward could not understand. He wanted to be accepted as a student. The press could only ever see him as a Prince.

Having attacked him for uncivil behaviour, when he celebrated his twentieth birthday that same month those who had denounced him now offered him flowery compliments, calling him 'the world's most eligible bachelor' and highlighting his acting talents. Edward could not understand how journalists could despise him one week and praise him the next. Faced with a large contingent of press representatives when he embarked on a sponsored crawl for Rag Week, he looked straight in their direction and announced to onlookers, 'You have probably the most professional crawlers in the world standing in front of you.' He later confided 'I've been wanting to say that all week' but it did nothing to improve relations. 'A snooty supercilious little princeling' wrote Alix Palmer in the *Daily Star*, and in what was to be the first of many damning attacks on him over the years, Jean Rook, late First Lady of Fleet Street, and columnist for the *Daily Express*, wrote that 'stripped of his birth, Edward is an undistinguished lad with no obvious potential for being anything but the Duke of Something'. Having once deliberately shot above the heads of reporters at Sandringham in January 1981 when Prince Charles was being hounded and wished editors 'a particularly nasty New Year', Prince Edward must now have felt like aiming his gun even lower.

The Prince was nevertheless satisfied with the publicity his taxi stunt received – 'I wanted to promote the show and do something that would be a crowd-stopper,' he explained. Photographs of him wearing a flat cap and driving the balloon-decorated car while a couple danced the Charleston on the roof appeared in the *Cambridge Evening News* and the show duly sold out. Some £600 was raised for children in Botswana and reviewers praised the show which the Prince produced. 'I have to make sure everyone gets their cues right,' he revealed when interviewed on local radio and said that he would be on stage 'but not visible, I hope'. In November of that year he made a much more visible appearance in a revue called *Captain Curious and his Invincible Quest*. Edward played a variety of comedy roles, most notably that of a giant, for which he sat on the shoulders of his detective, Andrew Merrylees. 'A very novel way to guard him,' the Queen is said to have commented when she heard about it. In the same show Edward dressed up as a royal court jester, but admitted afterwards that 'Comedy is far harder to play than something serious.'

The Queen, Prince Philip and Prince Charles visited Edward privately during his third term at college, though there was a great deal of public comment when he and Charles were seen kissing each other on the cheek as they met. A much more public royal visit, however, took place the following spring when the Queen and Princess Margaret arrived to see Edward in a revue called *Catch Me Foot*. Just eight weeks earlier Princess Margaret had been unexpectedly admitted to the Brompton Hospital in London, where it was revealed that she had been suffering from chest pains for several weeks and had developed an abnormal cough. To the Royal Family's great relief, a biopsy on the Princess's lung revealed that the tissue sample taken was non-malignant. Margaret's first public appearance after the operation was to see her nephew, on the eve of his twenty-first birthday, in the revue.

As she watched Edward sing, dance and act his way through the show, Princess Margaret must have been reminded of the wartime pantomimes at Windsor. Although Prince Edward was nervous during the show he was aware that media attention was more likely to be focused on his aunt than on him, as indeed it was. During the interval Princess Margaret opened her evening bag, fished out the familiar tortoiseshell cigarette holder and lit her first cigarette in public since her cancer scare. The boredom of recuperation had led her to smoke even more. It is because of Princess Margaret, and the fact that his grandfather King George VI died of lung cancer, that Prince Edward has never smoked.

Now more experienced on stage, *Catch Me Foot* was considered to be one of Edward's best performances and is a show he remembers with great affection. In one scene he staggered drunkenly across the stage swigging noisily from a gin bottle, his cheeks red, his clothes askew. 'I'm sure I've seen that face before,' said one of the other actors to the audience. '*Spitting Image* perhaps?' It was the kind of humour the student audience loved and there were numerous references to the Royal Family in the script which Edward had helped write. In another sketch he played a spy and had the line, 'It's HM here from BP.' Aware that his bodyguards were as much a part of the student scene as he was, the audience erupted with laughter as they chased him around the stage dressed as the Keystone Cops. It was the perfect opportunity for Edward to send himself up and poke fun at his royal status, and his fellow undergraduates admired him for it. Whether wiggling his hips as a macho toreador or dancing in a skin-tight Edwardian-style bathing costume, the Prince entered energetically into the spirit of revue. 'The dancing sequences are the hardest part,' he admitted. 'It is difficult to concentrate on what you are singing and remember where to put your feet at the same time.' The show raised more than £1,000 for charity.

If Edward was unpopular with the press, the same could not be said for his fellow students. 'He has fitted in really well since he arrived,' said one of his contemporaries. 'He doesn't put on any airs and graces and everyone calls him Edward. Quite simply, he is very popular on his own merits.' The Prince could not have hoped for any greater compliment. After the show the cast brought an enormous birthday cake on to the stage and even the Queen seemed moved as the audience sang her son

'Happy Birthday'. That night Edward danced through the streets of Cambridge wearing a bowler hat, surrounded by the cast and friends, carrying his birthday presents. It was a scene of sheer unadulterated pleasure, and he was like a man released from a lifetime's imprisonment. Rarely would Prince Edward experience such a feeling of freedom and acceptance again. That night he was Edward Windsor, student.

For his degree course Prince Edward had chosen to study archaeology and anthropology, as Prince Charles had once done, with the option of changing to history in the second year. Known as 'arch and anth', it was considered by many to be an easy course, but Edward still had to put in the full quota of work. Throughout May 1983 he revised hard for his first-year examinations. If he did not achieve a creditable pass he would be asked to leave the university. Having already been admitted with low 'A' level grades it would have been impossible to justify his continuation if he had failed. Fortunately he passed, but only with a lower second grade. Gavin MacKenzie, his senior tutor, called it 'respectable' but figures showed that more than 50 per cent of the students had passed with a more respectable upper second. As part of the degree course in August 1984 the Prince went on an archaeological dig on the site of the ancient Roman city of Viroconium in Shropshire, spending a week of his summer holiday working on the site with his fellow students. Like Prince Charles, Edward changed in his second year from archaeology and anthropology to history. That same summer holiday Prince Edward went back to Gordonstoun.

Broadcaster Julian Pettifer had been making a documentary about the school with a BBC Scotland film unit. As one of Gordonstoun's better-known pupils, Prince Edward agreed to return to the school for his first ever television interview. He was filmed in the library of the Round Square where he had spent so many hours studying for his 'A' levels. Among those waiting to meet him was his old housemaster, James Thomas. The film unit had visited the school on and off for a whole year and Prince Edward naturally spoke diplomatically about his own experiences. 'As long as the person who is weak has the determination to go on he'll get all the help he wants,' he said of Gordonstoun's tough education system. His greatest revelation was that his brother, the Prince of Wales, had 'hated' his five years at Gordonstoun. This was the first public confirmation of a fact that had so often been hinted at in the past. Prince Edward also, rather surprisingly, expressed his approval of corporal punishment in schools, saying, 'A beating or a thrashing, if used in the right context, is, I think, very valuable.' When the programme was first broadcast on 14 August 1984 there were many who disagreed with his view.

At Gordonstoun Prince Edward had played rugby for his house and he chose to continue playing at Jesus College. Within two weeks of his arrival at Cambridge he played his first match for the second team, against Prince Charles's old college, Trinity. Wearing red socks, white shorts and royal blue shirt, Edward played an energetic match, but Jesus College still suffered an humiliating defeat, losing 26-3. His rugby career was never illustrious. 'He must improve his technique in the attack, and particularly his binding in the scrum. But he's very fit,' said his coach, admitting that there was much room for improvement.

For those who had only seen an apparently mild-mannered Prince in public, his behaviour on the rugby field was often unexpectedly aggressive. The sport offered Edward a welcome opportunity to release his tensions. (This is also one of the reasons why he enjoys playing squash so much – he can slam the ball as hard as he likes.) In his second rugby match Jesus College played against Girton College and won 18-4, although little of the victory could be credited to the Prince. He was beginning to find himself the target of attack by opposing players and after a painful 'below-the-belt' hit during a scrum the angry Prince punched the offending player, Hugh Bethell, a Girton medical student. Bethell apologised afterwards, admitting the foul. 'I got what I deserved,' he said. Successive games seemed to be eventful for Edward for the wrong reasons. He had his shirt badly torn in a match against Selwyn College, and in a game with St John's College he suffered concussion after colliding with an opponent and had to be carried off the field for medical treatment. This led to a later remark that he had given up the sport because he 'got fed up with being beaten up all the time'. He would, however, have joined the University's Rugby Club on a tour of Canada, but had to withdraw when he developed glandular fever, which was to leave him debilitated for many months.

Prince Edward has always been a keen sportsman, coming from a family with a background of enjoying outdoor pursuits. In New Zealand he had gone 'white water rafting' – shooting the rapids – and he has never been afraid of attempting something new, whether it be archery or abseiling. Most mornings at Cambridge Prince Edward was out very early jogging along the banks of the River Cam with his detective. When possible he would cycle through the streets, and in his spare time he would go swimming to keep himself in good shape. After giving up rugby he started playing real tennis, a game popularised by Henry VIII and much more difficult than modern lawn tennis. Edward represented the University in matches and it is now his favourite sport. By early 1992 he was training twice a week with a professional coach, ex-champion Chris Ronaldson, and began playing in open tournaments.

Edward's participation in sport was not merely due to his desire to keep fit. As a second lieutenant in the Royal Marines his studies at Cambridge were punctuated by Marine training courses. In September 1983, just before going to Jesus College, he had attended his first two-week course, and the following September he undertook a more intensive five-week course at Lympstone (which involved getting up at 6 a.m. for speed marches, carrying an 85 lb back pack). In December 1985 Edward spent two weeks in Belize with 40 Commando Royal Marines in order to gain experience of their operational role and later spent time with 539 Assault Squadron and the Brigade Air Squadron.

When Prince Edward turned twenty-one, the Queen held a party at Windsor Castle for the 'royal quartet', as he, James, Sarah and Helen were called, which Edward helped organise. 'It was a marvellous night,' said Lady Elizabeth Anson of Party Planners, who dealt with the arrangements. 'Edward had lots of lovely original ideas.' He had already organised the Jesus College May Ball that year, for which he had booked magician Paul Daniels, marking the start of their long friendship. At the event itself Prince Edward, wearing a trilby and a raincoat, rubber-stamped ticket holders's hands as they entered, to prove they were genuine guests.

Reaching the age of twenty-one meant another series of official photographs, for which Tim Graham was chosen once again. No press photographs had been allowed at the official birthday party, as it was classed as a private function. An official photograph was later released of the four royal cousins together and Prince Edward posed informally for Tim Graham at Cambridge, the photographer noting how much more relaxed Edward was at twenty-one than he had been at eighteen. Graham photographed the Prince in his room at Chapel Court, working at a very cluttered desk, with a book entitled *The British Empire 1558-1983* placed strategically to indicate a study of history. The cluttered walls behind him showed a poster for his production of *The Crucible*, and a photograph of himself in rugby kit with the Jesus XV, emphasising the fact that Edward was living and working like any student. He was photographed both formally in a jacket and tie, and informally in a college sweater, in the university library, as well as riding his bicycle and walking outside the college in a walled area known as 'The Chimney'. Conservatively rather than fashionably dressed, Edward was still dubbed 'The Handsome Prince' by newspaper editors.

Twenty-one also brought additional royal responsibility as the Prince officially became a Counsellor of State, which meant that he could deputise for the Queen in certain situations. He had already represented Her Majesty at the state funeral of the former Prime Minister and Governor-General of New Zealand, the Right Honourable Sir Keith Holyoake, at Wellington in December 1983, but as a Counsellor of State Prince Edward could now attend meetings of the Privy Council and even hold investitures in the Queen's absence. The Regency Acts of 1937 and 1943 provide for the appointment of Counsellors to 'prevent delay or difficulty in the despatch of public business'. In the event of absence (through overseas tours), or temporary or partial incapacity on the part of the Sovereign (due to illness), a Counsellor of State in effect becomes temporary monarch. The Act allows for six Counsellors – the Queen's husband, the Queen's mother, and the four qualified persons next in line of succession to the throne who are twenty-one or over. Thus, when Prince Edward became eligible in 1985, Princess Margaret had to relinquish her position to him. No further changes will now occur until the year 2003 when Prince William of Wales turns twenty-one and Princess Anne will have to relinquish her position to him. Because males always take precedence over females in the line of succession, Prince Edward takes precedence over Princess Anne even though he was born after her (see Appendix IV).

On returning to college for his final year, after his twenty-first birthday revels, Prince Edward threw himself into his studies. Both sport and drama had to take a back seat, but during his holidays he was present at the Trooping the Colour ceremony on 15 June 1985 (travelling in a carriage with the Queen Mother and the Princess of Wales), and also took part in family celebrations for the Queen Mother's eighty-fifth birthday. To mark the occasion, Norman Parkinson took an official photograph of the Queen Mother with Charles, Andrew, Anne and Edward. This was released as a picture of her 'with her four grandchildren', which is said to have upset Princess Margaret whose son and daughter, Viscount Linley and Lady Sarah Armstrong-Jones, are also the Queen Mother's grandchildren and should, she felt, have been included.

Between his studies Prince Edward embarked on a series of promotional fund-raising activities for the Duke of Edinburgh Award Scheme Thirtieth Anniversary Tribute. The project was one that appealed to him as it gave young people, whether able-bodied or handicapped, an opportunity to participate in challenging activities to earn a medal. There are three levels of award: bronze, silver and gold. Each level consists of four sections – service, expeditions, skills and physical recreation – with an additional residential project at the gold award level. In July 1986 Prince Edward achieved a gold award himself, but he first became involved a year earlier. In 1985 he began chairing a committee to organise fund-raising events and appeared on a TV-AM children's programme *Wideawake* to encourage young people to participate in the scheme.

In April 1986 he undertook a series of engagements in Cardiff and London to raise funds and on 27 April took part in a sponsored bicycle ride through the streets of Cambridge, just a month before taking his finals. Today Prince Edward is International Trustee of the Award, as well as Chairman of the associated Pegasus Project which helps fund overseas trips for those participating in the Award Scheme. The whole scheme is now Edward's pet charity and he is almost synonymous with the cause, as Princess Anne is with Save the Children.

Prince Edward left Jesus College at the beginning of June 1986, a parting tinged with sadness. Once the early controversies of his arrival had died down he had settled easily into student life. He had quickly been accepted by his contemporaries and it seemed the only period of his education that he had genuinely enjoyed. He achieved a Second Class Honours degree (2:2) in History, his papers having been marked anonymously once again so that there could be no accusations of bias. Equally, having been awarded the degree, Edward had the satisfaction of knowing he had achieved it through his own efforts. The qualification will never be of any practical use to him, but it gave him considerable satisfaction and was one more stab at normality. Most important, the Prince had acquired social skills at university and had learnt the art of communication which is so crucial to the life he now leads. Equally, however, some might argue that he could easily have achieved exactly the same result at a less prestigious university. In this way he would not have deprived someone else of the chance to study at Cambridge, someone whose career and social standing might have been significantly enhanced as a result. Likewise, a lower-profile university might well have benefited from royal patronage.

As soon as his finals were over Edward threw himself into organising the celebrated Luton Hoo Ball to raise money for charity. On 22 June he started off a 'walkathon' from the forecourt of Buckingham Palace where hundreds of hikers set out on an eight-week walk to raise money for the Duke of Edinburgh Award Scheme, the walk ending at Balmoral in mid-August, for which he was present once again. In July the Prince flew to Jersey and the Isle of Man to make presentations to those who had achieved the Award, and then attended the island's Tynwald Day Ceremony – their Opening of Parliament – before flying off for a brief visit to New Zealand to publicise the Award Scheme. He also undertook other engagements, such as attending a motor show and visiting a cattle ranch. On his return he attended an Award Ceremony at St James's Palace where he received his own award from the Duke of Edinburgh, a proud moment for both father and son. Throughout August

Edward visited various Scottish venues associated with the scheme, and the thirtieth anniversary celebrations culminated on 4 September with a charity ball at Broadlands, the former home of his late uncle, Earl Mountbatten of Burma. Prince Edward's royal career had begun in earnest.

On the home front Prince Edward was present at Windsor earlier that year for a service to mark the Queen's sixtieth birthday on 21 April. Forty-four members of the Royal Family attended the service, and that same evening Prince Edward donned his dress suit and black bow tie to attend *Fanfare for Elizabeth*, a special gala show at the Royal Opera House, Covent Garden. Just three days later the Queen declared a period of family mourning when the Duchess of Windsor, formerly Wallis Simpson, died at her home in the Bois de Boulogne, aged 89. Her death ended more than ten years of acute illness and suffering. For the last six years of her life she had been confined to her room, paralysed and scarcely able to speak. Exiled from Britain for almost half a century, she had been denied the title 'Her Royal Highness' in life, but in death, was granted a funeral at Windsor and was buried with her husband and members of the family at Frogmore.

The Queen Mother's presence at the funeral was seen as a final act of reconciliation, for it was Wallis Simpson who had caused the abdication and changed the course of British history. Prince Edward was not present at the funeral himself but as he watched his family on television he must have reflected on how dramatically his own life had been affected by that one woman. Had Edward VIII remained on the throne and married someone else they could well have had a child of their own who would now be the reigning monarch. Equally, if Edward VIII had reigned but produced no heirs of his own then by the time he died in 1972 his brother the Duke of York (George VI) would have been dead for twenty years and experts suggest that the present Duke of Gloucester would now be King Richard IV. Fanciful speculation perhaps but certainly without Wallis Simpson, Prince Edward's place in the world would be very different.

On 23 July 1986 a far happier family occasion saw Prince Edward as the supporter (best man) at his brother Andrew's wedding. Prince Andrew married Miss Sarah Ferguson in

Westminster Abbey and on that day they were also created Duke and Duchess of York. It was a significant day for Prince Edward as he calmed his brother's nerves by telling jokes while they rode in the state landau to the Abbey. Sarah's entry into the Royal Family led to an even stronger interest in the younger members, whose workload, dress sense and general behaviour would from that moment on be relentlessly compared. The wedding left Prince Edward as the only one of the Queen's children still unmarried (which would heighten media interest in his love life) and the only son without a title. The subsequent collapse of Andrew's marriage in 1992, after only six years, placed even greater pressure on Edward to find the right partner. That July day in 1986 marked the first public occasion on which Prince Edward was seen wearing the ceremonial dress uniform of the Royal Marines. It was also one of the last few times he would wear it.

On 7 September Prince Edward travelled to Lympstone Barracks in Devon to join the Royal Marines full-time. His future in the services seemed assured.

Chapter 4

AN HONOURABLE RETREAT

And three times to the child I said,
'Why, Edward, tell me why?'

WILLIAM WORDSWORTH,

Anecdote for Fathers

When Prince Edward first signed up for a potential officers'
training course in May 1982 he wanted to be a Royal Marine.
He had turned eighteen two months earlier, and the decision to
join the services was entirely his own. This fact is pivotal, for
many have wrongly assumed that Edward subsequently
resigned his commission because he was pushed into the Marines due to his father being Captain General. However the
choice was his, without any pressure. He selected what was
potentially the most physically punishing military career open
to any Prince. The decision was made in his salad days and it
took courage in adulthood to admit that he had made a mistake.
Contrary to popular belief, however, joining the Marines was
not the mistake.

As the baby of the family, Edward was keen to prove that he
was not the weakling many imagined him to be. Prince Charles
had once been known as 'Action Man' because he had served in
the Royal Air Force and the Royal Navy, and when Prince
Edward signed up for his first course with the Marines his
second brother Prince Andrew was already being hailed as a
hero for piloting a Sea King helicopter in the Falklands conflict.

Edward knew that if he steered clear of the services himself he might be branded a coward, and if he followed in the footsteps of either brother he would be continually compared with them. His own pride made him want to prove that he could be just as strong as Prince Charles, and just as brave as Prince Andrew. So he opted to join the regiment whose training course offers the most notoriously demanding test of physical and mental endurance – the Royal Marines.

Whilst most people will now always associate Edward with the élite corps, Prince Charles had also undertaken a training course with the Marines in 1974 at Lympstone. At the time he was training to be a helicopter pilot, and as the pilot's duties partly involved carrying Royal Marines, it was felt that they should undergo a course to appreciate the Marines' work. In a major interview with Stuart Kuttner for the London *Evening Standard* on 8 January 1975 Prince Charles described his experiences on the course:

> *A most horrifying expedition where you have to swing over small chasms on ropes, slide down ropes at death-defying speeds and then walk across wires and up rope ladders strung between a pole and a tree. And all those sort of ghastly things. Anyway, I survived that and came out with my knees trembling in fear and trepidation. Then we had to do a form of survival course this afternoon which involved crawling through tunnels half-filled with water, then running across the moor and back.*

Prince Edward was only ten at the time, but his brother's experiences did nothing to dampen his enthusiasm. On his own first training course Edward was literally thrown in at the deep end. 'We give special treatment only to the enemy,' said recruitment officer Lieutenant Canning. 'I didn't pull any punches about what he was letting himself in for.' Consequently Edward was woken up unexpectedly at two o'clock in the morning and forced out on to the assault course, which ended with him being immersed, fully clothed, in a tank of cold water. Later he had to go on two lengthy cross-country runs. Throughout his years at Cambridge the Prince went on periodic training courses, was speed marched across Dartmoor in all weathers for 9 miles with a heavy pack on his back, waded through icy lakes, abseiled

Prince Edward with the Prince and Princess of Wales at The Collegiate in Wanganui, New Zealand in 1983. Prince Edward had been made an Honorary Chieftain of the Ngati Awa tribe and greeted them in his ceremonial cloak of kiwi feathers. (Jayne Fincher, Photographers International)

Prince Edward whilst a student at Jesus College, Cambridge, 1983-86.
(Tim Graham, London)

down cliffs, climbed up the vertical faces of ruined buildings, swam down water-filled tunnels and was put through periods of almost unendurable physical training. According to his sergeant, the Prince showed 'grit and determination'. Having experienced so much of this over four years, he could easily have opted out quietly while still at Cambridge with no publicity and little comment. As it was, he *chose* to continue.

Prince Edward arrived at the Lympstone training centre on 7 September 1986, complete with the inevitable bodyguard. This very simple fact of royal life did not go down well with the Marines, who consider that nobody is better qualified to offer protection than themselves. It was 'stupid and insulting' wrote former Commando Nigel Foster in his book *The Making of a Marine Commando*, claiming that Edward was doomed from the day he arrived, as 'The Palace never understood the Marines' view that the unit is a lot more important than one young Prince.'

Prince Edward was officially a Second Lieutenant, an automatic appointment as a graduate in the Marines University Entrance Scheme, and was given a salary of £7,391 per annum. He neither asked for nor expected preferential treatment. 'He will have six weeks' leave a year – and at the Government's convenience,' said a spokesman for the Royal Marines. 'There may be special leave occasionally but he can expect a nine-to-five existence and it is *much* tougher than the Royal Navy. Prince Edward will be treated as any other Royal Marine Officer.' Like the other yo-yos (Marine slang for Young Officer recruit), Edward was given his own spartan room, less than 12 feet square, and ate in the officers' mess. Although the spokesman implied that Edward would get special leave only occasionally, on 6 November the Prince was at Westminster Abbey accompanying his father at a service to mark the thirtieth anniversary of the Duke of Edinburgh's Award Scheme, and on 19 December he secretly visited Northern Ireland as Chairman of the Award Scheme. The suggestion that Edward could expect 'a nine-to-five existence' also proved to be way off the mark.

Edward's day began at 6 a.m. and frequently ended late. Some nights the recruits were out in the field under canvas, occasionally they did not see a bed at all. Each day included gymnastics and fitness exercises, assault courses and weapons training which could mean mock SAS style battles. Commandos have to learn survival, which involves punishing military manoeuvres and self-defence, as well as rock-climbing and canoeing. Besides the rigorous physical demands of the course the new recruits could also spend up to six hours a day in the classroom studying anything from map-reading to economics, British law to the British Constitution, for which they were given homework to complete. The ultimate aim was to earn the coveted Green Beret, the hallowed symbol of a Marine officer. 'It will not be handed to Prince Edward on a plate,' said his commanding officer, Ian Moore. 'He will have to earn it.' Possibly the worst aspect of Marine training was the much-feared endurance course which generally begins with a speed march across Dartmoor, followed by a crawl through a pitch black 30 foot long tunnel, then across 'Peter's Pool', crawling along a thin rope. If they manage to cross without falling into the icy water they still face being pushed through a 10 foot long concrete pipe filled with water after which they are required to speed march for what is understandably termed 'Heartbreak Mile' back to barracks. Once back, Edward and his fellow recruits were given just ten minutes to wash and change before lining up on the parade ground in clean uniform.

Prince Edward proved that he had the physical stamina to survive such gruelling tests of physical endurance, but having known a special kind of freedom as a student, he found the regimented lifestyle difficult to come to terms with. At the time false reports circulated in the press that the Prince had been bullied while in the Marines, but he had actually experienced more bullying on the rugby field at Jesus College. He was one of fifteen new recruits who formed a close-knit group. They were in it together and this fact helped them survive. Prince Edward became particularly friendly with two fellow recruits, Peter Fraser and Quintus Travis, both of whom had known the Prince at Cambridge. Both later confirmed that Edward had not been bullied, nor had he found the physical training difficult. What daunted him was the austerity of his surroundings, the lack of freedom and individuality as a recruit, and the fact that this was intended to be his lifestyle for five more years. He had spent eighteen years of his life being educated and wanted to be able to go to the theatre and socialise in the evenings, not spend all his time studying.

One of the mistakes he had made was going to university before the Marines. At Gordonstoun he was used to a regimented lifestyle and could have coped with service life much more easily then. But having spread his wings and tasted freedom at Cambridge, his small room at Lympstone suddenly seemed like a prison. It was no coincidence that he reached a crisis point during his first holiday when he saw Windsor and Sandringham again. In the security of his family the very thought of returning to his 'cell' in Devon filled him with dread. Edward knew then that he had made a mistake – not the mistake of going into the Royal Marines but of going into the services in the first place. If he had gone into *any* of the services, *any* regiment, he would have felt the same and openly admitted this in an interview the following June.

When he had first gone to Cambridge, Edward had been able to assert his individuality for the first time. His studies were more tailored to his own interests than at school. He had also enjoyed a varied social life, carved himself a niche in the Light Entertainment Society, and in many ways found himself leading quite a cosy existence. He was part of the real world, yet he could quite literally still hide in a crowd of students. It was an environment of gentle academic tradition where the worst he ever had to face was a recalcitrant press photographer and the greatest demands made on him were in examination papers.

Immediately after leaving Jesus College he had experienced his first taste of adult life, but not in the harsh world of any other graduate seeking employment. For two months he undertook his first official royal engagements in his own right, not simply as a hanger-on watching his mother and father at work but as a fully fledged Prince. He enjoyed being in control. His duties took him from the beauty of Jersey in summer to a nostalgic return to New Zealand, no longer as a student travelling incognito but as a member of the Royal Family, with all the status that that entails. He was cheered on walkabouts, greeted with enthusiasm by Duke of Edinburgh Award Scheme participants, and generally had fun at the charity balls and fundraising events. Then, quite suddenly, he was plunged into the muddy, cold world of Lympstone. His smart suits and colourful

Fair Isle sweaters were replaced with more practical denim. The safe warm life of just three days earlier when he had been dancing at Broadlands seemed a million miles away. It was little comfort to be told that he should think himself lucky that Marines now had sheets on their beds!

In 1982, when he had first gone on training courses for the Royal Marines, Edward was like a teenager on an adventure holiday. Swinging across lakes on a narrow rope or climbing up the face of a ruined building presented an unusual challenge with an element of danger, and no matter how tough the exercises, he undertook them in the certain knowledge that within days he would be back at the hub of student life. Arriving at Lympstone full time in 1986, however, was very different. All too quickly he realised that it was no longer a game but a way of life and one that he did not really enjoy. Most worrying of all, he was expected to stay with the Marines until at least 1991 – five years away.

During the first twelve weeks Prince Edward was able to summon the strength to cope with this alien environment, his morale boosted by his fellow recruits who all at some point suffered feelings of depression and self-doubt. Edward might well have settled into the training and remained with the Marines had he not returned home so early for Christmas. There could be no greater contrast than going straight from the barrack huts at Lympstone first to Buckingham Palace and then on to Windsor Castle. The training centre was bordered on three sides by the dark hills of Dartmoor, a barren area of heathland, and the bleak River Exe – all very beautiful to holiday-makers but hell on earth to a cold, wet, muddy soldier on a bleak December morning. At Windsor Castle Prince Edward could relax in the comparative luxury of room 126 in the Queen's Tower overlooking Home Park. There was a valet to lay out his clothes and run his bath. There were fresh flowers, the aroma of Roger & Gallet soap, and a box of Charbonnel et Walker chocolates. There was no early call at 6 a.m. and if the Prince wanted freedom he could ride in Windsor Great Park to his heart's content.

In her first ever Christmas broadcast in 1952 the Queen described the pleasure she felt at having her family around her: 'There is nothing quite like the family gathering in familiar

surroundings . . . when it is night and the wind and rain beat
upon the window . . . the family is most truly conscious of the
warmth and peacefulness that surrounds the pleasant fireside.'
These sentiments must have echoed in Prince Edward's mind
that Christmas. As he sat in his private sitting room he would
have thought about not wanting to return to Lympstone. Re-
membering the physical torture of military training, he must
surely have questioned whether it was really necessary for him
to suffer such agonies. The Marines' motto *Per mare, per terram*
means 'By land and sea', and many Commandos are ultimately
sent overseas to fight in conflicts or control riots, as on the
streets of Belfast. Indeed, part of the actual training programme for officers included a period in Northern Ireland. As
a Marine officer, however, Prince Edward would be excluded
from any such exercise. His royal status would make him a
prime target for the IRA and place the whole regiment in
unnecessary danger. He could never, therefore, be looked
upon as a true Marine, a situation that also caused Prince
Michael of Kent to quit Army training. The very fact that, as a
Prince of the Realm, Edward needed protection himself
seemed to make a mockery of his being a soldier.

Some 35 per cent of new recruits dropout before their
training is completed and Prince Edward knew this option was
open to him, though he also realised that his release from
commission would be higher-profile than any other officer's.
In addition he was acutely aware that anyone who resigns from
the Army or Navy might encounter difficulties in finding
alternative employment. While Edward had expressed doubts
about his suitability for the services early in December, it was
not fully confirmed in his own mind until Christmas. Then he
knew without a shadow of a doubt that he did not want to
return. Ahead lay some agonising decisions – not whether to
resign or not, but how to tell the Marines, how to tell his family
(especially Prince Philip) and how to face the media. He knew
that he had made a terrible mistake and that there would be a
price to pay. There is a misconception that Edward was too
weak to cope with the life of a Marine; he was in fact too strong.
In the Marines there is no room to be an individual; the
emphasis is on working as a team. The Prince's character and
royal training had not prepared him for a future in a rifle

platoon. He needed to be centre stage. The problem was how to break the news.

The Prince decided to let Christmas and New Year pass quietly before talking to his family about it, not wishing to spoil the celebrations. Obviously subdued, he may well have intimated his unhappiness to Princess Anne in whom he has always felt able to confide, but it was not until early January at Sandringham that he spoke to the Queen and Prince Philip about his decision. The conversation was private and can therefore only ever be conjectured, but whatever the reaction it cannot have been an easy meeting for the Prince. Tabloid sources like to suppose that Prince Philip was furious and an 'insider' at Sandringham revealed that he was 'in a foul mood. We have all suffered.' Certainly there have been some well-documented rifts between the Duke and his eldest son, Prince Charles, whom he has sometimes considered to be too sensitive, and Prince Philip can hardly have been enthusiastic about his youngest son's news. After nine months at Wanganui he had returned saying, 'I don't want to teach.' Now, after barely four months' full-time training with the Marines, he was saying 'I don't want a career in the services.' It is not difficult to imagine the impatient Duke asking, 'Well, what *do* you want to do?'

This would not have been an unreasonable question under the circumstances, and to Edward's chagrin it was not one he could answer at the time. Certainly the Queen and Prince Philip asked Edward to reconsider. After such a short period of training they did not feel that he had given himself sufficient time to make up his mind and, after a family Christmas, it was easy for the Queen to see why her son did not want to go back. However the Prince was adamant. He had made his decision and nothing was going to change it. However bad the public reaction might be the consequences could be no worse than five years in the Marines. Although many newspapers later wrote of a rift between Prince Edward and the Duke of Edinburgh, the two were spotted together walking through the grounds of Sandringham deep in conversation. Ahead, Prince Edward now faced one of the toughest weeks of his short life.

Sunday 4 January 1987
Prince Edward was missing when the Royal Family went to church at Sandringham. When questioned, the Press Office replied that it was simply because he was driving back to Buckingham Palace to prepare for his return to the Marines.

Monday 5 January 1987
Prince Edward had been expected back at Lympstone to join the YO (Young Officers) Batch 86 on a route march across Dartmoor, in what would have been sub-zero temperatures. Buckingham Palace told officers that the Prince was suffering from flu and would therefore be remaining in London for a few days. Prince Philip had, however, as both father of the Prince and Captain General of the Marines, been in touch with Sir Michael Watkins, Edward's Commanding Officer, about the situation. Prince Edward wrote out his letter of resignation.

Tuesday 6 January 1987
The Commandant Sir Michael Watkins travelled to Buckingham Palace for a two-hour private meeting with Prince Edward, during which he tried to persuade the Prince to change his mind. Sir Michael suggested that, at the very least, Edward should do eight more months of training so that he could leave after a complete year with the Marines. It would then be a simple matter of stating that he had decided not to pursue any further training. Prince Edward formally handed over his letter of resignation but, to placate Sir Michael and, one suspects, the Duke of Edinburgh, he agreed to return to Lympstone the following day to talk to the other officers. Possibly it was hoped that, once back at barracks amongst his colleagues, the Prince might change his mind.

Wednesday 7 January 1987
A letter from Prince Philip to Sir Michael Watkins was leaked to the press and the *Sun* revealed that Prince Edward intended to resign from the Royal Marines. In the letter Prince Philip expressed his regrets, but made it very clear that the final decision had been Prince Edward's alone. The letter also stated that Prince Philip felt that Edward would now face a very difficult period of readjustment. That morning a grim-faced

Prince Edward, dressed in civilian clothes, was driven out of Buckingham Palace to begin the 200-mile journey to Lympstone. On arrival in the afternoon he smiled and raised his hand to the guard on duty. He was greeted by Major Paul Bancroft, his training officer, and had subsequent meetings with his Commanding officer, Colonel Ian Moore, and the officer in charge of training, Captain Robert Fanshawe. Each tried to persuade Edward to remain, but suggested that if he did resign it would be wise to undertake a counselling programme designed specifically for resigning Marines. Prince Edward chose not to spend the night in his small 12 foot by 8 foot room, but was seen that evening driving out of the barracks in his own Rover car, trailed by his detective in a car behind.

That day the Prince found himself the subject of numerous television and newspaper reports, all speculating on his future. Even his former tutor, Dr Gavin MacKenzie, appeared on the Jimmy Young programme on Radio Two to discuss the young Prince's situation.

Thursday 8 January 1987
Prince Edward's friend, Lieutenant Peter Fraser, revealed that he too was resigning from the Royal Marines, but stated that he had not been influenced by the Prince's decision, nor had Edward ever discussed the matter with him. 'From my observations of Prince Edward he has the makings of becoming a Green Beret,' Peter Fraser told reporters. Asked why he thought Edward had decided to resign he said, 'I would not put it down to the physical side of Marine training. It is far more likely that his three years at university have broadened his horizons. That explanation is much nearer the mark.'

After spending some time at Buckingham Palace, Prince Edward returned to his family at Sandringham.

Friday 9 January 1987
Prince Philip ordered an enquiry to find out who had leaked information to the press about Prince Edward's resignation. He also began proceedings for breach of copyright because one of his private letters had been published. Eventually the *Sun* newspaper had to pay an undisclosed sum to one of Prince Philip's charities. Prince Edward was seen that day riding his

horse as he so often did when he needed to be alone. Although obviously exhausted and distressed he nevertheless spoke calmly to the press saying, 'I'm here until Sunday. Then I'm going to Lympstone and I'll be making my decision on Monday. That's all. There's nothing more to be said.' That day he joined the Duke of Edinburgh on a shoot at Wood Farm. Although no official announcement had yet been made, the media knew that his resignation was a foregone conclusion. His training officer, Captain Robert Fanshawe, diplomatically told reporters, 'I sincerely hope to see this young man on Monday morning bright-eyed and bushy-tailed and full of motivation for life as a Marine.'

An unconfirmed story that Prince Edward had 'wept while making his decision' led the *New York Post* to dub him 'The Weeping Wimp of Windsor', Meanwhile biographer Anthony Holden defended him in the *Daily Mail*, writing:

> *Edward is no wimp . . . the first four months of a Marine officer's training course, through which he has apparently come with flying colours, are by far the most physically arduous. No, Edward's problems are more psychological. He has merely had the good sense to question the value of a military career* per se, *particularly for someone in his own unique position. He has shown that he wishes to be his own man and thus to choose his own career, not have it chosen for him, nor to live his life merely by tradition or precedent.*

Sunday 11 January 1987

Prince Edward returned to London to prepare for his final visit to Lympstone, and many hoped that he would have a final change of heart. Every national Sunday newspaper discussed the Prince's problems. Sir John Junor wrote in the *Sunday Express*:

> *It is said that Prince Edward wept for hours after taking his decision to quit the Royal Marines. I feel like weeping for him too. If he had been an ordinary young man of middle-class parents it would still have been an awesome decision to make . . . but no one outside his own family and friends would ever have known about it. Now the whole world knows. And even if, under pressure, he has*

a last minute change of mind, it will not lessen the damage. For all the rest of his life his irresolution is going to be remembered.

A *Sunday Express* opinion poll proved that the country was solidly behind Prince Edward's decision. The poll was conducted by the Northampton and London based Telephone Surveys Ltd, and from a sample of 1,000 adults, 80.7 per cent were on his side and only 12 per cent against. Of the women who supported Prince Edward, in the 55 to 64 age group 99 per cent voted in his favour. Surprisingly it was people in his own age group who offered less support. Of the 16- to 24-year-olds, only 63 per cent agreed with him. Overwhelmingly, though, the nation seemed to accept that the Prince had to act in accordance with his own feelings.

Monday 12 January 1987
Prince Edward spent his final day at Lympstone, packing up his kit and collecting the few belongings he had left in his room. He met once more with his senior officers and once again confirmed his decision. During his time with the Royal Marines he had been known as 'Rock Steady Eddie' and he was now living up to his nickname.

As the Prince viewed the barracks for the last time he could not have had any regrets. He looked out across Woodbury Common where he had once twisted his ankle badly on a speed march; he saw the gymnasium where in his second week he had received a bloodied nose and a black eye in the boxing ring (wounds which had caused the rumours of bullying); he thought of the freezing mud and the painful blisters from swinging over icy lakes deep enough to drown a man. Then, with what must surely have been a sense of relief, he finally drove away from Lympstone to the sanctuary of Gatcombe Park with his sister, Princess Anne. If Prince Philip was as angry as many would have us believe, this brief separation gave him some time to cool off, and Edward an opportunity to gather his thoughts.

Tuesday 13 January 1987
An official statement was issued by Buckingham Palace:

*After much consideration HRH The Prince Edward has decided
to resign from the Royal Marines.*

*An announcement about his future plans is not expected for
some time.*

*Prince Edward is leaving the Marines with great regret but has
decided that he does not wish to make the service his long-term
career.*

At last the truth was confirmed and the media speculation
could end. It was no coincidence that Prince Edward went to
stay with his sister, for she was the only member of his immediate family who had not been in one of the services herself.
Prince Charles had experienced the Air Force and the Navy,
which his brother and father had chosen as a career, and even
the Queen had once been a second subaltern in the Auxiliary
Territorial Service. Princess Anne could look at the situation
from a more impartial point of view. She applauded his decision to go his own way and not be dictated to by convention. She
was also the one person who could be down to earth about the
matter. She would tell Edward to pull himself together if he
started to feel sorry for himself, but she could also offer
support and advice. Together they looked at the available
options. He could take up teaching, something he did not want
to do. He could take up the offer of work in industry from Sir
Terence Beckett, the Director-General of the Confederation of
British Industry, or he could pursue a career in the arts as
suggested by Sir Roy Strong. Alternatively he could follow
Anne's lead and embark on a full-time career of royal duty.
Anne had herself shunned the idea of going to university,
considering it to be of no practical use to her, and had carved
out her own niche. Edward could do the same, but whatever
path he chose he knew that he could count on his sister's
support. She sympathised with her brother, knowing that the
stigma of the Royal Marines episode would haunt him for the
rest of his life, but strongly believed that everyone should enjoy
their work. Edward was not happy with what he was doing, so
he gave it up. In her eyes it was as simple as that.

Prince Edward came through the episode a stronger and
wiser person, having gained much respect on the way for not
giving in to convention. Prince Charles, for example, had not

always been happy in the forces but did not want to set an awkward precedent by giving it up. His admiration for Edward increased as a result of his decision. Sending Princes into the services had become a tradition, but it was by no means an obligation. Prince Edward has now broken that tradition. It is unlikely, for example, that Prince William or Prince Harry will enter the services unless, of course, they really want to. They have Uncle Edward to thank for terminating that obligation. Alan Hamilton, Royal Correspondent of *The Times*, wrote:

> *Most will applaud his decision to quit rather than chain himself to nine years of misery. And most will applaud him for breaking a convention which is perhaps becoming outdated . . . The next generation is likely to find other ways of proving its character and its worth.*

Of the four royal cousins born in 1964 Prince Edward had been the only one expected to go into services, simply because his mother is Queen. When Princess Alexandra's son, James Ogilvy, *chose* to join the Army at the age of eighteen it surprised his family. Always keen on new experiences James joined the Scots Guards, his father's old regiment, on a short-term commission and was stationed in Hong Kong. It was never intended to be a full-time career and simply filled a gap before James embarked on a four-year history of art course at St Andrew's University. Although it had been Prince Edward's own decision to join the Royal Marines, in his case it always had to be considered a long-term commitment. He did not have the option of dabbling as his cousin James did. In retrospect, had Edward joined the Marines for a year before going to university he would have known then that he was not cut out for a service career.

Despite stories that Prince Edward was unpopular with the Marines, many of his colleagues were sorry to see him go. He had tried hard to integrate himself into their community and had received no special privileges. He had to fit in with their lifestyle, from making his own bed to polishing his own boots, but once again his status, upbringing and Scotland Yard protection meant that he could never be just one of the boys. Certainly after his resignation there was no obvious animosity. In May

1987 Prince Edward was officially invited to watch a display by the Marines unarmed combat unit in North Devon and met one of his former instructors 'Nobby' Hall. The two chatted amiably for fifteen minutes with much laughter. 'It was lovely to see you again,' said Edward, shaking his hand at the end of the conversation. If Edward was haunted by the memory of his time with the Marines, he did not show it. Later he agreed to take the salute at the 1987 Royal Tournament, whose theme for that year was the Royal Navy, to which the Marines are attached. Edward agreed, however, on condition that he could take the salute in 'civvies'. He did not want to be seen in his Royal Marines uniform.

For a while the media inevitably poked fun at Prince Edward's situation. A Mac cartoon in the *Daily Mail* showed the Duke of Edinburgh dropping a teacup in horror as the Queen calmly says, 'While we're on the subject dear – Andrew is starting to feel that his naval career is getting in the way of his flower arranging classes . . .' Cummings of the *Express* portrayed the Queen bent double under the weight of a massive crown, accompanied by Margaret Thatcher, the then Prime Minister, burdened down by the Government, above the caption, 'Take heart, Prince Edward! Look at what WE carry on our backs and look how WE enjoy it!'

Contrary to speculation that there had been a family rift, Edward revealed in an interview four months after his resignation that he had received only support from his family. Although he was unlikely to say anything to the contrary, once Prince Philip had overcome the disappointment, the episode actually seemed to bring the two closer together. It also revealed how very similar Prince Edward and his father are. Prince Philip has always been an individual, never frightened of speaking his own mind or of following his own desires, and if he had had to follow convention he has done it in his own way. He has gone to the Ascot races to please the Queen, but has discreetly, almost defiantly, listened to cricket on a small radio. He is President of the Worldwide Fund for Nature, who aim to conserve wild animals, yet because he enjoys hunting he has not once bowed to criticism that shooting and killing animals is incongruous with his position. As a man's man, Prince Philip enjoyed the camaraderie of the Royal Navy and was suited to life on a destroyer during wartime, but had a naval career been incompatible with his character he would have had no qualms about opting out. Irritated he might well have been by his youngest son's resignation, but he finally came to admire Edward's strength of character in admitting that he had made a mistake. An episode which looked as if it might destroy the relationship between father and son irrevocably, actually brought them closer together. It is no coincidence that the cause with which Prince Edward is now most closely associated is the one that bears his father's name, the Duke of Edinburgh's Award.

The whole experience of the Royal Marines was a very short but painful chapter in Prince Edward's life, and as the furore died down he faced a new and unnerving situation. He was about to celebrate his twenty-third birthday but the secure future he had once envisaged had evaporated. 'What can Edward do now?' screamed the headlines, and it was a question he must also have asked himself. Opening his engagement diary that spring he faced page after blank page. For the first time in his life he was in control of how each day should be filled. It had been his decision to quit the Marines and now it was up to him to consider the next move.

Chapter 5

RESTING

Fate finds for every man
His share of misery.

EURIPIDES,

Iphigenia in Aulis

Prince Edward reached for his pen before sending a plate of half-cooked pasta swiftly back to the Palace kitchens.

'Would you like me to come and show you how to cook this?' he wrote angrily.

This was not the first time Edward had complained about his meals, and his sometimes sarcastic notes did not endear him to the long-suffering staff.

Often alone for long periods at Buckingham Palace, Prince Edward felt frustrated. He had technically left home fifteen years earlier when he first went to Heatherdown boarding school. Now, in 1987, at the age of twenty-three he was suddenly back home with Mother. While his family went off on their usual round of official engagements, Edward often vented his feelings on those closest to him, the Palace staff. On Canada Day, when a group of Canadian dancers and musicians put on a display in the courtyard in the presence of the Queen Mother, staff who stood watching the free show glanced up at the windows of the second floor and saw the sad figure of Prince Edward looking down – in his own home, yet strangely isolated. Somewhat ironically, in retrospect, they likened him to the Phantom of the Opera.

Although the media had been almost universally compassionate towards the Prince following his resignation from the Royal Marines, sympathy does not last for ever. Already certain newspapers were calculating that Princess Anne, now with a reformed image and only weeks away from being honoured with the title Princess Royal, had undertaken 704 engagements in the previous year, spending sixty-seven days overseas, whilst Prince Edward had only fulfilled thirty-seven engagements, attended twenty-two dinners or receptions, and spent a mere twenty days overseas. What they did not take into account was that from January to June 1986 Edward had been studying for and taking his finals, and from September to December he had been in the Marines, but the figures looked low enough to warrant a story. Eager to discover the Prince's next career move, the press accused him of procrastination. It did nothing for Edward's confidence.

The media did not understand that even the simplest of royal engagements involves precision planning. During the early part of 1987 Prince Edward's availability had not been anticipated and so his official diary remained empty. Until he had turned eighteen Prince Edward had shared a Private Secretary and Equerry with Prince Andrew, a role first taken by Squadron Leader Adam Wise and later by Lieutenant Colonel Sean O'Dwyer. When Prince Andrew married in 1986 and his wife became a full member of 'the Firm', he began to establish his own compliment of staff to handle their ever-increasing duties. During their six-year marriage the Yorks had a Private Secretary and Treasurer, a Comptroller and Assistant Private Secretary, an Equerry and an extra-Equerry for the Duke and four ladies-in-waiting for the Duchess. This was in addition to their private domestic staff. During the same period, as a single man Prince Edward at first simply took on Lieutenant Colonel Sean O'Dwyer as a Private Secretary and Equerry, and in the last five years has only added to his staff an Assistant Private Secretary and two part-time clerks.

During this apparently inactive period, invitations for the Prince to attend functions at the Palace arrived daily, including requests for his patronage. Edward gave great thought to the organisations with which he would be associated and opted for those that fell within his sphere of knowledge and personal interest so that his patronage would be of some practical advantage. He did not want to be a mere figurehead, but was determined to be actively involved with anything he put his name to. The theatre was never far from his thoughts and he agreed to become Patron of the Haddo House Hall Arts Trust which had been established by a family friend, the Marchioness of Aberdeen, as well as the National Youth Theatre of Great Britain and the National Youth Orchestra of Scotland. The same year he took on the Presidency of the National Youth Music Theatre. He had already been appointed Patron of the Cambridge Youth Theatre and the Cambridge Symphony Orchestra during his time at university. Perhaps the most significant role that Edward accepted in 1987 was that of International Trustee of the Duke of Edinburgh's Award International Association for which he began to chair regular monthly meetings at the Palace.

As it took time for his Private Secretary to organise a diary of official engagements, and the Prince was seldom seen in public, there was a natural assumption that he was idling his time away. Through his close involvement with the Duke of Edinburgh's Award and his interest in the arts, Edward was, however, formulating projects which would give the Scheme a higher public profile. Having been established for thirty years there was a very real danger of complacency, and the Award risked being over-shadowed by more actively self-promoting causes. Yet the Prince saw that the Scheme could still offer young people much-needed challenges and opportunities. (Skills that young people have acquired in obtaining the Award have frequently resulted in a career for life.) Having enjoyed his brief experience of television while making the programme on Gordonstoun in 1984, and his appearances on TV-AM's *Wideawake* and BBC1's *Saturday Super-store*, the Prince saw the medium as a perfect way of bringing the Scheme to a wider audience. Not surprisingly, he did not find it difficult to interest the BBC in his ideas, and he spent the first part of 1987 writing the script for a two-part film. Eventually Edward was involved in the actual filming and narrated the documentaries himself.

When the programmes were broadcast in April 1987 the Prince was praised for his relaxed manner and informative approach, with critics hailing him as 'a natural communicator'. The films fulfilled a dual purpose. They achieved their main aim of publicising the Duke of Edinburgh's Award and encouraged new participants, but from the Prince's own point of view the exercise also gave him valuable television experience and a higher public profile. This was indelible evidence that he had not been idling his time away. Also, for someone contemplating a career in the arts, the programmes gave Edward media credibility. BBC producer Michael Begg commented:

> *The Prince was a lot less trouble than 90 per cent of the presenters I work with. He's no dilettante and had obviously taken pains to find out what this TV business is all about. He knew how scripts were put together, and he understands interview techniques, though he'd be the first to concede he's not yet a perfect master at it. He even threw himself into boring bits like dubbing.*

Three times for the cameras Edward was made to catapult in a canoe from the quayside into the Solent. Wet and cold after completing the feat, he got his own back on the producer by pushing him, fully clothed, into the water. 'You bugger, your Royal Highness,' spluttered Michael Begg. It was kept in as the final line of the film.

Spurred on by the success of these programmes, Prince Edward conceived a much more ambitious television project, a programme which, if it worked, could do much to enhance the Royal Family's reputation, especially amongst the young. If it failed there was an equal chance that their image could be tarnished. For several months Prince Edward was to walk a tightrope, with many critics simply waiting for him to fall.

A successful television game show which Prince Edward had enjoyed as a child was the BBC programme *It's a Knockout*, originally invented by the French. Introduced to British viewers in the early 1970s by sports commentator David Vine, it was eventually taken over by the broadcaster whose name will always be synonymous with it, Stuart Hall, and the programme became a national institution. Each week the crew filmed in a different venue so that participants from all over the country could dress in outrageous costumes while being put through all sorts of undignified physical challenges. A man dressed as a banana might have to climb over a wall, while someone dressed as a melon had to squeeze through a tunnel. It was pure custard pie throwing slapstick in the guise of a game show. In 1977, when the programme was filmed in Windsor Great Park, a slim blond thirteen-year-old boy joined the crowds to watch the frolics. It was a rare opportunity for Edward to mingle with spectators unnoticed. 'I was at the age when I could still do that sort of thing,' the Prince later said, lamenting the fact that he cannot now go anywhere unrecognised.

Prince Edward's idea was to put on a royal version of *It's a Knockout*, with four members of the Royal Family each leading a team of celebrity competitors. The money raised through the event could be split between four charities of their choice. It was to be Edward's first venture as an impresario. As such, he had to convince members of his own family to take part and, more importantly, gain the Queen's permission. Naturally the Queen did not want to see the monarchy cheapened so she made the proviso that younger members of her family could only participate as team leaders, they were not to take part in the games themselves. Edward admitted to being 'rather disappointed' that they could not compete but tactfully acknowledged that 'these things are decided by the powers that be'. The powers in this instance were certainly not the BBC, who were keen to involve the younger royals as much as possible. 'The games aren't in fact custard pies and greasy wraps,' said Edward at a press conference. 'In that sense it's slightly different from the old *It's a Knockout*, but we've deliberately kept a sense of decorum to suit the people involved. It's an atmosphere of heroism and gentility.'

It was not considered seemly for the heir to the throne to join a game show which might appear too much like a sketch from *Spitting Image*. Edward's sporting sister the Princess Royal was, however, prepared to do almost anything to raise money for the Save the Children Fund, and the Duke and Duchess of York were happy to captain the other teams for, respectively, the Worldwide Fund for Nature and International Year of Shelter for the Homeless. 'Charity tends to be rather a cut-throat business, with everyone competing for the same money,' Prince Edward told Nicki Household of the *Radio Times*. 'This event sets a good example because we're pooling our resources and sharing the proceeds. If nothing else, it proves that charities can work together.' The Prince's own share of the proceeds were naturally intended for the Duke of Edinburgh's Award Scheme.

Prince Edward was involved in every stage of planning. The initial problem was finding a suitable venue. Not only was a large open space required but one that could offer catering facilities, dressing-room space and, most important of all, tight security. Alton Towers in Staffordshire was eventually selected as having all the necessary facilities, as well as providing an ideal backdrop for the event. On the day of recording itself, because four members of the Royal Family were present, security arrangements were so tight that even the press were confined to a room with a television monitor.

Prince Edward had been made Patron of the Royal Tournament in 1986 and was thus able to seek expert advice from the organisers who each year have to arrange a public display with a different theme. For what was eventually to be titled *The Grand Knockout Tournament*, Prince Edward needed to find a suitably royal theme for the costumes and games. Possibly inspired by the stately portraits which adorn his family's residences, he settled for a Tudor theme and decided to present the whole tournament as if the year were 1587 when Queen Elizabeth I was on the throne. As a historian, Edward should have known that this was not his ancestor's happiest year, for she was facing anguish over the execution of Mary Queen of Scots as well as the threat of Spanish invasion. His own return to 1587 was not to prove the happiest of experiences either.

Just as when he produced and acted in plays at Cambridge, Edward threw himself heart and soul into organising the *Knockout Tournament*, but at times he was in danger of being over-confident. Only twenty-three and still relatively inexperienced, he would get irritated if his plans did not fall easily into place, and as the date of filming drew closer he lived on 'snatched sleep and the occasional sandwich or Mars Bar'. In typical royal fashion he sought advice from all quarters, from historical costumiers for the outfits, to Charity Projects for fund-raising details. He enjoyed the challenge but he had to learn to delegate.

To raise funds for the tournament Prince Edward persuaded well-known retailers to sponsor the players. He received sponsorship money from Harrods, MacDonalds and Asda, and held fortnightly meetings in the run-up to the event with accountants Price Waterhouse, the public relations company Good Relations, and the solicitors Harbottle and Lewis. There were also meetings with the Staffordshire police and fire brigade to discuss security and safety arrangements. Edward not only selected celebrities as potential contestants but personally telephoned each of them to discuss their availability. Finally he had many long sessions with BBC producers and designers to discuss everything from props to camera angles. It proved an excellent apprenticeship for the would-be production assistant and Andrew Lloyd Webber may perhaps have been taking note.

In an interview for *Woman's Own* Edward admitted:

I've had doubts about it – one always does when one is trying to put on any sort of show. I thought that maybe we were taking on too much in too short a time. Also the event has the active involvement of members of the Royal Family in a way that hasn't been done before . . . All sorts of people have been concerned that so many members of the Royal Family are heavily involved . . . but I would like the public to view it in a generous way . . . We're not superstars and, I hope, at the end of the competition the Royal Family will come out of it much better.

Prince Edward also held a general press conference for the media at which he explained, 'We felt that there is too much seriousness in the world. People were forgetting that they should let their hair down and have fun.' As if to emphasise the point, at rehearsals he wore a T-shirt printed with the words: 'NO, I JUST LOOK LIKE HIM!' Asked if the tournament meant a new departure for the Royal Family, he replied that they were not, in his opinion, making themselves 'more accessible. It's just that we're more active these days.'

Although Prince Edward made himself available to the media before the event he was particularly selective, using them to his own advantage, just as he had done at Cambridge. For example, he allowed only one photographer to record the proceedings – royal favourite, Jayne Fincher. The gentle Miss Fincher has often photographed Prince Edward and by this time had built up a good rapport with him. At the tournament itself she admitted that even she was surprised by Edward's professional approach and described him as 'mature and bright with ideas no matter whether they concerned costumes or picture lay-out. The Prince is extremely adept at chairing committee meetings. He was always up at six o'clock, if not before.' Julie Ticehurst of Good Relations said that Edward proved to be 'a brilliant organiser, who kept an enormous amount in his head and managed, with expertise beyond his years, to keep together the various organisations involved.'

During the run-up to the event Edward became adept at fielding questions, and his answers were frequently tongue in cheek. Had he signed a contract for the programme, many were curious to know. 'I didn't sign any actual contract with the BBC,' he grinned. 'Just a piece of paper promising that I wouldn't get married this year!'

The culmination of months of hard work came on Monday 15 June when the event was filmed at Alton Towers Leisure Park in front of 4,000 spectators, many of whom had entered into the spirit of the occasion by dressing in costume themselves, ranging from cardboard armour to Elizabethan-style dresses. Prince Edward's one big hope for the event was that it would be 'a lovely sunny day' but he awoke after only a few hours sleep to find a very wet, windy June morning. He arrived at Alton Towers at 6.30 a.m. and later said, 'It was literally the worst day of my life as I surveyed the soggy scene.' They call it 'Queen's weather', for royal occasions are invariably dogged by rain.

Prince Edward had spent much of the previous day making final preparations, although some of the star performers did not arrive until the actual day. 'Superman' Christopher Reeve, for example, flew in on Concorde on the very day of filming. 'It's been a bit of a nightmare making sure everyone's costume fits,' said Prince Edward. 'Some of the Americans were a bit baffled when we asked for their measurements to make a period costume.' For most of the players the proceedings began on the eve of the tournament with a banquet at the Isaac Walton Hotel in nearby Dovedale. Already in boisterous spirits, the Duchess of York threw after-dinner mints at her husband, sparking off a mock battle. Prince Edward must have been relieved that the Queen was 150 miles away.

The four teams were made up of many illustrious names from the world of entertainment and sport. All had been carefully hand-picked, many were personal friends. Stuart Hall was, quite naturally, Master of Ceremonies for the day, assisted by Les Dawson and Su Pollard, with Aled Jones as Herald. The entertainer, Paul Daniels, acted as Judge, and the Prince's own team included athletes Steve Cram and Tessa Sanderson, champion swimmer Duncan Goodhew, and champion boxer Barry McGuigan. There were also comedy actors John Cleese and Nicholas Lyndhurst, Prince Charles's favourite singer Dame Kiri Te Kanawa, plus singer/actress Toyah Willcox whom Prince Edward had worked with in the National Youth Theatre. The Princess Royal's team included old friends Anthony Andrews and Jackie Stewart, her sparring partner Emlyn Hughes (who she had once hit over the head with a handbag on the TV quiz pro-gramme *A Question of Sport*), singers Cliff Richard, Tom Jones and Sheena Easton, and actress Jenny Agutter. The Duke of York had amongst his Tudor lords and ladies TV action girl Anneka Rice, footballer Gary Lineker, motor racer Nigel Mansell, actors George Lazenby, Griff Rhys Jones and Michael Palin, actress Fiona Fullerton and American heart-throb John Travolta; while the Duchess captained comedienne friend Pamela Stephenson, Jane Seymour, Chris de Burgh, Meatloaf, Mel Smith, Ben Cross, Michael Brandon, Viv Richards and Steve Cauthen. All together over fifty celebrities took part in the royal spectacle.

The team captains seemed eager to join in the games, but contented themselves with shouting encouragement from the sidelines. Hearing the Duchess of York screaming, it was difficult to believe that she was still recovering from laryngitis. Continuing where she had left off at the previous night's banquet, she now threw apples, oranges and pears at her husband. Finally she kissed him on the cheek for the benefit of the cameras to prove that there was no ill-feeling. Possibly having second thoughts on the day itself, Princess Anne looked grim and severe on arrival, but soon warmed to the event and cheered on her 'Red Perils' team. Uncharacteristically, the Princess playfully tweaked Stuart Hall's eyebrows, which were almost singed when the Duke of York fired a cannon. It was that sort of day. Prince Edward took off his T-shirt, and peaked cap bearing the slogan 'Operation Deep Freeze', to don a doublet and hose, offering to play the fool and put his head in the stocks in return for a £50 donation.

The Duchess of York won the audience's affection with her boisterous antics spurring on her team, the 'Blue Bandits', but it was the Princess Royal who eventually led her team to victory. At the outset she had admitted that she was 'cool, calm and collected'; her team would 'only get excited if they won'. It was an approach that paid off, and Anne also succeeded in retaining her dignity throughout. Ultimately there were no losers, for over a million pounds was raised for charity through the event. For the competitors, the day was rounded off with a barbecue and a fireworks display. A very tired Prince Edward thanked everyone who had helped raise money and make the day a success. Finally, at the end of a fourteen-hour day, Prince Edward made his way to the press tent.

Edward may have been exhausted, but some fifty journalists had been confined for fourteen hours in a tent on a wet day, yards from an event they were supposed to report but only allowed to watch the proceedings on a television monitor, being shown only what the cameras wanted them to see. Not surprisingly tempers were frayed. It was now past 8 p.m., they still had their copy to write for the following day's papers, and many still had to make the journey from Staffordshire back to London that night. The Prince had admitted that he was 'incredibly nervous' about the event and at the end of a long day the adrenalin was still flowing. Edward arrived at the press tent as an obligation, not in the mood to face journalists, wanting only to collapse into bed. He had already written a short speech about the day, which he duly delivered. As he paused towards the end, Independent Television News reporter Joan Thirkettle interrupted with a question, fully believing the speech to be over. Was the Prince pleased with how the event had gone, she asked. It was a perfectly reasonable question, but Miss Thirkettle had picked the wrong moment to ask it.

'I haven't finished yet,' Prince Edward replied firmly, and continued with his speech. Then, turning to his captive audience, he asked, 'I only hope you have enjoyed yourselves – have you?'

There was absolute silence. It was not the reaction he had anticipated, and an expression redolent of Prince Philip crossed his face.

'Great. Thanks for sounding so bloody enthusiastic,' he snapped. 'Well? What have you been doing all day?'

The reporters refrained from telling him. Again he met with a wall of silence.

Edward kicked back his chair, growled, 'Right, that's it!', and walked out. The ice thawed. The journalists now had their story.

Edward returned to the firework display, not anticipating the sparks that would fly the following day.

'What happened was not rudeness on his part,' explained Mike Smith, one of the *Knockout* directors, trying desperately to defuse the situation. 'He'd been up since six o'clock this morning and was extremely tired. He probably wanted someone to say "Well done".'

Nobody was placated, least of all when a still angry Prince Edward was confronted by a group of press photographers as he left Alton Towers: 'One of these days you people are going to have to learn some manners,' he warned. It was another drop of oil on the flames. For those who had previously expressed doubts that the Royal Family would come out of the episode very well, Prince Edward was the last person they had expected to end the day on a sour note.

After he had calmed down, Edward later said that he had been thrown by the unexpectedly 'hostile' reception he had received. 'I was tired and lacking in patience,' he confessed, admitting that he could kick himself for giving the press an 'opportunity to get their knives into me'. But it was too late for regrets. The pens of Fleet Street had already been sharpened. 'It's a Walkout' screamed the next morning's headlines, 'Edward storms out After Game Show'. For one who had tried so hard to make the *Grand Knockout Tournament* a success, it was ironic that Prince Edward was the one member of the Royal Family who received the most criticism. 'The free press has little to fear from finger-wagging Princes,' wrote Peter McKay of *The Times*. 'To wear a T-shirt saying, "No, I just look like him" might invite ridicule . . . Prince Edward is so conscious of his own celebrity that he carries a derisory joke about it on his back. Self-mockery is a dangerous trick best left to experts,' and suggested that the Prince found 'some thespian undertaking slightly more uplifting than *It's A Knockout*.'

Prince Edward's credibility was tarnished. Those who had been sympathetic about the Marines saga now classed that and the *Knockout* tournament as his failures. Had it not been for an emotional display of intolerance Prince Edward would have been hailed as a hero. He would have been applauded for his comic T-shirt as his own sister was when she wore a sweat-shirt with the slogan 'Menial Tasks Division' at the Gatcombe Park horse trials. It was a sign that they do not take themselves too seriously. The inexperienced Prince unfortunately not only lost his temper, but lost it in front of people that matter – those who influence his public image. If Prince Edward had wept after leaving the

Marines, he must now have shed tears of frustration at how a sudden lack of control had destroyed all that he had worked so hard to achieve. The press were understandably annoyed at seemingly being kept apart from the entertainment, but Prince Edward should have explained that they had been segregated deliberately. The rights of the programme had to be kept exclusive for the benefit of charity, which is why only one official photographer was allowed. At the end of the day the press needed a whipping-boy on whom to take out their own frustration and, for them, Prince Edward said the wrong thing at the right time.

Broadcast on Friday 19 June, the programme received a positive reaction from television audiences and in America was nominated for an ACE Award, the television equivalent of an Oscar. In December the Prince was able to reveal that more than the targeted £1,000,000 had been achieved when he went to the fourth-floor of Harrods in Knightsbridge to launch a *Royal Knockout* book and board game, the proceeds of which would swell the charitable funds even further. Looking less confident and faltering slightly under the barrage of photographers' flash-bulbs, he made a short and uncontroversial speech. He posed willingly with the producer and some of the contestants to promote the book and then departed quietly. From the *Knockout* saga the Prince had learned some valuable lessons, not least in media relations.

In theatrical terms Prince Edward was considered to be 'resting' during 1987, to the uninitiated a euphemism for being out of work, but it was very much a period of learning and taking stock. Certainly the Prince was not by any means inactive, he was carefully laying the foundations for his future. He admitted that the *Knockout* competition 'took nearly four weeks to recover from' and it was an event which dominated his life for the early part of the year. Nevertheless he knew there was a limit to how long he could continue to receive an annual Civil List allowance while performing only the minimum number of duties. Many already believed – quite wrongly – that the allowance was a private income, so the time had come to try and prove his worth.

To find out more about the British Constitution, which forms the basis of the monarch's role, the Prince spent a day at the Palace of Westminster, learning about the workings of Parliament at first hand. He had a private lunch with three members of the House of

Lords, and later in the afternoon had tea with Bernard Weatherill, MP for Croydon North East and at that time Speaker of the House of Commons. For several hours Edward acquainted himself with the day-to-day workings of Government, looking at how Bills went through Parliament. He learned about different types of legislation and the stages that must be passed through before they become law, from the First Reading (when the Bill is formally introduced) to the point of Royal Assent (when the Queen finally agrees to it becoming an Act of Parliament). He spent another day visiting the Old Bailey Central Criminal Court to watch a trial and had lunch and discussions with the Lord Mayor and Sheriffs of the City of London. Neither of these visits were classed as official, they were part of the Prince's own research to improve his background knowledge of government and legislation. Although we will never know the Prince's political leanings – he is eligible to vote in a general election but chooses not to exercise his right – it was not long after these visits that he began to take the Conservative Government to task on certain issues.

Through *Knockout*, for example, the Prince had contacted the group Charity Projects. This later led to him being asked to become President of the Holborn Great Investment Race, a scheme in which ten of the top City stockbrokers were given £500,000 to use on the Exchange. Through dealing they raised £800,000 for the homeless. As part of the Investment Race, Prince Edward was able to visit various projects and met many homeless people himself. When he handed over the £800,000 cheque he used his speech to make a case for the homeless and attacked the Government for its policy over housing benefits. It was a way of using his position to get people to sit up and take notice. When his sister-in-law Diana met and shook hands with AIDS sufferers, her simple act was said to have done more for their plight than thousands of pounds worth of advertising. His own secure accommodation may have made Edward feel particular compassion for the homeless, and possibly a twinge of guilt.

That same year, as Chairman of the Duke of Edinburgh's Award Project '87, the Prince travelled all over the United Kingdom visiting regional centres and those participating in the Scheme and made two official overseas tours to Canada and Portugal. On 25 June, barely a week after filming the *Knockout* programme, Prince Edward left Heathrow Airport to undertake engagements in Nova Scotia and Prince Edward Island. He had a full and varied schedule of official duties, but tempered with many informal moments. Crowds lined his route and the Canadian press christened him 'The Heart-throb Prince'. The Prince's warm, unassuming style quickly endeared him to the Canadian people who were keen to involve him in as many sporting activities as possible. On his first day in Halifax, the capital of Nova Scotia, he was invited to take the helm of a schooner, *Bluenose II*, which he steered across the harbour; and, more formally, he handed out awards at the Maritime Museum of the Atlantic Dock. At Nova Scotia Agricultural College he watched displays by athletes and at a youth day on Prince Edward Island he visited thirteen activity stations and met several Canadian Duke of Edinburgh's Gold Award achievers. At the youth day he was applauded by the crowds as he showed off his golf swing, gave a display of archery and played a game of bowls. On the fifth and final day he was taken lobster fishing in the open sea off Malpeque harbour in extremely strong winds. During his five-day visit the Prince met Nova Scotia's premier John M. Buchanan, inspected a guard of honour mounted by the 78th Highlanders and toured Halifax Citadel National Historic Park. Each day he made speeches, went on impromptu walkabouts and presented medals to new achievers of the Duke of Edinburgh's Award, before returning quietly to London on 30 June. Two weeks later an official visit to Canada by the Duke and Duchess of York filled the newspapers. Few people in Britain were even aware that Edward had been there. His visit had been uncontroversial and consequently un-newsworthy. It was a galling fact of life that he would take time to come to terms with.

Two weeks after his return from Canada, Prince Edward took part in a Fun Day at Ascot on 12 July to raise £100,000 for charity. The *Knockout* tournament was still being discussed, and unconfirmed reports claimed that the Queen was so upset by it that she had forbidden any such royal group activity again. Yet, as if to contradict the rumours, four members of the Royal Family were once more competing in teams to raise money. Appearing to cock a snook at critics, Princess Anne captained a team including Prince Edward and the Duchess of York (just days away from her own Canadian tour), who called themselves 'Three Quarters of a Knockout'. If the Queen really had been that upset even these rebels would not have been so insensitive as to rub salt in the wound so blatantly.

Princess Michael of Kent captained the opposing side with a team which included the Princess's friends Rosie, the Marchioness of Northampton, and horse-rider Pamela Hutton. They called themselves, less controversially, 'The Leaping Lypiatts' after the Kents' private house in Gloucestershire, Nether Lypiatt. Unlike the undignified televised sports a month earlier, however, the Royal Family confined themselves this time to the more conventional 'sport of Kings', negotiating fences on horseback. The event attracted thousands of spectators at the world-famous racecourse and raised money for the British Racing School and the Police Convalescence and Rehabilitation Trust.

Princess Anne's team at first looked like surefire winners, the Princess's skills at three-day eventing and flat racing being well known, but it was not their day. Princess Anne took 1 minute 43 seconds to complete the course, knocking down one fence; whereas Princess Michael of Kent completed a clear round of twenty-five fences in 1 minute 24 seconds. Just as Prince Edward had suffered a bad day at Alton Towers, his round as Ascot proved unspectacular. He knocked down five fences and was disqualified for not completing the course in the allotted time of 2 minutes. The Duchess of York fared better with only one fence down and a time of 1 minute 55 seconds, but it was not enough. Princess Michael of Kent's team were declared the outright winners. Fortunately the grim-faced Edward did not have to hold a press conference, but it seemed as if everything was conspiring against him.

Although now saddled with the image of a petulant Prince because of his one outburst at the press, the second half of 1987 was nevertheless an industrious time when Edward tried to improve his public persona. He presented the 1987 Schools Design Prize at the Science Museum in London, launched the Summer Proms at the Barbican Centre, took the salute at the Royal Tournament, and in November switched on the Regent Street Christmas lights. His more serious engagements ranged from fund-raising functions for the Muscular Dystrophy Group and the Mobility Trust to attending the funeral of Prince Ernest Augustus of Hanover in December. Amongst his many other official duties he chaired fortnightly meetings for the Duke of Edinburgh's Award.

His days may have been occupied but inwardly the Prince still felt unfulfilled. He had long discussions with Prince Charles who was himself facing something of a mid-life crisis. He was on the verge of his fortieth birthday and still had no practical role other than as heir to the throne. In February 1987 Charles told a group of journalists:

> *You cannot understand what it's like to have your whole life mapped out for you a year in advance. It's so awful to be programmed. I know what I'll be doing next week, next month, even next year. At times I get so fed up with the whole idea.*

After nearly forty years he was implying that he wanted to break the fetters of royal life. In February he stayed on at Klosters skiing after Diana returned home with the children, knowing that without her the press would go and he would have some space. In March he spent a long weekend in Gstaad with friends, and in April he went into the Kalahari Desert with his mentor, South African writer Sir Laurens Van der Post. In May he went salmon fishing alone on the River Dee and later in the year spent three days alone on a remote island in the Hebrides to experience the life of a crofter, as far removed as you can get from public life. Even some of his official visits that year were not on the list of engagements submitted to the press. From mid-September to mid-October Prince Charles remained in Scotland without his wife to take stock and gather his thoughts.

Having a difficult year himself, Prince Edward was very aware of his eldest brother's plight. He could see how Charles was trapped by his royal birth, only able to break free by taking refuge in some remote part of the world, which only incited media speculation about the state of his marriage. Queen Elizabeth II has hinted many times that hers is 'a job for life'. If she lives as long as her mother Prince Charles will be in his seventies before he succeeds to the throne – almost a lifetime of waiting in the wings.

With Prince Charles's example in mind, Prince Edward knew that he could not devote himself solely to royal duty, no matter how worthwhile the cause. There had to be something more to life. After his return from Canada that summer Edward began rehearsing for an amateur production of Shakespeare's *The Winter's Tale* in which he was cast as Florizel, Prince of Bohemia. The play was publicly performed in Aberdeen by the Haddo House players, sparking off false rumours of a romance between him and the girl playing his shepherdess, Glasgow University student Hannah Welfare. As he stepped on to the stage that August, Edward was reminded of happier days in student productions at Cambridge. Most of all he remembered a simple show he had written, produced and performed for a senior citizens club in Suffolk. It was not a high-quality drama, but they had listened and joined in with the show, and Edward had experienced the thrill of entertaining an appreciative audience. They were not like his usual audience of students who watched and cheered but could mock and jeer at the same time; they were not a crowd who came just to see if a member of the Royal Family would fall flat on their face, but a group of people who genuinely wanted to have a good time. According to the President of the Light Entertainment Society, 'The old people just loved Prince Edward and he was very good with them. I remember him teaching them a routine he'd devised for "Oh What A Luvverly Bunch of Coconuts" and it was *brilliant.*'

At Haddo Hall, with an audience of mostly local people, Edward again experienced the approbation of an audience who had come to see the play rather than him. He knew at that moment that he wanted a career in the arts. On a royal engagement he had no script, no rehearsal, just a one-off performance, with success or failure resting entirely on his shoulders. In the theatre he enjoyed the team effort, the fun of watching a production come together and its success being proved by sell-out performances. Although much of the *Knockout* programme had been a nightmare to produce, Edward had been involved at every stage. He had conceived the original idea, brought the people together, and, having planned every minute detail, watched the show come to fruition. His media relations skills may have been called into question, but his organisational abilities were not. Everyone involved with the project praised the Prince's command of the situation, his wealth of ideas and enthusiasm. Prince Edward knew that a career on the stage as a professional actor was a practical impossibility, but there was nothing to stop him having a managerial position.

There were suggestions that Prince Philip wanted his son to go into the diplomatic service or follow James Ogilvy into banking. Other members of the Royal Family have managed to combine royal duties with a career of their own. The Duke of Gloucester is an architect, the Duke of Kent works for the British Overseas Trade Board, and Prince Michael of Kent has had a career with the Ministry of Defence Intelligence Staff and as a non-executive director of Standard Telephones and investment advisers Aitken Hume. Of the royal quartet born in 1964, Edward was at that time the only one of the cousins without a career of his own. He was, however, the only one included in the Civil List and thus expected to fulfil royal duties. Whilst Prince Philip may have preferred his son to enter a respectable low-key career, if Edward was ever going to be a director in a company it would be theatrical rather than financial. On leaving the Marines he had already admitted to friends that he would like a career in television as a producer or director. He preferred a more glamorous career, like his relatives Lord Lichfield and Lord Snowdon, rather than a discreet life in the City.

In April 1986 Prince Edward met the composer and impresario Andrew Lloyd Webber and his then wife Sarah Brightman. The Lloyd Webbers had been invited to a party at Windsor Castle to celebrate the Queen's sixtieth birthday, for which the composer had devised a musical entertainment. The piece was a mini-musical written in collaboration with Tim Rice and called *Cricket*. The sixtieth birthday show had been organised by the Queen's youngest son.

As one of the most commercially successful composers of modern times, the Prince was naturally intrigued by Andrew Lloyd Webber's talent and subsequently went to see his hit show *Phantom of the Opera* on more than one occasion. Equally Mr Lloyd Webber was impressed by Edward's knowledge of the theatre and organisational skills. Prince Edward accepted an invitation to dine with the Lloyd Webbers on their 100-acre Berkshire estate in *Watership Down* country, and through relaxed conversations came the original idea that the Prince might join the Really Useful Theatre Company in some capacity. For the Prince it would mean joining an established and reputable company. For Andrew Lloyd Webber it would be excellent publicity and a royal seal of approval for his work. The proposal appeared to be mutually beneficial, and after lengthy discussions, it was agreed that the Prince would join the company in February 1988 as a production assistant.

The Queen gave her permission, on condition that Edward could still undertake royal duties. Of all professions the theatre offered some of the most flexible working hours and Andrew Lloyd Webber appreciated the Prince's obligations. 'You won't believe it – they are both thrilled,' Edward told a close relative, when asked about his parents' reaction to the news. He was less certain how the world media would take it. On 23 December 1987 Prince Edward ended his difficult year on a theatrical note. In black tie he walked on to the stage of the Barbican Theatre in London and, backed by the London Symphony Orchestra, narrated Prokofiev's *Peter and the Wolf*, a work in which timing is of paramount importance. The show raised money for the Beethoven Fund for Deaf Children and won Edward some rave reviews.

The timing of his next theatrical appearance would be studied equally closely by the critics. Exactly one year after his resignation from the Royal Marines, Buckingham Palace announced Prince Edward's next career move with trepidation.

Chapter 6

A REALLY USEFUL CAREER

On the stage he was natural, simple, affecting,
'twas only that, when he was off, he was acting.

OLIVER GOLDSMITH,

Garrick

Having accepted Andrew Lloyd Webber's offer of employment, the Prince faced a dilemma. He had insisted that he wanted to learn the profession from the bottom, and was prepared to work hard to prove that he was a worthwhile member of the team and not just a high-status passenger. However the job did carry a certain amount of responsibility and he would need to use his own initiative. The problem was how to present his new career to the public. If it appeared that he had been given a high-powered position, sceptics would say that it was for no other reason than *who* he was. It was therefore necessary to play down the job description. In typical tabloid style the Prince was represented not as a trainee but as a tea boy. Fully aware of the jokes that were being made about him, Edward decided that it would be wrong to arrive on his first day wearing a suit, and felt that the best approach was to play up to it. He arrived at the theatre in smart casuals, carrying a box of PG Tips tea bags. It was a guaranteed hit with waiting press photographers, and the fact that Andrew Lloyd Webber happened to own the *Palace* Theatre inspired even more jokes at Edward's expense.

'We all had reservations,' said Biddy Hayward, the company's Executive Director at the time. 'The fact of who he is will inevitably raise the question of why we're employing him. But that could lead to reverse discrimination. He's bright, he's intelligent and he has made it clear that the theatre is not just a passing whim.' As if to affirm his interest in the theatre, Prince Edward attended the prestigious Laurence Olivier Awards Ceremony just a few days before starting his new job.

On the morning of Monday 15 February 1988 Prince Edward became the first child of a reigning monarch to take up a full-time career other than the services. His arrival at the theatre, however, was unlike that of any other employee. First the building had to be searched by members of the Royal Protection Squad with sniffer dogs, looking for IRA bombs. Police outriders preceded Edward's limousine, not the usual mode of transport for back stage staff, and a crowd watched from the pavement as if this were an official visit. One admirer even handed him a rose. Press photographers crowded round an apparently benevolent Prince, whose only hope was that the novelty of his having joined the Really Useful Group would quickly wear off, allowing him to do his job quietly.

When his favourite relative Princess Alexandra undertook a nursing course at the Great Ormond Street Hospital in 1956 she too wanted no preferential treatment. Dressed in her regulation pink and white uniform with starched apron and cap, it did not please her to be greeted by hordes of photographers, cheering crowds and a bouquet from the matron on her first day. Like Prince Edward, she worked hard to break down the royal barrier that surrounded her, but her status always set her apart. The more menial the tasks she undertook to show that she was just one of the girls, the more impressed people seemed to be. Before his arrival at the Palace Theatre the staff were told to treat the Prince like any ordinary employee. They were to call him 'Edward' and there was to be no bowing or curtseying. Through no fault of his own it was impossible for anyone to forget who he was, not least because of his ever-present police bodyguards. They were all very aware of the danger of giving him orders and appearing either patronising or bullying; equally there was the risk of praising everything he did simply because of who he was. At first nobody wanted to appear too forward or sycophantic. It would take time to build up a close circle of friends who could respect the privacy he needed but also treat him like a normal twenty-four-year-old man.

It was with Prince Edward's immediate boss Biddy Hayward that the 'tea boy' image originated. When questioned by the press about her new employee's role she insisted that he would be 'starting on the bottom rung of the ladder' to play down any suggestion that Edward had been shown favouritism. 'He'll make himself useful by answering the phones, allocating tickets and even brewing up,' she said. Asked by a *Daily Star* reporter what status Edward would have, she replied, 'None whatsoever. It is the lowest rung. He's got to learn a lot and meet a lot of people. Until he's done that we can't expose him to a production.' Will he be making the tea, the reporter queried. 'I make the tea, *everyone* makes the tea,' Miss Hayward insisted. If Edward was 'on the lowest rung' this implied he would be making the tea. To Kevin O'Sullivan of the *Sun* she reiterated, 'Sure, he'll make the tea, but we're a very democratic outfit and it's not unknown for even me to make the tea. We all muck in.'

Prince Edward did indeed have to muck in, but his duties were far more varied than making refreshments. Andrew Lloyd Webber had not employed Edward for his tea-making abilities. He worked in a small office with five other employees, his day starting at 9.00 a.m., though he invariably arrived earlier. At first his duties were fairly simple: opening the mail and dealing with applications for auditions, bills and administrative problems. Each morning there were production meetings to discuss the shows currently being staged and those in rehearsal. In 1984, for example, Andrew Lloyd Webber had seven shows running simultaneously in London and Broadway, earning him an estimated $1 million a week. There was always re-casting to be arranged; designers, publicists, financiers, journalists, printers, set builders, sound technicians, lighting designers, and so on to be co-ordinated and briefed. Edward described his job as 'putting it all together'. Once he had been taken into the fold, he and the one man and four women with whom he worked became a close-knit team. Even before he started work, Biddy Hayward said, 'All his colleagues have met him and have said that they like him. If they did not like him as a person they would not work with him.'

Each lunchtime Edward would either have a sandwich at the theatre with his colleagues or go to Gulp!, a local sandwich bar in Soho, with his detective. With many good restaurants in the area the Prince would often choose to visit a local Chinese or Italian restaurant. On one occasion Andrew Lloyd Webber took him to The Last Days of the Raj in Drury Lane for an Indian meal with other employees. There were no special privileges for Edward. 'We require the staff to be responsible about their jobs,' said Biddy Hayward, 'so there are no three-hour lunch breaks.'

Prince Edward's days were not short either. He seldom arrived back at Buckingham Palace before 7 p.m., and would then often have to change for an official evening function. He tried his best to confine his royal duties to weekends, but this was not always possible. Shortly after joining the Really Useful Theatre Company for example, as a Prince he was present at the BAFTA North's Craft Awards Ceremony at the BBC Studios, Liverpool (Sunday 13 March); attended a 'Youth Makes Music' concert at the Royal Festival Hall to mark the fiftieth anniversary of the Schools Music Association (7.15 p.m., Monday 14 March); went to the Wales v. France International at Cardiff Arms Park at the invitation of the Welsh Rugby Union (Saturday 19 March); attended the Mayor's Banquet and Ball given by the Mayor of the Royal Borough of Windsor and Maidenhead at the School Hall, Eton College (7.35 p.m., Friday 25 March); attended the King's Head Theatre Royal Gala Performance at Sadler's Wells to launch the Club's Appeal (7.20 p.m., Sunday 10 April); was guest of honour at the Annual Dinner of the National Association of Youth and Community Education Officers at Hatfield House (evening of Wednesday 13 April); visited Loch Lomond to inaugurate the Loch Lomond Park Authority and visited the Boys' Brigade Senate 88 (Saturday 16 April). He also fitted in several film premiers, presented awards for the Stars Organisation for Spastics, went to a Garden Party in Cambridge for the Duke of Edinburgh's Award Scheme, and one weekend undertook engagements in both Aberdeenshire and Berkshire. For Edward there was a division of loyalties. He received £20,000 a year from the Civil List towards his royal duties and £20,000 a year from Andrew

Lloyd Webber for his theatrical obligations. He wanted to keep both of them happy.

Occasionally unforeseen circumstances took their toll on the Prince's time. His twenty-fourth birthday on 10 March 1988, which should have been a time of celebration, will always be remembered as a day when public tragedy befell the royal circle. Because of his career Edward had been unable to join his brother Charles and sisters-in-law, Diana and Sarah, on the ski slopes at the Swiss resort of Klosters. That day an avalanche killed a close family friend and former Equerry to the Queen, Major Hugh Lindsay, and seriously injured Mrs Patti Palmer-Tomkinson. Prince Charles escaped death himself, it has been said 'more by luck than judgement'.

Prince Edward had known Hugh Lindsay for five years since he first became an Equerry in 1983, and his wife Sarah Lindsay, then expecting their first child, worked in the Press Office at Buckingham Palace. With tragic irony it was she who took the call in the Press Office that told her that her husband had been killed. Prince Edward was shocked to hear the news. By coincidence, the fourteen-week pregnant Duchess of York had fallen heavily in the snow that day and had returned early to their holiday chalet with the Princess of Wales. Had this not happened, both Sarah and Diana could well have been part of the six-strong party headed by Prince Charles who decided to ski off-piste on one of the steepest and most dangerous runs in the Alps, the Gotschnawang, nicknamed 'The Wang'. It was a bright clear winter's day and despite avalanche warnings the party ventured further afield to find deeper fresher snow. Prince Charles had skied there before and they were all skilled sportsmen. This was their first full day skiing and as they paused to take breath an avalanche rumbled towards them, apparently caused by snow that they had themselves disturbed. Major Lindsay and Mrs Palmer-Tomkinson were swept away in a whirling maelstrom as the entire mountainside appeared to vanish.

Although deeply shocked and distressed by the disaster – eye witnesses say that Prince Charles broke down and wept when he learned of Major Lindsay's death – he played a vital part in the rescue operation, digging frantically in the snow with his bare hands despite the intense cold, while shouting orders to his companions. Not only was Prince Edward upset at the death of Major Lindsay, he was equally alarmed at the thought of what might so easily have happened. Had his sister-in-law Sarah not slipped that morning she and Diana might easily have been killed; his own brother had escaped death by a miracle. Had he not taken up employment himself, Edward too might have joined the party as a birthday treat. The Royal Family spend their lives being guarded, yet nothing can save them from natural disasters. Edward had himself experienced an earthquake in New Zealand and might have been killed by falling masonry. No amount of armed protection could save them from the forces of nature. Quite naturally public sympathy lay with Prince Charles who had been present at the tragedy, but Prince Edward was equally concerned about his brother's mental well-being. In discussions a year earlier he had learned of Charles's frustrations and feelings of inadequacy and he knew this incident would not help his state of mind. Prince Edward took time off from the Really Useful Theatre Company to attend the funeral of Major Hugh Lindsay, not just to express his own condolences but to give his brother moral support. After the funeral Prince Charles flew back to Switzerland on his own.

Although Edward's colleagues expressed their sympathy, the Prince could not discuss his fears or worries about his family. Anyone else could say that they were concerned about their brother, but Edward had to bottle up his emotions simply because the relative concerned happened to be heir to the throne. Prince Charles's sanity had already been questioned when the media ridiculed him for talking to his plants; Edward could not risk unleashing further public probing into the Prince of Wales's inner feelings.

After six months with the Really Useful Theatre Company the newest Production Assistant was making progress. Andrew Lloyd Webber's latest musical *Aspects of Love* was in rehearsal and Edward helped make demo tapes for the cast recording. He was now fully accepted as a member of the team and was gradually being given more behind-the-scenes responsibility. As hit shows such as *Evita, Cats, Starlight Express* and *Phantom of the Opera* were already firmly established in the West End, the Prince was able to concentrate on putting *Aspects of Love* into production. After his apprenticeship he was eventually to be promoted to Production Administrator, specifically looking after *Cats* and *Starlight Express*, and later Overseas Coordinator on Andrew Lloyd Webber's productions around the world. The Prince was closely involved with putting on *Phantom of the Opera* and *Aspects of Love* on Broadway and in the course of duty travelled backwards and forwards between London and New York, Los Angeles, Paris, Tokyo, Toronto and Vienna. Sadly, to the British public, he was still only making tea.

Although Prince Edward was fulfilling a worthwhile role within the Really Useful Theatre Company it was far more of a personal achievement to him than people realised. Yes, he had to have round-the-clock security protection and, yes, I do know of someone who actually used to curtsey to the telephone whenever they received a call from him, but the job still meant freedom. He had an independence he had never before experienced and it was the closest he would ever come to an ordinary life. He genuinely looked upon himself as a wage earner and, perhaps surprisingly, he needed the income. The Civil List allowance he received went entirely on royal duties, paying the wages of his small staff and the running costs of his office. If he travelled in a helicopter of the Queen's Flight for an engagement or used the royal train or an official car, it had to be paid for out of his allowance. Divide his Civil List quota by the number of engagements he fulfilled in 1987 and it works out at £296 a visit. Bearing in mind the cost of administration, planning, staff wages and travel, this does not seem by any means excessive. More importantly, he did not receive a penny of the Civil List for his personal use, which made the income from Andrew Lloyd Webber significant. It may not have been vital to his security – the Queen would hardly have thrown him out on the street if he had been unable to pay his way – but it gave him independence. The job also enabled him to walk through the streets of London unrecognised, a rare experience for someone in his position, eat in restaurants, visit shops, all the things that non-royals simply take for granted. Edward had much to thank Andrew Lloyd Webber for.

One incident which brought home to Edward what it is like to be non-royal occurred exactly a week after he had started full-time employment. He had agreed to attend a committee meeting of Charity Projects, an organisation with which he had been involved since the *Knockout* tournament. The meeting was set for 6 p.m. so that Edward could attend after work and was held in the organisation's D'Arblay Street offices, barely five minutes walk from the Palace Theatre. As a new employee Prince Edward did not feel able to rush out of the theatre on the stroke of 6, and conscientiously completed his tasks for the day before leaving. This meant that he was late. He walked quickly through the dark streets of Soho, down dusky alleyways that anyone might have second thoughts about, let alone a member of the Royal Family, yet no one noticed him. Finally he arrived at the Charity Projects offices and pressed the button on the intercom to be let in. The ten-strong committee was, however, so deep in discussion that nobody heard the buzzer and Edward was left standing unceremoniously on the doorstep. Eventually he could do nothing but go home. Anyone else might have been irritated, but it afforded the Prince some wry amusement. Members of the Royal Family usually arrive on even the most private of visits with a certain amount of pomp and ceremony, but he had been late and was thus left standing on the doorstep. It must have been a royal first.

For his day-to-day duties Prince Edward was based in offices at the Palace Theatre in Cambridge Circus where Shaftesbury Avenue and the Charing Cross Road divide. The large Victorian theatre, built in 1891, was originally an opera house, its opening production being Sullivan's *Ivanhoe* under the D'Oyly Carte management. Over the years it has been home to many prestigious and long-running productions, such as *No, No Nanette*, *The Sound of Music* and *King's Rhapsody*. Although Prince Edward was the first royal employee, the Palace Theatre had been the scene of the very first Royal Command Performance in 1911. Andrew Lloyd Webber's association with the theatre went back to 1970 when it became the home of his first major success *Jesus Christ Superstar*. Eventually Lloyd Webber bought the theatre which, since December 1985, has housed one of the most successful musical shows of all time, *Les Misérables*. The theatre cost him £1,300,000.

In the very week that Prince Edward joined the Really Useful Theatre Company, Andrew Lloyd Webber's personal fortune was estimated to be £25 million by *Money Magazine*. He was positioned only 115th, however, in their top 200 richest people in Britain list – the Queen considered the richest person in the country because of her portfolio of stocks and shares. Prince Charles ranked fourteenth, but no other member of the Royal Family appeared. Prince Edward's own personal investments amounted to no more than 800 British Telecom shares which he had purchased in 1984.

Despite his enormous success, Andrew Lloyd Webber's background was of course rather humbler than Prince Edward's. Born in 1948, the same year as Prince Charles, he is the son of the late Dr William Lloyd Webber, a director of the London College of Music. His father was a renowned organist and played regularly for church services at the Methodist Central Hall in Westminster. His mother, Jean Lloyd Webber, also taught the piano, so it was a very musical background. (His brother is the celebrated cellist, Julian Lloyd Webber.) It was while he was at Oxford that Andrew collaborated with fellow music scholar Tim Rice. They wrote *Joseph and the Amazing Technicolour Dreamcoat* in 1968, originally as a short piece for schools. The expanded musical has been continually revived over the last twenty-five years and was a major success for Jason Donovan at the London Palladium in 1991/92, swelling the Lloyd Webber coffers even more. Amongst his many shows, from *Evita* to *Song and Dance*, there has only been one failure, a musical called *Jeeves*, written in 1975 with Alan Ayckbourn.

With this sort of track record, Prince Edward knew he could get no better training in the theatre, even though many struggling drama students criticised him for not acquiring some academic training in the profession first. Equally Andrew Lloyd Webber knew that he would gain a great deal of prestige from having a Prince on his staff. He also knew from the outset that he was taking on an honest and enthusiastic worker.

On a day-to-day basis Prince Edward rarely came into contact with Mr Lloyd Webber, seeing him only on first nights and at high-powered production meetings. His immediate boss was Bridget 'Biddy' Hayward who had originally been employed as Andrew Lloyd Webber's secretary when she was twenty. Forthright, creative and efficient, she was to remain in his employment for seventeen years, working her way up to Executive Director. Many called her Lloyd Webber's right-hand woman.

Certainly she was extremely competent and had a passion for musicals, but she also had ambitions. While working for the Really Useful Theatre Company she produced *Lend Me a Tenor* and the play *Shirley Valentine* on Broadway, and ultimately planned to set up her own company. If she had been granted the talent to write musicals as well, Andrew Lloyd Webber would have had a formidable rival.

Prince Edward always had a good working relationship with Biddy Hayward and learned a great deal from her. Like Biddy, he could not see himself as a humble Production Assistant all his life but was intelligent enough to use his training to his own advantage. It was his own skill at putting on a show which had attracted Lloyd Webber in the first place and Edward was keen to develop those organisational skills. His own family saw evidence of his talents in November 1988 when Edward arranged the celebrations for Prince Charles's fortieth birthday. Far closer in spirit to Prince Charles than to the tougher Prince Andrew, Edward knew that his eldest brother had suffered an unsettled twelve months and he was eager to give him an evening to remember.

With Windsor Castle undergoing an extensive rewiring programme, Edward had to select one of the 600 rooms at Buckingham Palace as a venue for the party. He eventually settled on the 155-foot-long Picture Gallery which occupies the whole central area of the first floor at the back of the Palace. It is reached by the magnificent Grand Staircase. Leading off the Gallery are the Blue Drawing Room, 68 feet long and originally a ballroom, and the Music Room, into which the 600 guests could drift. The Picture Gallery itself has a glass roof which gives the feel of a conservatory during the day, but can look cold at night. Prince Edward decided to drape the glass ceiling with a silk canopy, borrowed from the Sultan of Brunei, to give the impression of a huge marquee in the heart of the Palace. It proved to be a great talking point. Originally dark, gloomy and overcrowded, it is Edward's great-grandmother Queen Mary who must take the credit for brightening up the Picture Gallery during her residency. Although today it is used to display paintings from the Queen's collection, Edward was not the first to realise the Picture Gallery's potential as a party venue. In June 1852 it was the scene of a full state banquet to mark the christening of Prince Leopold, Queen Victoria's eighth child. The haemophiliac Prince was later created Duke of Albany and Earl of Clarence, two titles which have frequently been suggested for Edward when he marries.

At the party the royal families of Britain, Europe and Spain mingled with celebrities from the world of entertainment. Prince Charles's favourite comedians Barry Humphries (also known as Dame Edna Everage), Spike Milligan and Billy Connolly were in high spirits, as was pop superstar Elton John and 'Mr Fix It' himself, Jimmy Savile. After a private family celebration the main party began at 10 p.m. with entertainment provided by Phil Collins. Prince Edward had also managed to acquire the services of a band called the Dark Blues who had performed at Prince Charles's twenty-first birthday party in 1969. The Queen was seen dancing La Bamba and joined in a rousing chorus of 'Happy Birthday'. At one point the sound system failed. 'What kind of a gig is this?' joked rock singer Phil Collins. The Queen roared with laughter. Many guests were still dancing at 3.30 a.m. and eventually left, declaring it the best party they had ever been to. Much of the success was due to Prince Edward. On the guest list was Andrew Lloyd Webber with Sarah Brightman, who conceded that the Prince need not arrive for work as usual at 9.00 a.m.

By his own twenty-fifth birthday in 1989 life with the Really Useful Theatre Company had settled into a pattern and Edward was working towards the opening of the musical *Aspects of Love*. It was to be premiered at the Prince of Wales Theatre where Lillie Langtry, a mistress of Edward's great-great grandfather, had once appeared. The Prince had no difficulty in arranging for the Queen and the Duke of Edinburgh to officially attend the premiere on 10 April. It was the kind of string that only one of Andrew Lloyd Webber's employees could pull.

In private Prince Edward was seen at events such as the Windsor Horse Show with the Duke of Edinburgh, any past animosity clearly forgotten. In 1988 they went on a three-day private visit to Australia together, spending time in Brisbane at a forum about the Duke of Edinburgh's Award. Edward made history by taking with him a handwritten copy of the Magna Carta. It had been made in 1215 and this was the first time that such a copy had been taken out of England. The visit proved the strength of the relationship between father and son. Now a mature twenty-five-year-old, Edward also seemed much closer to his brother Charles, the age gap far less apparent. During weekends at Windsor the two were seen out walking and riding together, sometimes sitting in silence while the Prince of Wales sketched and Edward played with Charles's Jack Russell dog. In May 1984 many newspapers had a field day when Charles and Edward had publicly kissed and embraced on meeting. The display of affection, however, merely reflected the very real closeness between them.

In the autumn of 1989 when both Charles and Edward had royal engagements in Scotland they stayed quietly at Holyrood-house together. On a free weekend they amused themselves by doing an archaeological survey of the house, which had originally been built in 1501 by James IV. This was a year when Edward appeared at his most relaxed. If spotted out riding with the Queen at Sandringham he had a smile for the photographers and seemed equally nonchalant if captured on film in the streets of Soho near the theatre. The collapse of Princess Anne's marriage was finally made public that year, followed by a supposed relationship with Commander Timothy Lawrence, so the spotlight was temporarily off Edward and focused on his sister. The Duchess of York had now been cast as the Aunt Sally of the family, always setting herself up to be knocked down, which released Edward from the pressure of media attention. Now in his second year in the theatre, the novelty of writing about his Really Useful work had worn off, and he was undertaking a sufficient number of royal duties to avoid criticism.

For Prince Edward the highlight of 1989 was in April when he visited Moscow, becoming the first member of the Royal Family to visit Russia for more than a decade. Although Princess Anne had been to Kiev in 1973 to take part in the European Three Day Event Championships, and Prince Philip had been in 1979 for meetings as President of the International Equestrian Federation, Prince Edward's own visit was seen as more significant, for it appeared to pave the way for a state visit by the Queen. No member of the Royal Family had actually made a state visit to the country since the Bolsheviks had murdered their cousins, the Imperial Family of Romanov, at Ekaterinburg in July 1918. President Gorbachev's planned visit to Britain in 1988 had been cancelled due to an earthquake in Armenia, but he finally made a state visit in the spring of 1989 and on 7 April formally invited the Queen to visit Russia. The invitation was provisionally accepted but no one could have anticipated the speed with which political events would move within the country, leading to the eventual collapse of the Soviet Union and the swift removal from power of President Gorbachev. Prince Edward's visit was followed by one from his sister in May 1990 but the Queen was unable to take up her own invitation in the light of the political difficulties.

Although Prince Edward flew to Moscow exactly one week after Mr Gorbachev's visit to Windsor Castle the invitation had been received in January and three months of planning had ensued. The invitation itself came from the Russian Ministry of Culture to Edward as Patron of the National Youth Theatre to see a production of T. S. Eliot's *Murder in the Cathedral*. Members of the National Youth Theatre were to visit as part of a cultural exchange which would also bring young Russian actors to Britain. Edward's visit was to be classed as strictly cultural with no political overtones, as a display of closer Anglo-Soviet relations. However there were weeks of discussion beforehand between Buckingham Palace, Downing Street and the Foreign Office because of concerns that Edward's presence in the country could be used as political propaganda and portrayed as a state visit. The detailed preparations were not solely for Edward's benefit, but were made very much with the Queen in mind. If she did visit in the future she would be the first British sovereign ever to set foot on Russian soil. It would be history in the making.

So as not to interrupt his work with the Really Useful Theatre Company, Prince Edward made only a brief three-day visit to Russia over a weekend. On Saturday 15 April 1989, he flew from RAF Northolt on board a BAe 146 jet of the Queen's Flight. For security reasons the craft and crew had already made a dummy run of the eight-hour journey to plan diversionary routes and emergency landings in the event of terrorist activity. He emerged from the plane in Moscow wearing a full-length herringbone tweed coat as protection against the bleak weather but without the Russian fur hat that was packed in his suitcase. Waiting to greet him was Gury Khilchevsky, the Deputy Minister of Culture, who had been instrumental in arranging the visit, and together they drove in a long black Chaika limousine as used by Soviet Presidents to the British Embassy. The Prince was to be the guest of the British Ambassador Sir Rodrick Braithwaite and his wife Gillian, and spent two nights at the Embassy. Because the visit was only a short one Edward was given less than an hour to change and freshen up before being driven to the famous Bolshoi Theatre to see a performance of the ballet *Giselle*. If this was a cultural visit his Russian hosts were determined that he would see some culture. Less tactfully, perhaps, the Prince was placed in the royal box once used by his murdered ancestors. This provoked much comment amongst both British and Soviet journalists. Many speculated as to whether Queen Elizabeth II might one day occupy the seat in which the ill-fated Tsar Nicholas II once sat.

Although great curiosity surrounded Edward's visit his was not a familiar face to the people on the streets of Moscow. When he stood in Red Square in front of St Basil's Cathedral the next day scarcely any of the passersby knew or cared who he was, and there was no reason why they should. None of President Gorbachev's children would have received a second glance on the streets of London. On Sunday morning Edward was driven to Kolomenskoye where he attended a service at the Church of Kazan Icon of the Mother of God. Although he was greeted warmly by the parish priest Father Sviatoslav and the Secretary to the Patriarch Father Matvei, and given a bouquet of a dozen red roses, many members of the congregation had no idea who he was. 'Is he a Catholic?' asked one onlooker, a remark which made Edward smile, in view of the fact that his mother is Head of the Church of England. Like his aunt Princess Margaret, Edward has a deep seated faith, and found the service moving. He was given bread and salt, the Church's traditional gift to strangers, and a breakfast of smoked meats in the Church crypt afterwards. (He declined the Russian caviar.) As he departed, Father Matvei embraced and kissed the Prince on the cheek. Again, members of his entourage could not help wondering how the Queen would react to such a gesture. She was visibly surprised when she was unexpectedly hugged by a very large female admirer on a trip to America, and her hackles were raised when Prime Minister Paul Keating put his arm around her waist during her 1992 tour of Australia.

Following the church service Prince Edward was driven the 12 miles back to Moscow for a sightseeing tour. In the Kremlin he was reminded of Peter the Great who had himself tried unsuccessfully to bring Russia and the West into closer harmony. The Prince commented:

> *That was a long time ago and it didn't work. In that sense I am very aware of the history and the great experiment that is going on. It will be interesting to see what happens, how it continues and if better things develop. From the British side, or from an outsider's point of view, we will always see the positive aspects. People within the Soviet Union are exactly the same as people in Great Britain who are too willing to grumble about anything that means change.*

Of his own visit the Prince said, 'This is the beginning of building a solid bridge between us. I feel that we are not just exchanging plays and theatre companies – we are exchanging our thoughts.' While in the Kremlin he told journalists. 'It is a fascinating place, and holds a special fascination for me. I am not that distantly related to some of the former occupants. The thing that is surprising is that it was not really that long ago.'

That night came the main reason for his visit, the performance of *Murder in the Cathedral* at the Moscow Arts Theatre, a play which before *perestroika* would not have been seen or even allowed in Russia because its central theme is discord between the church and state. Although he had seen the play before, Prince Edward said afterwards that having visited a Russian Orthodox Church himself that very day made the production even more poignant. He was struck, he said, by the parallels between the play and events in the present-day Soviet Union. Directed by Edward Wilson, the National Youth Theatre Director who had helped set up the tour, and with young actor Conor Grimes as Archbishop Thomas à Becket, the production played to full houses for its week-long run. The Russian audiences cheered towards the end of the play when the first knight's final speech included the words, '. . . disperse quietly to your homes. Please be careful not to loiter in groups at street corners, and do nothing that might provoke any public outbreak.' It was a sentiment they could all identify with.

On his final day Prince Edward visited the Anglo-Soviet Month Exhibition at Moscow's International Trade Centre, where many British companies had stands, before attending a reception in the Union of Theatre Workers Headquarters, the Russian equivalent of the British actor's union, Equity. Here he was able to talk with many young actors about the theatre and his own passion for plays. That afternoon he was driven to Sheremetyevo Airport for the eight-hour flight back to London to prepare for the official opening night performance of Andrew Lloyd Webber's musical *Aspects of Love*. In Russia he was a Prince, in the theatre he was merely 'Production Assistant: Edward Windsor'. What would he tell the Queen about his visit, both Soviet and British journalists asked as he departed, but Edward was not giving anything away. 'It will be a secret between us,' he grinned.

Although Soviet officials were reported in *The Times* as saying that 'the Prince's visit had been of great value in improving bilateral relations', some sections of the British press criticised Edward for 'costing the tax payer £100,000'. The visit was in fact funded by the National Youth Theatre's official sponsor, Sainsbury's. Through sponsorship, eighty-two members of the Youth Theatre were able to make the trip of a lifetime to Russia and in return young Russian actors had the opportunity to visit London. A *Daily Mail* columnist wrote:

> *Questions are likely to be asked in Parliament over the efficacy of splashing out a small fortune on a low-key visit by the sixth in line to the Throne, especially when British Airways runs a splendid daily service – £976 first class return.*

Echoing these sentiments five days later, *The People* declared that Prince Edward had posed for a photograph in Red Square

> *. . wearing a fur hat that made him look an even bigger prat than usual. Eager Eddy could have gone there and back for less than £1,000 travelling first class with British Airways . . . such inexcusable waste of taxpayers' money makes Edward appear more like a ponce than a prince.*

133

Once again, Edward's efforts had been misrepresented; the cost of sending more than ninety people to Russia had been attributed to him alone. Not one penny of taxpayers' money had been spent on the venture. Undaunted by adverse publicity, Prince Edward later paid a similar visit to Poland with the Cambridge Youth Theatre. Although still hurt by press criticism, especially when it was unjustified, Edward was beginning to develop a thicker skin.

Once *Aspects of Love* had been successfully staged in London (after numerous backstage problems, including the withdrawal of its original star, 'James Bond' actor Roger Moore), Prince Edward was promoted to Production Administrator. He was specifically asked to look after the musicals *Cats* and *Starlight Express*, both in the West End and overseas. He also organised the licensing for these shows in other countries, which involved foreign travel to solve any administrative problems that arose. Eventually he was part of the team involved with staging *Aspects of Love* on Broadway, and even though he was present as an employee, the very fact that the cast could say 'Prince Edward is in the audience' gave each first night a royal touch.

In the offices at the Palace Theatre, however, there was growing disillusionment. Since 1988 much of the production team's work had been geared towards putting on *Aspects of Love*. Now there was a sudden sense of anti-climax. These days most of the productions were already being staged, and once the teething troubles had been resolved the work began to lose its sparkle. There were rumours that Andrew Lloyd Webber was not writing any more stage musicals but wanted to concentrate instead on films. For any years he had been trying to launch a film version of *Evita*, without success. At any one time there had been rumours that Elaine Paige, Madonna or Meryl Streep had been cast as Eva Péron, but nobody really knew which. Another film project that seemed to undergo years of discussion was the life story of the musical star Jessie Matthews, for which Andrew Lloyd Webber's wife Sarah Brightman seemed perfect casting. Not only did she have the talent to sing and dance, she was facially not dissimilar. However first there were problems over the actress Evelyn Laye, who did not want the story of Jessie Matthews' love affair with her husband Sonnie Hale dragged on to the big screen in her lifetime. Then the collapse of the

Lloyd Webber's own marriage put the film on hold. Finally a film version of *Phantom of the Opera* was mooted, to star the original London phantom, Michael Crawford. Again the years seemed to pass without any major development, but the discussions occupied a great deal of Andrew Lloyd Webber's time. With new productions of current shows and constant revivals of older works, such as *Joseph and the Amazing Technicolour Dreamcoat*, he had no need to rush into his next venture. For Biddy Hayward, however, the apparent move towards the film industry had little appeal. Her first love, like Edward's, was the theatre. Although the Royal Family are all great lovers of film, and have private showings at Windsor, Sandringham, Balmoral and even on *Britannia*, Edward has never expressed any desire to produce films and still prefers live performances.

Biddy Hayward might have been the first to feel that there was life outside the Really Useful Theatre Company, but some of her colleagues shared her fears. The first sign of any practical move was in April 1990, immediately after *Aspects of Love* had opened on Broadway. All together seven of Andrew Lloyd Webber's employees appeared discontented and at first, almost lightheartedly, joked about the possibility of setting up their own company to produce their own shows. Why swell the Lloyd Webber coffers further when they had the combined talents necessary to form a new enterprise? What initially started out as a fantasy suddenly began to look like a viable proposition. It was not something that could be discussed openly at the Palace Theatre and Edward's moves during the day were carefully monitored by the press. He eventually decided that a meeting should be arranged at a venue where they would not be spotted, at a time when they would not be expected.

Edward himself selected the Scandic Crown Hotel near Victoria Station, just a short walk from Buckingham Palace, a hotel popular with Scandinavian tourists who were unlikely to recognise him. He booked two boardrooms on the ninth floor, one in which to have refreshments, the other in which to talk. Just before midnight on 20 April the Prince and his bodyguard Andrew Merrylees walked the short distance from Buckingham Palace to the hotel. The foyer was almost empty when they arrived, apart from six other people waiting to meet him. Quietly the hotel manager led them up to the ninth floor where a meal and drinks were served, after which they adjourned to the second room where secret talks took place until 2 a.m. when the meeting ended and a jubilant group emerged. Whether it was a member of staff or one of the guests, somebody recognised the Prince and by the time he left the hotel the press were waiting. Edward was clearly angry at being discovered after such careful planning, but neither he nor his conspirators would comment. The press could only speculate as to why Edward and six others had held a clandestine meeting at midnight in a backstreet hotel. The next day the Prince travelled to Windsor to celebrate the Queen's birthday. Exactly two months were to pass before the secret was revealed.

First, at the beginning of June Biddy Hayward resigned from the Really Useful Theatre Company. Unconfirmed reports say that Andrew Lloyd Webber gave her a £300,000 pay-off. Then, more dramatically, on 20 June six other employees handed in their notice: Harold Dagnall (General Manager); Robert Eady (Box Office); Anne Simpson (Merchandising Coordinator); Trevor Jackson (Production Administrator); Clare Vidal-Hall (PA) and one Edward Windsor. In a statement issued from Buckingham Palace, Prince Edward said:

> *I am particularly grateful to Andrew Lloyd Webber and the Really Useful Theatre Group for their support and encouragement over the last couple of years and especially for giving me the chance to work in the theatre professionally. I hope to use this experience to progress further into production and explore new areas.*

It was no coincidence that the group resigned together, nor that Biddy Hayward left in advance. If all seven had resigned at once it might have looked as if Miss Hayward was deliberately stealing Andrew Lloyd Webber's staff. By leaving first it looked as if her colleagues had independently chosen to follow her. In the Scandic Crown Hotel in April they had decided to set up a new production company called Theatre Division. The seven people who formed the basis of the company each had vital experience in a different area. Biddy Hayward, for example, had worked on many aspects, from secretarial to mounting a full-scale show on Broadway. Bob Eady was experienced in the box office side, Clare Vidal-Hall in publicity. Prince Edward was appointed Technical Administrator and his presence ensured the sort of media coverage which many new enterprises have to struggle to achieve. However he was also a liability because, as with the Marines, there was no room for failure. Any other new theatre company could start in a small way in the provinces and gradually build up a reputation, whereas the company Prince Edward worked for had a reputation from the outset. Nothing less than a West End success to rival Andrew Lloyd Webber's would be expected of them, but his is a hard act to follow.

'It is not a bitter split, just a desire to move on,' said one of the group, despite the fact that Andrew Lloyd Webber was said to be 'deeply offended' by the move. The first the impressario/composer knew of the resignations was a phone call from Really Useful's Managing Director, John Whitney. It came at a difficult time, when he was attempting to buy back his company from public ownership. Irritated by interventions from shareholders, it is said that Andrew Lloyd Webber wanted complete control of the company once more. Some reports claimed that the gang of six left because they thought Biddy Hayward had been treated badly, but theirs was no protest walk-out. All had very definite plans and ambitions. Certainly Andrew Lloyd Webber's apparent move towards films influenced their timing; maybe his bid to buy back total control of Really Useful also had some bearing on their decision. At the beginning of 1990 there were rumours of possible redundancies and Prince Edward's future was said to be 'in the balance', even though a senior executive claimed the Prince was now 'an indispensable part of the team'. If any employees were to be sacked it was unlikely that Prince Edward would have been one of them.

After Prince Edward's resignation had been announced, Really Useful spokesman Peter Qunard said:

> *Mr Lloyd Webber is very relaxed about it all. He does not think it is worth spending any time over. He's too busy to talk about it. These things happen in any business and it is a good move for the people concerned and he wishes them well.*

Prince Edward tried to avoid reporters as he worked out his notice at the Palace Theatre, saying only 'Who knows?' when one managed to ask him what the future held. Biddy Hayward found her private life under the microscope for no other reason than that she had been the Prince's boss. All tried to play down any suggestion of animosity towards Andrew Lloyd Webber. Even the meeting at the Scandic Crown Hotel was dismissed as 'an ordinary production meeting about *Starlight Express*.' In a backstreet hotel? At midnight? Few were convinced.

Leaving the Palace Theatre for the last time in July 1990, Prince Edward made what was now becoming an annual pilgrimage to Aberdeen to play Lord Darlington in Oscar Wilde's comedy *Lady Windermere's Fan* for the Haddo House Players, giving three performances. Meanwhile, in London, Biddy Hayward found West End premises for Theatre Division, and made plans for their first production. However political events had been moving faster than anyone had anticipated, and despite having the prestige of a royal Technical Administrator, there was no guarantee of success for the new company. With the recession starting to bite, and the threat of war in the Gulf, West End audiences were already dwindling and each month promising new shows were closing. World-famous impressario Harold Fielding went out of business after forty-five years. A £3 million musical about Martin Luther King had to be axed. A stage version of the Marilyn Monroe film *Bus Stop* with Jerry Hall and Petula Clark's musical *Someone Like You* both flopped. *Vanilla* starring Joanna Lumley, Jeffrey Archer's *Exclusive* and the Michael Frayn comedy *Look Look* were all victims. It was a difficult climate in which to begin any new venture, let alone one which could not afford to fail.

For Theatre Division's first production, Jean Anouilh's 1950 comedy *The Rehearsal* was chosen. The leading French dramatist described his work as a 'pièce brilliante', a comedy with sparkle. Nobody had expected a full-scale musical to rival *Starlight Express*, but it was an unexpected and not obviously commercial choice. Some felt that the burlesque comedy of the same name, written by a former Duke of Buckingham, would have been more appropriate. The leading roles were taken by Nicola Pagett, Christine Kavanagh and Juliet Ormond – all excellent actresses but even they would admit that they were not internationally known names. The play opened at the Garrick Theatre in November 1990 to mixed reviews and managed to struggle on while more notable productions fell by the wayside, but it was not the sell-out success that Theatre Division needed. Perhaps if Prince Edward had been allowed to tread the boards himself, more tickets would have been sold. Not a member of the actors' union Equity, he could not have appeared if he had wanted to. It was an uncertain month for the British economy with the resignation of Prime Minister Margaret Thatcher after eleven years in office and the Gulf crisis, both of which were blamed for poor audiences.

For a brand new company, obtaining the prestigious Garrick Theatre in Charing Cross Road had been quite a coup. The cost of staging a West End show, however, is in excess of £250,000 and soon Theatre Division were making a loss. One insider told me that one of their problems was initially spending too much on 'plush offices to rival Andrew Lloyd Webber's instead of sinking more money into the show.' While *The Rehearsal* struggled on, they began mounting the next ambitious production – *Same Old Moon* by Geraldine Aron, which was destined for the Globe Theatre – even though they were at that time £150,000 in debt. Theoretically Prince Edward was an employee not a director of the company and may have been oblivious of the financial problems. On the telephone he would promise cheques to costumiers and set constructors and was left embarrassed and apologetic when they did not arrive. Edward may have been a good organiser but he proved to be less adept at practical matters. This was never more obvious than when the stage crew began to erect the set of *Same Old Moon*, according to Prince Edward's ground plans, only to discover that it was far too large for the stage. In a complicated profession the Prince's two years with the Really Useful Theatre Company had been a relatively short apprenticeship and Edward frequently found himself way out of his depth.

The conflict between Edward's royal duties and theatre did not help matters. The family firm always had to take priority. This was less of a problem in a large organisation, but in a smaller company like Theatre Division everyone was expected to pull their weight and the stage management team were left open-mouthed when the Technical Administrator had to leave in the middle of a technical rehearsal to go to Windsor Castle. 'He used to drive me up the wall,' said Roger Penhale, stage manager for *Same Old Moon*. Edward may have been very keen on the theatre, but as anyone who works in it knows, it is a profession which requires 100 per cent dedication. Edward could only ever offer 50 per cent, which was insufficient. 'It was our livelihood,' said one of the backstage staff at the Globe Theatre, 'but at times it seemed as if he was only playing at theatre. He did not always take things as seriously as he might.'

One incident that those involved remember all too clearly is the smoke bomb disaster. A crucial part of the plot for *Some Old Moon* involved a bed catching fire. The effect was achieved with a smoke bomb, which at one performance refused to go off. Without it the script made no sense. Whilst the professionals panicked, the Prince laughed. 'It might be funny at a Windsor Castle pantomime,' said a colleague, 'but it's no joke in front of a paying audience.' Clearly Edward still had much to learn, although he may have laughed more out of embarrassment than amusement.

By sheer coincidence the setting up of Theatre Division coincided with a review of the Civil List, which was usually increased annually below the rate of inflation. To avoid the criticism that inevitably occurred whenever there was an increase, it was decided that a fixed rate would be established, to last until the end of the century. Whilst allowances for every other member of the Royal Family had been raised each year, Prince Edward's had been fixed at £20,000 since he had turned eighteen. To cover his ever-increasing costs, and to allow for the fact that he might marry before the year 2000 and would have a wife who would also have to undertake duties, Edward's allowance was increased to £100,000, a rise of 400 per cent.

Inevitably he received the full force of the subsequent media attack, inspiring such headlines as 'The Queen's Son Should Do Something Really Useful For His Princely Sum'. In the wake of this he felt bound to increase his royal workload even more. While Theatre Division was being established Prince Edward had to fit in a visit to Poland with the Cambridge Youth Theatre; he became Patron of the London Mozart Players who then required his presence at various functions to mark the bicentennial year of Mozart's death in 1991; and he toured Wales to see the Duke of Edinburgh's Award projects. From opening the Dame Alicia Markova Theatre in Tring to attending the World Greyhound Racing Federation Conference, he was constantly in demand as a Prince. All this did nothing to help his career as Technical Administrator in the theatre.

Six weeks after opening, *Same Old Moon* was forced to close in July 1991, and Theatre Division collapsed with debts of £600,000. There had been small audiences and very poor reviews. A spokesman blamed the recession and the shortage of American tourists who had temporarily stopped visiting Britain for fear of planes being attacked due to the Gulf war. More realistically, the company had probably not chosen the best plays to attract audiences and had bitten off more than they could chew by launching straight into the West End where competition is intense. Because of Prince Edward's involvement there were critics who wanted to see him fall. In the same month that Theatre Division collapsed, Andrew Lloyd Webber donated £100,000 to save the Almeida Theatre in North London from closure.

For Edward the end of Theatre Division was the death of yet another dream. Insiders wondered if he could ever work in the theatre again. Having Prince Edward as part of the company had proved to be no guarantee of success. Once more his career seemed to be in limbo.

Chapter 7

BEHIND THE SCENES

I sighed as a lover, I obeyed as a son.

EDWARD GIBBON,

Autobiography

During a charity gala celebrating the work of composer Lionel Bart at the Dome Theatre, Brighton, in January 1992, theatre critic and raconteur Jack Tinker mentioned the National Youth Theatre and their admiration for Mr Bart's music. 'They also have Prince Edward as their – I was going to say *Fairy* God-mother – I should say President,' the evening's host joked. The 1,500 strong audience erupted into laughter and applause at the innuendo. That same week when a member of the back-stage crew at another theatre heard that I was writing about Prince Edward he exclaimed, 'Oh, Dockland Doris.' Others referred to the Queen's youngest son derisively as 'Mavis'. Until he is married with children the Prince knows that his sexuality will be called into question – rumours of homosexuality have been common since he first displayed an interest in the arts.

Due to his own late marriage, Prince Charles's sexuality was also a subject of discussion at many a society dinner, but his 'Action Man' image saved him from public ridicule. With Prince Andrew being cast as 'Randy Andy', Prince Edward has always suffered from comparison with his obviously heterosexual elder brothers. Research has established that one in four people are homosexual. The Queen has four children, three of whom are not gay . . .

Many of the rumours surrounding Edward have been circulated to counteract the images built up for his brothers. When Prince Charles was in his twenties he was called the 'Daredevil Prince' by the media. Through spending time in the forces, he was constantly photographed parachuting, driving, mounting climbing and even deep-sea diving. Like his father at that time he was frequently seen on horseback playing polo. It was a very masculine persona and more than a hundred different girls were said to be romantically linked with him (though he only had to meet a girl once for the press to call it a romance). In private, however, Prince Charles was very shy and withdrawn, and in his teenage years at Gordonstoun displayed no obvious interest in the female sex. While other boys sneaked off to a café in Elgin to meet the local girls, Prince Charles stayed behind and watched television with his detective, Michael Varney. The latter felt that there was a paradox about the Prince: he was actually aware that he was a lonely person, yet he enjoyed his own company most of all. Not only did he feel unable to have a girlfriend for fear of how the papers would blow it into a story, he actually showed no real desire to have one. Many of his supposed romances only occurred in other people's imaginations.

Prince Andrew, on the other hand, enjoyed the company of girls from an early age and his playboy image was bolstered by friendships with Koo Stark and Katie Rabett. As a teenager there were frequent pictures of him playing rugby. As he grew older it was the Navy and fighting in the Falklands – all very macho.

What a contrast to Prince Edward. Having been kept out of the limelight in his early years, when he eventually went to Cambridge the majority of press photos of him were taken on stage, dressed in tights and codpiece for Shakespeare, or clowning it up in a revue. In adulthood the Royal Marines episode left many thinking that he could not cope with the phsyically tough world of the services. On one occasion in the Marines Edward tried on his new cap and said to an NCO, 'How do I look?' The NCO winked at his colleagues and replied, 'You look lovely, sir, just lovely,' and kissed the embarrassed Prince on the cheek.

Edward was apparently teased mercilessly afterwards, and when the story came out it did nothing to enhance his masculine image. After the services he seemed to go to the opposite extreme by entering the theatrical profession, which few would deny has a large proportion of gay men and women. Edward's behaviour and appearance at the *Grand Knockout Tournament*, wearing a brocade yellow cape with tassels and feathered hat, did little to promote a picture of manliness either.

The issue came to a head in April 1990 when Prince Edward was in New York for the Broadway premier of Andrew Lloyd Webber's *Aspects of Love*. Earlier a newspaper gossip columnist had hinted that the Prince had a 'touching' friendship with the show's male star, Michael Ball, implying that the two were having a relationship. The story angered Prince Edward and amused Michael Ball who later admitted that he had only ever spoken to the Prince 'five or six times and that was about work . . . Yes, I did once say that he made tea for me – and about twenty others!' At an after-show party in New York Prince Edward was approached by a journalist from the *Daily Mirror*. Their conversation prompted a 'World Exclusive' headline. 'QUEEN'S SON POURS HIS HEART OUT TO THE MIRROR – I'M NOT GAY'.

Although Prince Edward was well aware that he was talking to a reporter, his main aim was to deny the unfounded allegations made by certain sections of the British press. He was accurately quoted, saying 'I am not gay', but it was in answer to a skilfully worded question along the lines of, 'Is it difficult being a member of the Royal Family and gay?' Answer: 'I am *not* gay!' Result: one newspaper headline. It was rather like the Archbishop who stepped off a plane in New York and was asked, 'Will you be visiting any nightclubs while you're in New York?' Not wishing to be trapped, the Archbishop feigned innocence and joked, 'Are there any nightclubs in New York?' The next day's newspaper headline ran, 'Archbishop's first question as he steps off the plane: Are there any nightclubs in New York?' When Prince Charles was a student at Cambridge, a French journalist asked his bodyguard Michael Varney an equally loaded question. 'Do you know when Prince Charles lost his virginity?' If Varney had said that the Prince had not, there would have been a story. If he had replied in the affirmative, then it would have been equally newsworthy. Tactfully the bodyguard refused to answer either way.

Possibly, being on the other side of the Atlantic, Prince Edward did not realise that his words would be published. Or perhaps he saw it as an excellent opportunity to put the record straight. 'It's just outrageous to suggest that sort of thing,' he said. The *Daily Mirror* of 10 April 1990 quoted him as saying:

It's so unfair to me and my family. How would you feel if someone said you were gay? The rumours are preposterous. I am not gay but what can I do about it? . . . The press has to be a lot more responsible. I just wish I could be left to enjoy what I do. I love the theatre.

It was the first time any member of the Royal Family had made such candid remarks about their sexuality, and a rare public denial of any inaccurate story. Prince Edward had been dogged by gossip for so long that maybe he had reached the end of his tether. The Michael Ball story was simply the straw that broke the camel's back. In 1989, for example, Harry Arnold of the *Sun* had written an article headed 'WHY ONE IS ALWAYS THE ODD ONE OUT. EDWARD FAILS TO MATCH UP TO HIS TWO REAL-MAN BROTHERS.' Although the word 'homosexual' was not used, suggestions that he was trying to be like the 'darlings' and 'dear boys' of theatreland and needed to 'find a woman to make a man of him' were blatant in their implications. The *Daily Express* called him 'an outcast simply waiting for love'. In the wake of his cousin Viscount Linley's successful libel suit in which he sued *Today* newspaper for branding him a 'lager lout', Prince Edward considered taking legal action to put an end to the whisperings, but knew it would probably spark an even greater scandal.

Viscount Linley had been accused of something that was palpably untrue. A newspaper story stated that he had thrown beer in a London public house and had consequently been barred from the premises. 'It was an invention,' Edward's cousin told the high court jury. 'I was in the pub only once with another person about two years before.' David Linley went on to say that the false article could have a 'damaging effect' on his family and on his own reputation as a furniture-maker:

> *Say I was going to a meeting with a company who was about to place a large order, and in the morning they had read I was to be seen in the local pub splashing beer over workers. They perhaps would not place the order or take a very dim view.*

Viscount Linley won his case and was awarded £35,000 damages, but just as important he had destroyed the belief that the Royal Family never sue. All hoped that the press might be more responsible as a result. Viscount Linley waived his claim to the damages awarded; he merely wanted to clear his name.

Prince Edward might easily have followed his cousin into court but proving that you do not throw beer is one thing; proving that you are not homosexual is clearly far more difficult. Any trial, even if you are sure of your case, is demoralising and depressing. To have your private life laid bare is a humiliating experience. For Edward, having his own sexuality discussed openly in court would have been the very antithesis of the royal approach. In trying to scotch the unfounded rumours, he had already made himself the subject of public debate. Harold Brooks-Baker, editor of *Burke's Peerage*, praised the Prince for speaking out. 'It shows that Prince Edward has the courage he has never been given credit for,' said Mr Brooks-Baker. 'It is high time for people to realise that he is not a weedy person but a true member of the House of Windsor.' David Williamson, co-editor of *Debrett's*, also made a valid point. 'If it was ever revealed that a member of the Royal Family was homosexual, I don't think it would be a great blow to the monarchy. It is an entirely different age we live in now.'

There is a certain irony in the fact that there have *already* been six homosexual kings in England – William II, Richard I, Edward I, Richard II, James I and William III – so a gay prince would by no means be a twentieth-century phenomenon. It is also well known that there are a large number of gay men amongst the staff of the Royal household, and the Royal Family have been particularly tolerant during the present reign. King George V was less approving. 'I thought men like that shot themselves,' he exclaimed on hearing that an elderly friend was gay. During their lifetime there were rumours that the Duke of Windsor (Edward VIII) and Lord Louis Mountbatten had homosexual encounters and the late Duke of Kent had a liking for picking up blond boys at the Embassy Club in London's Bond Street. He allegedly had an affair with Noël Coward and the appearance of some love letters the Duke had written to a man in Paris almost created a public scandal, diverted only because he was able to buy the letters back. So, if Prince Edward were gay he would not be setting a royal precedent.

Judging by the courage he has already shown in following his own career choices, Edward has the strength of character to admit the truth if he was attracted to members of his own sex, but would his advisers really allow him to say it? Such an admission would do much for greater tolerance and acceptance of thousands of gay men and women in Britain, but Buckingham Palace would be too afraid of a scandal and the risk of possible damage to the monarchy to countenance such a thing. It might be seen to rock the 'home life of our own dear Queen'. Behind the Palace railings, it would seem, there are double standards. Homosexual employees are accepted, almost encouraged, just as long as it does not become public knowledge.

The Queen's former bodyguard Commander Michael Trestrail was forced to resign in July 1982 after a homosexual prostitute had tried to blackmail him. He had been the Queen's personal bodyguard for nine years, she had been very fond of him and tried to save his job. 'He has done his work excellently,' she said, but even the Queen did not have the power to save him. Commander Trestrail was considered to be a security risk and therefore had to go. As an astute woman, the Queen must have realised her bodyguard's proclivities and was unconcerned, but her advisers now doubted his integrity and suggested that he might pass secrets on to lovers. Michael Trestrail never once had access to state papers and the Queen must surely have asked herself why someone having an affair with a man should be considered more likely to pass on secrets than someone having an affair with a woman. If Michael Trestrail could have been honest about his homosexuality he would never have been open to blackmail in the first place. Sexual acts between consenting mails have been legal in Britain since 1967, but 'coercion of prostitution in any form is banned and homosexual acts by members of the Armed Forces and of the Merchant Navy remain illegal.' Forced to hide his feelings, Commander Trestrail made the mistake of having an affair with a male prostitute and had to pay with his job.

Because the Royal Family promote an image of security and respectability, achieving their greatest popularity when there is a wedding or a baby due, even in the late twentieth century it still would not seem acceptable for any of them to rock the boat in this way. When the Duchess of York's father was found to have visited a Soho massage parlour it caused a national outcry, even though he wasn't even royal. If any member of the family were homosexual they would be forced to keep their private life under wraps. Prince Edward, however, has publicly stated that he is not gay and he must be believed. The fact that he was forced into making the comment in the first place is a sad reflection on modern tabloid journalism.

Acutely aware of the playboy images his brothers were saddled with, Edward has been exceptionally discreet about his relationships, only to have his discretion backfire on him. If he had openly flaunted his female escorts, the media would have been continually marrying him off, but having gone out of his way to keep his girlfriends out of the spotlight people have jumped to the wrong conclusion. Seen talking more than once to Michael Ball, who was unmarried and around the same age as the Prince, in tabloid terms meant a relationship. In reality, since 1990 Michael Ball has been romantically linked (at his own admission) to sixties pop star Cathy McGowan. In 1992, the year in which Michael Ball represented Britain in the Eurovision Song Contest, the couple purchased a house together and began contemplating marriage. At the same time the world waited to see if Prince Edward would settle down too.

Prince Edward knows that marriage is the only thing that will put an end to gay gossip. He might have set the record straight by speaking out to the *Daily Mirror*, but his comments did far more harm than good. Princess Anne once said that there is no point in replying to such rumours because it only makes matters worse. Many of the *Daily Mirror*'s four million readers had not even considered the possibility that Edward might be gay, but the article put the thought in their minds. As with so many articles, readers remember the gist. 'There was something in

Prince Edward whilst a Second Lieutenant in the Royal Marines, in Autumn 1986. (Rex Features, London)

Prince Edward appearing with Hannah Welfare in a production of A Winter's Tale *at Haddo House in Aberdeenshire in 1987.*   (Syndication International)

the paper about Prince Edward being gay,' people will say. Those who either began or believe the rumours are unlikely to be swayed by the denial. 'Methinks the lady doth protest too much,' is a common reaction. Prince Edward's outburst also did little to endear him to the large homosexual community in Britain. 'How would you feel if someone said you were gay?' the Prince had demanded, showing little sympathy for those who are. As when he walked out of the *Knockout* press conference, Prince Edward has again had cause to regret his action. Prince Philip, who has also made his fair share of publicity gaffes, has called it 'dentopedology' – putting one's foot in one's mouth.

Prince Edward has always been aware of the difficulties of having a relationship when you are royal. 'You become conscious of the feeling that if you try to get to know anybody they are going to suffer for the rest of their lives,' he said when he was a student at Cambridge. At an official luncheon he later revealed to a guest that the female sex were a mystery to him. 'It's extraordinary,' he said. 'You find them really interesting and everything is going well. Then they say something and you don't like them as much anymore.' All too often he has discovered that girls have only been interested in him because of his status. That knowledge is always guaranteed to dampen any spark of friendship. Those who want to know him as an individual hold back. It is an eternal dilemma.

When asked about marriage during a phone-in on a BBC children's television programme in 1987 Prince Edward said that he was in 'no hurry at all' and has never made his eldest brother's mistake of suggesting an age at which he would like to settle down. Prince Charles had once said that he thought thirty was a good age to marry and the quote haunted him until the day of his engagement. 'Royal men are only interesting to the tabloids when they're with women,' a well-known journalist has said. 'Edward conducts his romantic life with far too much discretion.' Being circumspect the Prince has had to pay the price in scurrilous gossip.

Those in royal circles like to think that Prince Edward is earmarked for Lady Rose Fitzroy, the youngest daughter of the Duchess of Grafton, the Queen's formidable Mistress of the Robes. Whilst she may be eminently suitable from a social point of view there has never been any evidence of an emotional entanglement. As a teenager the Prince appeared to be particularly friendly with Princess Anne's stable girl at Gatcombe Park, Shelley Whitborn, who used to go out riding with him, but it was not until he reached nineteen that Edward really seemed to develop an eye for the girls. Even so, he was extremely conscious that he was not free to sow his wild oats at random and had to take care to choose girlfriends who would not kiss and tell. 'The Prince is like a lot of young men who wait until they fall in love and find the right person before embarking on a sexual relationship,' said royal expert Margaret Holder in 1990. Such restraint on the Prince's part has always been tantalising for the media.

The one female who did receive a lot of publicity was model Romy Adlington, who met Edward at the Cowes Regatta in 1983 just before he went up to Cambridge. The beautiful brunette fashion model from Micheldover in Hampshire was later invited to stay at Balmoral and subsequent reports gave the length of their friendship as varying from between five months and three years before they drifted apart. In 1990 Romy Adlington, then living with her boyfriend Nic Sunnucks and expecting his baby, claimed to be still 'very, very good friends' with the Prince, but if this were true she later committed the ultimate sin by telling her story to a Sunday newspaper.

Earlier, in a royal exclusive for the *News of the World*, a 'friend' of the model's gave details of the relationship which led to the headline 'THE NIGHT PRINCE EDDIE WAS READY HE TRIED TO GET INTO MY BEDDIE'. The main article, headed 'LUSTY PRINCE KNOCKED ON MY DOOR AT MIDNIGHT,' was based on an interview with an unnamed person who claimed that Prince Edward had knocked on the model's door at midnight wanting to make love to her. 'He was very anxious to prove he was a red-blooded male,' Romy had 'told a pal' according to the article, 'but I thought trying it on at Balmoral with the Queen so near was a bit much.' It is no coincidence that the piece was published just five days after the 'I'm Not Gay' headlines. The newspaper, and presumably the anonymous source of the article, were confident that Prince Edward would take no legal action to refute the story. To have categorically stated that he was not gay and then to have publicly denied that he tried to bed an attractive fashion model would have been counterproductive. If Romy Adlington was angered by the article there was little she could do either, for it had shown her to be honourable. 'I felt very touched by his attention, but I told him to go back to his room, which he did,' she was quoted as saying.

For seven years she had refused to speak to the press about the Prince, but perhaps moved by the *News of the World*, four months later Miss Adlington decided to put her side of the story. She made no mention of a midnight visit to her room by the 'lusty Prince' but alleged that Edward had dated her in disguise, wearing a false nose and moustache which was set on fire by a candle in a restaurant. In her 'exclusive' for the *Sunday Mirror* she told of how the Queen was waiting to meet her 'at the front door' of Balmoral Castle when she arrived. 'She was just as I imagined her but less formal and more smiley than on public engagements.' Miss Adlington went on to mention how she had been shopping with Princess Anne and bought her a pair of Union Jack boxer shorts, how she had cooked sausages on a barbecue while the Queen and Prince Philip argued over the washing-up, and that when she was cold on a shooting-party 'the Queen Mother came over to me and offered me a sip of some sloe gin. She said "This will warm you up from the inside." It was a lovely gesture.' If Prince Edward ever saw the article it is more likely that it caused him laughter than anger. Miss Adlington in no way blackened the Prince's character – 'He is very sensitive, which some people don't make allowances for,' she said.

At Cambridge Prince Edward formed a closer attachment to fellow student Eleanor Weightman. Although they were studying different subjects (her area was languages), the two are said to have met once over a crowded lecture hall and were mutually attracted. They were frequently seen working together in the university library sitting side by side, and the Prince nicknamed her 'Munchkin'. They shared the same sense of humour, which is an essential factor for Edward in any friendship. On her door at college Eleanor had a card saying 'Appreciate me now – avoid the rush later.' Contemporaries at Cambridge remember them looking rather comical together, for Eleanor was only 5 feet tall while Prince Edward had already reached his towering height of over 6 feet. Perhaps Miss Weightman's diminutive size led to her nickname, the munchkins being dwarf-like characters in the Judy Garland film *The Wizard of Oz*. Cruelly, those who even then speculated that the Prince could be gay, called him 'a friend of Dorothy's' – a phrase that has its origins in the film. When Prince Edward stayed with Eleanor at her parents' home in Cheshire royal-watchers read more into the relationship than there actually was. For 'romance' read 'friendship'. A decade on, the two still keep in touch occasionally.

While Romy Adlington and Eleanor Weightman were girls Prince Edward had seen privately, the first time he ever appeared with a female escort in public was in July 1987 when he was twenty-three and had just returned from Canada. He arrived at the Henley Ball with the Scandinavian TV-AM weathergirl Ulrika Jonsson. Later he took her to see *Three Men and a Horse*, a play at the Vaudeville Theatre in London. For someone who wanted to keep their love life private, Prince Edward suddenly seemed to be flaunting it in public, but those in the know were well aware that if Ulrika had been intended as the future Mrs Edward Windsor she would not have been seen so openly in the Prince's company.

That autumn the Prince entertained a 'mystery blonde' at Windsor over a weekend. Many believed it to be Ulrika but her mother strongly refuted this and denied any rumours of romance with the standard, 'They are just good friends.' Prince Edward's guest would have remained completely secret had they not been romantically toasting crumpets over a log fire and accidentally set off the Castle's alarms. Within minutes the Berkshire Fire Brigade were thundering towards the Castle and found an apologetic but red-faced Prince. The news that the Prince had not been alone spread as quickly as the imagined fire, but Edward was too discreet to reveal his companion's identity. Possibly frightened off by the fire scare, the girl was not seen again. Friends of the Prince have a much more likely answer to the mystery, believing that Edward was simply having afternoon tea with his cousin Lady Helen Windsor, daughter of the Duke and Duchess of Kent. Others speculate that it was Gail Greenough, a blonde Canadian showjumper who had taken part in the *Knockout* tournament as a member of the Duchess of York's team. It is one secret Prince Edward has not revealed and in any case the weekend was certainly innocent, for by this time he had formed a far more romantic attachment.

At the Royal Yacht Squadron Ball in Cowes on the Isle of Wight, during the annual regatta in August, Edward had met Georgia May. A year younger than the Prince, she is the daughter of millionaire David May who owns the Bethon Boat Company of Lymington. Dark-haired Georgia lived with her divorced mother Catherine in Fulham, just a short distance from Buckingham Palace. Prince Edward enjoyed Georgia's company so much that he invited her to join the Royal Family on their summer cruise on *Britannia* to the Western Isles, the first time he had made such an offer. With Prince Andrew now married, the spotlight had been turned on Edward as the world's most eligible bachelor, and he may have felt under pressure to settle down. What he needed was someone like his cousin Viscount Linley's escort, Susannah Constantine. For a decade now this daughter of a Mayfair haulage millionaire has been Viscount Linley's companion. Rumours of an imminent marriage have prevailed since 1984. They holiday in Mustique together, are seen out at the theatre and in nightclubs, and give the media just sufficient interest to allow them to live their lives without too much intrusion. So accepted have they become as a couple that they are no longer newsworthy, even though to date they appear no nearer to making a permanent commitment to each other.

Prince Edward felt that he too would like a long-term escort who could be accepted by the press without them continually marrying him off to any girl he spoke to. There is a significant difference between the two cousins, however. Viscount Linley undertakes no official duties. His mother Princess Margaret once said that her children are 'not royal. They just happen to have an aunt who is the Queen.' For this reason, as plain David Linley, he has been able to build up a highly successful furniture-making business by devoting himself to it full-time. Prince Edward, on the other hand, has to undertake royal duties, a division of time which prevents him making a total commitment to a career of his own choosing. His status also means that undue pressure is automatically placed on any potential girlfriend. Both the wives of Prince Charles and Prince Andrew suffered intense trauma and long periods of adjustment, ill-prepared for the task ahead, unaware of the total lack of privacy and all the restrictions that are part and parcel of royal status. Diana learned to fit in, but Sarah was never comfortable with her royal role. A square peg in a round hole, she was eventually pushed out. Because of their well-publicised experiences, any girlfriend of Prince Edward's knows what to expect, and this immediately overshadows any budding friendship. Again Prince Edward suffers because of his brothers' marital problems.

It cannot be classed as a love match but Prince Edward was certainly keen on Georgia May. This year – 1987 – had been a traumatic one for him. He was desperately trying to find his way in life and Georgia was able to offer companionship and words of support. The Queen is said to have liked her, and Georgia was invited to spend New Year with the Royal Family at Sandringham, a rare honour only previously afforded to Lady Diana Spencer just a few weeks before her engagement to Prince Charles was announced. The Sandringham New Year holiday is almost always strictly a family affair, a chance to recharge the batteries before embarking on another twelve months of official duties. On New Year's Day 1988 Georgia travelled with the Queen Mother from Sandringham House to the Queen's shooting lodge where they joined Prince Edward and Prince Philip on a pheasant shoot. The next day Georgia was seen wearing a green anorak and headscarf, being driven around the estate by Prince Philip as if she were one of the family. Arriving to watch the day's shoot she was greeted warmly by the Queen, and later stood in the pouring ran with Princess Anne and the Duchess of York while Prince Philip, Prince Andrew and Prince Edward shot pheasants, partridges and wood pigeons. The three women looked like royal wives watching their husbands at sport.

During the visit Edward and Georgia were spotted out walking and holding hands, engrossed in conversation. Edward took her to see the Queen's kennels where the twenty gun dogs are kept, they went riding together, and when the Royal Family went to church on Sunday a crowd of over 10,000 people gathered in the hope of seeing a future royal bride. They were to be disappointed. Although Prince Edward was smitten, Georgia had a career of her own as a financial adviser, and did not relish the prospect of relinquishing her freedom. A five-month taste of media interest proved too much for her. 'She is getting cross – she might crack,' said her father David May at a press conference, revealing that he felt that Edward and his daughter were 'both too young to get married'. Even if Georgia had seen herself as the love of Edward's life, her chances were finally scuppered when another boyfriend appeared on the scene. Another Edward, Ed Danby, who had crewed the New Zealand challenge in the America's Cup told journalists that he was Georgia May's 'real boyfriend', insisting that they were still going out together. Georgia May moved swiftly out of the royal circle.

Edward had no time to be disappointed because he immediately took up his post as Production Assistant for Andrew Lloyd Webber in February 1988, and for the first time had a much greater opportunity to meet girls who were not part of the usual social set and who shared a common interest in the theatre rather than hunting, shooting and fishing. Although he met up again with the Canadian showjumper Gail Greenough in Newfoundland, who told the press 'He's great company', during his time with the Really Useful Theatre the Prince's name was linked with several other girls. He was said to be dating Marsha Bland, a dancer from *Cats* (although there is no evidence that they ever discussed anything other than work and she was not invited to Buckingham Palace or Sandringham); Rhian-Anwen Roberts, a friend from university at Cambridge (she was invited to Sandringham but she had a boyfriend already and there is no evidence that her visit was anything more than that of an old acquaintance); and another dancer from *Cats*, Ruthie Henshall. The husky-voiced Ruthie told reporters, 'I go to Edward's parties, he goes to mine. I am desperate to be a star. I know I'll get there somehow.' Edward did not, however, help her to fame and fortune. Shortly before leaving the Really Useful Theatre Company he was accompanied to the Royal Tournament in June 1990 by Cosima von Bulow whom he had met while attending the first night party for *Aspects of Love* in New York. She was also known to have been entertained to dinner in Edward's apartment at the Palace, but shortly afterwards flew out of the Prince's life.

Whatever friendships the Prince might have formed in the theatre, he obviously had no intention of emulating his great-great-grandfather and namesake, Edward VII, who had a penchant for actresses. Desperate to re-enact *The Prince and the Showgirl* nevertheless, in October 1992 rumour-mongers paired Prince Edward off with former TV-AM journalist Anastasia Cooke who firmly denied the suggestions until the gossip died down. Prince Edward visited the studios to take part in a programme on truancy, but shared nothing more than a cup of tea with the attractive blonde. Edward would not have known at the time but there were certain points which in any case made Anastasia Cooke an unacceptable candidate for the royal marriage stakes. She smoked cigarettes, which the Prince strongly dislikes; she is also a journalist, a profession the royals distrust; but more importantly she is a Catholic. Prince Edward cannot marry a Catholic because his mother is Head of the Church of England and the 1701 Act of Settlement prevents a Catholic or anyone marrying a Catholic being in line of succession to the throne.

Both Prince Michael of Kent and Edward's cousin George, the Earl of St Andrews, had to renounce all rights of succession in order to marry Catholics. Sixteenth and seventeenth in line respectively at the times of their marriages, both were highly unlikely ever to accede to the throne anyway, but it would be acutely embarrassing for the Queen if her son were not to remain in the order of succession. Under the 1772 Royal Marriages Act Prince Edward also has to seek the Queen's permission to marry and it is highly improbably that she would agree to such a union. Whilst Prince Edward has always said he wants to marry for love, his choice is in fact restricted. He is allowed to marry a commoner, like his brothers, but equally she must be the *right* commoner. Notoriously Edward VIII fell in love with the wrong person, lost his throne and his home, and was forced to live in exile. Prince Edward cannot afford to make the same mistake.

By October 1990 it seemed that Prince Edward had at last found the right girl. Princess Martha Louise, the only daughter of King Harald and Queen Sonja of Norway arrived in England in September to spend ten months training as a showjumper at Waterstock Training School near Oxford, where she had already undertaken short training courses during the previous six summers while still at school. Alone in Britain, and having close ties with the Royal Family, she was invited to Windsor where she and Edward became very friendly.

As far as the Queen was concerned, Princess Martha Louise was the perfect candidate for her youngest son. Born a Princess herself, she was as used to the restrictions of royal life as Edward. They both shared a common great-great-grandfather in King Edward VII, whose daughter Princess Maud married King Haakon of Norway. Their son, later King Olav of Norway, was George V's cousin and retained close ties with the House of Windsor until his death in 1991. In April 1957 Olav actually proposed to Princess Marina, the Duchess of Kent, and would have liked to have married the Queen Mother. He was turned down by both, but remained a close friend of the Queen Mother's and always, for example, accompanied her to White-hall for the annual wreath-laying ceremony at the Cenotaph. Princess Martha Louise's father, now King Harald (Olav's only son), had once been considered as a possible husband for Princess Alexandra before she married Angus Ogilvy. If she had married Harald, Alexandra would now be Queen of Norway. During the Second World War the Norwegian Royal Family spent several years in exile in Britain.

Not only does Princess Martha Louise have the perfect background, she also has the ideal character and personality for Edward. Said to be as 'wholesome' as Lady Diana Spencer, Martha enjoys outdoor pursuits and shares the Royal Family's passion for horses. With her brother Haakon Magnus now Crown Prince and heir to the throne, Martha has far greater freedom than Edward, for according to current Norwegian law a woman cannot inherit the throne. In Britain, if there was a huge catastrophe which wiped out both the Wales and York families, Prince Edward would be heir to the throne and one day King, but Martha could never been Queen in her own country. For this reason she has been able to lead a far more normal life than her distant cousin, Edward. She went to a primary school and a mixed secondary school in Oslo, where she specialised in English and French. Like Edward she enjoyed sailing, skiing and riding, and is trying to establish a career of her own as a showjumper. Fiercely independent, she took a job in a laundry in order to pay for her training. Eventually it was agreed that she could spend ten months in a training school before going on to university. Both her father and grandfather studied at Baliol College, Oxford, and it was Martha Louise's ambition to follow them.

In February 1991 the Princess moved on to the exclusive Arena UK riding centre in Lincolnshire which is run by former showjumper, John Lanni. Having grown up in a family for whom horses are a favourite hobby, Edward has always enjoyed riding but has never particularly liked competitive events. Although he occasionally goes to Royal Ascot it is as much for the social life as the sport. He is seldom seen with the Queen in the royal box at the Derby or standing on the sidelines at polo, so it came as something of a surprise when he privately attended a very small gymkhana in June 1991, and remained there for five hours. One of the competitors was Princess Martha Louise on her horse Two Socks. Two weeks later, on 21 June, she returned to Norway for the blessing ceremony of her parents' coronation (King Olav, her grandfather, had died on 17 January that year). On 19 July, following the collapse of the Theatre Division, Prince Edward was on a plane bound for Oslo.

In Norway Princess Martha Louise's brother, Crown Prince Haakon Magnus, was celebrating his eighteenth birthday. Prince Edward went to Norway to join in the three days of celebrations which included a grand ball for European royalty on the Friday evening, a trip on the Norwegian royal yacht on Saturday, followed by a glittering celebration dinner that night, and a bus tour of Oslo on Sunday. Royal-watchers quickly seized on the fact that Edward had not made the effort to go to Norway for Martha's own eighteenth party. Was it because he was now romantically involved that he had used Haakon's birthday as an excuse to see her again? Buckingham Palace pointed out that Haakon was now Crown Prince and heir to the throne and therefore of much higher status than he had been six months earlier which was why a senior member of the British Royal Family had been invited.

Whether conscious of the speculation and keen not to add fuel to the flames, or because there was no spark of romance anyway, Prince Edward and Princess Martha Louise scarcely spoke to each other during the three-day visit. At dinner on the first night Martha flirted with Crown Prince Frederic of Denmark, the handsome twenty-three-year-old son of Queen Margrethe. In the European press Martha and Frederic had been romantically linked since October 1989. A daredevil Prince, Frederic is known to like fast cars and parachuting, and is currently a commando in the Danish army. He has a reputation for being rude on official visits and will even turn his back on photographers during photocalls, yet he seemed to score points over the more dignified British Prince. While Edward wore white tie and his CVO insignia, Frederic was vibrant in a red uniform swathed with gold braid, a sash and medals, as if costumed for an Ivor Novello operetta. Prince Edward could not compete.

As Princess Martha Louise laughed and joked with Prince Frederic at the Friday evening ball, Prince Edward sat on the sidelines talking to an elderly aunt. At the Saturday night dinner Martha and Frederic were seated side by side, while Edward was positioned next to Martha's mother. Edward eschewed the trip on the royal yacht and sat alone during the coach tour. Four rows behind him sat Princess Martha Louise and the Crown Prince. That night Edward returned alone to Buckingham Palace. If there had been any possibility of a serious friendship with Martha it seemed the Prince had been unlucky again, unless they both carried out a very convincing charade for the benefit of onlookers which seemed unlikely. On 10 March 1992 Prince Edward celebrated his twenty-eighth birthday apparently no closer to finding a soulmate.

Prince Charles was thirty-three the year he married, and had Prince Andrew waited until he was of a similar age, there would have been less pressure on Edward. As it was, Prince Andrew married at twenty-six, and it was exactly a month after his own twenty-sixth birthday that Edward found the 'gay' headlines appearing. When Prince Andrew's marriage collapsed, however, Edward suddenly gained some leeway. With two of the Queen's four children now separated, nobody wanted Edward to rush into an unsuitable union.

The difficulty facing Prince Edward on marriage is income. Most people look at the inherited property and art treasures of the Royal Family and assume they are wealthy, but whilst the

Windsors collectively have money, Prince Edward as an individual is not rich. He is fortunate enough to have security, but that is not the same as having money. Prince Charles has an income from the Duchy of Cornwall, Prince Andrew has a well-paid naval position, but Prince Edward has no personal wage. His Civil List allowance goes entirely on royal duties; not a penny is for his own use. The Queen and Prince Philip set up a trust fund for their children when they were young to bring them in an allowance and this money has been wisely invested for Prince Edward but he is by no means wealthy. In 1990 Prince Edward's Civil List allowance was increased to £100,000 per annum until the year 2000. A large increase at the time, it was explained as allowing for Edward to get married; yet his married brother the Duke of York received £250,000. Now that the Duke's marriage has ended, this financial arrangement will change; but had he remained married, by the end of the century Edward and his wife would have found themselves receiving £150,000 a year less than Andrew. Once again Edward seems to have been given a raw deal.

Being Royal, Prince Edward knows that he will have to share his wife with the world. The Princess of Wales and the Duchess of York both hoped that media interest in them would abate after their honeymoons. It did not in either case, and while in the early 1990s Diana found herself raised up as an icon, Sarah became the 'Aunt Sally' – by 1992 knocked down once too often. Prince Edward's wife can see from their examples how soul-destroying some of the criticism can be. The Duchess of York was attacked for being overweight, yet a considerable effort to slim sparked off headlines claiming that she was too thin and expressing fears for her health. Such petty sniping is difficult for anyone to tolerate and 'Fergie' must now be relieved in some ways that her days in the firing line are over. Whether or not she has any interest in fashion, the wife of Prince Edward will find her clothes scrutinised, her designers interrogated. Reams will be written on imagined rivalry between her and her sister-in-law Diana. If any children are taken on royal tours Prince Edward will be condemned; if they are left at home with a nanny they will also be attacked. Mrs Edward Windsor faces almost total loss of privacy; a member of staff will even know if she goes to the bathroom. If Edward spends time abroad for the Duke of Edinburgh's Award there will be hints of imminent divorce. In a sense marriage to Prince Edward can be seen as a life sentence in a gilded cage. Whilst there are many apparent benefits it is not a decision to be taken lightly. As Sarah Ferguson discovered, love alone can never be enough. Being royal is not a status but a way of life, an inescapable vocation.

It takes any member of the Royal Family a long time to make friends. You cannot choose to be close to them; they learn to confide in you. Ultimately they have to decide who holds the promise of true friendship. For somebody who has spent more than twenty years of their life with the freedom to talk to anyone they like, suddenly to become part of the small, closeted royal circle is very suffocating. Close courtiers of the Queen and their families are introduced to other members of the Royal Family and it eventually becomes a very insular, single-class world. For this reason finding a girlfriend has always presented a problem for Edward. When Prince Andrew became engaged to Sarah Ferguson her mother said, 'They met on the polo field. Doesn't everyone?' Prince Edward would disagree. He has tried the stable girl, the show girl and the showjumper without success, but is clearly attracted to girls outside his own social circle. Unlike Prince Charles he does not need a bride with 'a history but no past', but she will still have to meet certain criteria. Most important of all she will have to accept taking second place to her mother-in-law. This was the source of many a dispute between the newly married Prince and Princess of Wales when Charles had to leave Diana alone to have lunch with his mother. When Prince Edward worked for both Really Useful and Theatre Division he frustrated colleagues by announcing that he had to leave early to see his mother at Windsor.

Forever in the Queen's shadow, royal daughters-in-law also have to live up to her expectations. One member of the royal circle reveals that the Princess of Wales was for several years in awe of the Queen. It was not so much fear of the woman, but fear of what Her Majesty represents. Diana could never relax in the Queen's presence. She was always conscious of being watched and assessed. Not until Prince Andrew married did Diana feel able to mature into the role. When Prince Edward's wife is the newcomer she will probably feel the same, but as the last of the Queen's daughters-in-law she will always be in the shadow of Diana. For a long time she will feel an outsider. When Prince Edward marries he knows it will be the last major royal wedding this century. On 18 July 1992 his cousin Lady Helen Windsor married art dealer Tim Taylor, but it was a private family wedding at Windsor Castle, not a state occasion. After Prince Edward we will have to wait until the marriage of Prince William or Prince Harry to witness another such event, which means that Edward's wife will remain the newest addition to the family for a long time.

From the start of any relationship Prince Edward's friends are fully aware that he is no ordinary young man. They cannot telephone him without going through the Palace switchboard; they cannot write to him without putting a secret code on the envelope which will first go through a security scanner; if they visit him they have to be escorted to the Prince of Wales's door where they are met by Edward's valet and are escorted formally up to his apartment. Not having free access to him is intimidating for any girlfriend. When Lady Diana Spencer was being courted by Prince Charles she was once driven out of Sandringham at speed lying flat on the back seat of a Ford Cortina to avoid being spotted by photographers. Indeed she continually had to play cat and mouse with the press. On one occasion she packed up her car outside her flat with suitcases, a coat and shoes, and then walked around the corner as if going to a nearby shop. She returned three days later, having spent a weekend with Prince Charles in Scotland. Only then did the duped pressmen realise that Diana was playing them at their own game. Similarly in 1973 Princess Anne and Mark Philips were smuggled past photographers in the back of horseboxes. Having to carry out such a charade can be fun initially, but few can stand the pace for very long. Marriage to a member of the Royal Family can never be normal.

Edward has tried so hard to be 'ordinary', but it is a losing battle. One night, when they were still teenagers, Princess Anne and Prince Charles were being driven back to Buckingham Palace after a *son et lumière* show at St Paul's Cathedral. As their car approached the Palace they saw a young couple standing at the side of the road kissing passionately.

'I wish we didn't live such sheltered lives,' the Princess said regretfully. 'Don't you?'

'You mustn't ever say that,' replied her brother. 'I know it's true, but you mustn't ever say it.'

Psychologically the sheltered upbringing takes its toll. Even after more than eleven years of marriage Prince Charles still needs periods of total solitude away from his wife and sons to maintain his sanity; through following the royal path into the services Prince Andrew spent only forty days with his wife in 1991, said to be a key factor in their separation; and because of her own commitment to royal duty Princess Anne's marriage also collapsed. Such are the pressures that Prince Edward has quite deliberately bided his time before taking the final step. Better a lifetime of bachelorhood than to make the wrong decision. A false start in his career was easy enough to change, but to terminate a marriage contract would be viewed as a much more serious failure. As a Prince for whom so many previous choices appear to have misfired, matrimony could prove to be the making of him. Only time will tell.

Chapter 8

UNDER
THE SPOTLIGHT

*In practice it is seldom very hard to do one's duty
when one knows what it is, but it is sometimes exceedingly
difficult to find this out.*

SAMUEL BUTLER,

First Principles

Prince Edward staggered slightly as he rose to his feet to make a speech at the Duke of Edinburgh's Award thirtieth anniversary banquet. As he spoke his words slurred, his eyes appeared to be slightly glazed. Honoured guests at the Guildhall looked at each other uncomfortably, scarcely daring to believe that their International Trustee might be inebriated. The glassy stare changed in an instant to a wicked glint and the Prince roared with laughter. 'I thought that would get you worried!' he beamed. The diners applauded this impromptu performance, before the Prince embarked on a more serious piece of rhetoric.

Pretending to be drunk was an effective method of breaking the ice, but it was also a carefully calculated ploy designed to win the audience over and calm his own nerves. Undertaking official engagements has never been easy for Prince Edward. Far happier on stage with a script than having to improvise in public, he has always had to make a conscious effort at such times. Occasionally observers have found him reserved, wrongly attributing his sometimes sullen appearance to snobbishness rather than shyness. It seems strange that this most public of families should ever suffer from nerves, yet is is not uncommon. Visitors to Balmoral and Sandringham have found at times that if they wait for the Queen to start a conversation there will be a lengthy silence, like a shy schoolgirl. Princess Margaret, who on the surface seems to be one of the most outgoing members of the family, has learned to use her personality and humour to overcome a lack of self-confidence. Before the Windsor Castle pantomimes when she was a child her governess, Marion Crawford, wrote that the Princess looked literally green before a show. When Princess Anne was taken to Benenden School for the first time her car was forced to stop on the way because she was sick with fear. Prince Charles was acutely shy throughout his youth and today, like Prince Edward, can appear reserved and occasionally frustrated by duty, especially if his presence does not appear to serve any specific purpose.

All members of the Royal Family learn how to break the ice and lessen the formality of public occasions. I once watched Princess Anne begin to read what was clearly the wrong speech, meant for a different occasion entirely. She kept the charade going for just long enough before tearing it into pieces and announcing drily, 'Sorry, that was yesterday's!' Having poked fun at her own workload, she embarked on a genuinely witty and engaging speech as planned. After forty years of engagements, Princess Alexandra has mastered the art of winning hearts with her friendly, approachable manner. Inaugurating a new fountain dedicated to the Royal Alexandra Children's Hospital in Brighton during a visit to Sussex in March 1992, the Princess walked straight over to me and said, 'I bet people will splash about in this fountain in the summer!' Just before pulling the cord to unveil the plague she giggled, 'I do hope it works,' and having performed the ceremony she took off her glove and plunged her hand into the fountain to feel the temperature of the water. These may be innocuous comments, human reactions, but coming from a member of the Royal Family they completely won over the audience.

The stiff formality of former reigns, when the public were always over-awed in the presence of royalty has vanished with Edward's generation. The Royal Family are no longer required simply to honour us with their presence, they are also expected to entertain. Arriving at Westminster Abbey on the eve of the

Duke of York's wedding Prince Edward had his arm in a sling, causing his already anxious brother to panic. 'That fooled you!' he said to photographers, who dubbed him 'the Clown Prince'. Some may consider such humour infantile, but it serves a purpose putting people at their ease. Compared to Princess Alexandra, Edward is still a novice. Even the simplest royal visit takes months to set up and invariably involves many hundreds of people, but the responsibility for its success or failure still rests squarely on Edward's shoulders. If he fails to do his homework the organisers will feel short-changed.

As Prince Edward is driven to engagements in the official royal car, guided by police outriders, it is not surprising that he often suffers from stage fright. There must be an awareness that crowds line the route in his honour, and wait for hours, sometimes in the rain. Great things are expected of him simply because his mother is Queen. Experience makes it easier, but like an actor doing a lengthy one-man tour, the nervous energy is always there. The highly acclaimed British actress Dame Judi Dench once said that she feels:

> *Ill at the thought of having to make a speech. Or walking into a room full of people I don't know. Then I'll feel people are judging me on my choice of clothes and behaviour and speech . . . The stage is different. The audience aren't focusing on you up there, they're focusing on characters and a story. You're portraying a person completely different from yourself, saying words that aren't yours.*

Prince Edward can certainly identify with Dame Judi's sentiment. As he walks into a room the public and press alike are scrutinising his every move. They decide whether his suit is off-the-peg or tailor-made; they study the design on his tie and peer at the crest on his signet ring; they discuss his thinning hair and comment on his deep blue eyes. From his Mountbatten inherited bald spot to his Windsor nose, Prince Edward is studied like an exhibit at a freak show. He would far rather walk on to a stage in character or confront a television camera than enter a room full of strangers but it is a fact of life he is learning to live with. Being a member of the Royal Family can be very lonely, and in the course of a year Prince Edward meets many hundreds of people once and only once, invariably for just a few seconds. The conversation will be unrevealing, for much royal small talk involves asking questions to which the Prince already knows the answer. For this reason the Prince has deliberately accepted a number of presidencies and patronages which involve young people and children who are much more at ease in his presence and will talk honestly and openly to him. When Edward worked professionally in the theatre he was always behind the scenes, yet in real life he is centre stage, constantly expected to perform.

There is a poignant photograph of Prince Edward taken by Captain Voynovitch, a former Master of the Yugoslav Royal Household and one-time Private Secretary to King Peter. Under the alias John Scott he took several private pictures for the Royal Family's own albums including a photograph of Prince Edward aged about five, anxiously awaiting his first engagement, having to present a cup at a Windsor polo match. The fear is clearly apparent in the little boy's face. Another, taken around the same time, shows him being comforted by one of the crew on board the royal yacht *Britannia* while his mother went ashore to fulfil a public duty. Because the Queen has made a conscious effort to spend more time with Edward than she had been able to with her other children, he seemed to feel it even more keenly when they were apart. Although it was necessary to introduce him to public life from an early age, Edward was clearly frightened by the responsibility.

The Queen and Prince Philip had the difficult task of trying to shield him from the limelight for as long as possible while at the same time preparing him for his future role, and they therefore tried to initiate Edward gradually into official duties. At the age of fourteen, when in Canada for the 1978 Commonwealth Games, the Prince planted a commemorative tree at Lloydminster; and, accompanied by his father, made the 3,300-foot descent of the world's biggest potash mine at Cory, Saskatchewan. In June 1984, while he was still a student at Jesus College, Edward attended a garden party with Prince Philip to celebrate 400 years of the Cambridge University Press, the oldest press in the world. The Duke of Edinburgh was present as Chancellor of Cambridge University, but Edward tagged along to gain experience. That same month he accompanied the Queen and Prince Andrew to Gordounstoun for the school's golden jubilee celebrations, and in July Prince Edward again went with his father to the Royal Ascot Spectacular in aid of the Prince Philip Trust Fund. There the Prince entered into the spirit of the event by taking part in the tombola, insisting that he never had 'any luck'. He selected two blank tickets and received a small pink teddy bear as a consolation prize.

Not until he had left university in 1986 could the Prince really begin solo official engagements in earnest. That year he joined his family at annual events such as Trooping the Colour (travelling in a carriage with the Queen Mother and the Princess of Wales), and the Ascot Races. Even more publicly, he was a supporter at the wedding of the Duke and Duchess of York, but this was also the year that Edward took on his first official role. He became Chairman of the Duke of Edinburgh's Award Thirtieth Anniversary Tribute Project, aimed at publicising the Scheme. This marked the point at which his initiation ended and he became a working member of the family in his own right, undertaking engagements in London, Jersey, the Isle of Man and New Zealand.

Just as Princess Anne found her niche with the Save the Children Fund, so Prince Edward saw that he could be of benefit to the Duke of Edinburgh's Award. As the director Michael Hobbs said:

> *Prince Edward was the only one in the Royal Family still in the age group for the Award. He could go around and talk on equal terms to the young people doing it and find out what they thought and what needed doing.*

By 1988 Prince Edward had joined the Scheme's main board and was holding regular monthly meetings at Buckingham Palace.

The Scheme had been founded in 1956 by Prince Philip and Everest explorer Sir John Hunt in an attempt to fill the vacuum created by the ending of compulsory military National Service, but it had been originally initiated by Dr Kurt Hahn. As the founder and first headmaster of Gordonstoun, Hahn introduced the Moray Badge for personal achievement in extra-curricular activities. Prince Philip earned one of the badges himself and in 1954 he was approached by Kurt Hahn with a scheme to involve young people in personal challenges. Two years later the Award Scheme was officially launched and has to date involved more than two million young people. From the outset industries, schools, local education authorities, the armed services and voluntary youth organisations participated in the Scheme and within the first year it had 7,000 entrants. By 1977 the then Director Sir Alfred Blake said that 'one in ten of all young people in the United Kingdom now takes part in the Scheme at some time, and many thousands are involved in nearly all the Commonwealth countries.' Prince Philip described it as being:

> *intended to help both the young and those people who take an interest in their welfare. It is designed as an introduction to leisure-time activities, a challenge to the individual to personal achievement, and as a guide to those people and organisations who are concerned about the development of our future citizens.*

In practical terms young people between the ages of fourteen and twenty-five, including those with disabilities, are encouraged to gain an award through learning new skills within their own area of personal interest and in a non-competitive way. The emphasis is very similar to that which Kurt Hahn placed on individual sports and personal achievement for his pupils at Gordonstoun. There are three types of award – bronze (which can be achieved within six months); silver (which is for people of fifteen and over, and takes a year to earn); and gold (which takes eighteen months to achieve and for which participants must be sixteen or over). For each award, entrants have to complete four separate sections in which they are judged on personal progress, proficiency, and sustained effort. Each level sets new targets and widens the participant's horizons; and within each section there is a wide range of activities so that all young people, regardless of physical or mental ability, can be achievers.

The four sections for each medal are as follows:

169

Service
The aim is to encourage participants to serve others and develop both an awareness of the needs of their local community and a sense of their own responsibilities. Participants can train and give practical service in child care, first aid, hospital volunteer work, animal care, Oxfam, Samaritans, police service, youth work, being a canoe lifeguard, home nursing, conservation projects (such as woodland clearance, stone walling, footpath preservation), anything that will provide a service to the community.

Expedition
This is the most popular section, aiming to encourage a spirit of adventure and to teach the importance of working in a team. The social skills learned, such as budgeting, leadership, buying of supplies and developing working relationships, are all of great practical importance. Young people are trained in safety precautions, map-reading, cooking and the country code, and subsequently have to undertake a journey by foot, cycle, canoe, horse or boat. Expeditions last between two and four days, depending on the level of the award. For the gold award, for example, either 50 miles on foot or 100 miles riding must be accomplished within a four day venture, including three nights' camping.

Skills
The aim of this section is to encourage perseverance and the development of personal interests and practical skills. Participants have to select a hobby or topic to study and are required to show progress in the subject. There are over 200 different skills to choose from, including music, drama, archaeology, astronomy, librarianship, debating, writing, brass rubbing, photography, dog training, aeronautics, electronics and ornithology.

Physical Recreation
Participants are required to take part in some form of physical recreation and achieve individual fitness. Conventional sports are included but also activities such as dancing, riding, yoga, ballet, karate, rock-climbing and skate-boarding. Two points are awarded for each hourly session and between twenty-four

and thirty-six points must be attained. Only two points can be awarded per week, or four points per alternate weekend, to ensure a sustained effort.

In addition, for the gold award, participants have to complete a residential project aimed at broadening their experience through involvement with others. They must be in the company of others (who are not their everyday companions), for a period of five consecutive days, perhaps on an outward bound course or a National Trust acorn camp.

When all sections have been satisfactorily completed, participants receive a bronze, silver or gold badge and a certificate. Gold achievers receive theirs personally from Prince Philip or Prince Edward at St James's Palace or Holyroodhouse. By this point participants have increased their own personal skills and often, as a direct result, improve their career opportunities. In recent years award-holders have entered the worlds of education, medicine, community care and conservation by virtue of their experience on the Scheme. All those who have taken part agree that they have benefited from the experience and have grown in confidence. Prince Edward's own activities included an expedition in the Cairngorms, learning real tennis and training junior air cadets, and his interest in the Award Scheme has grown dramatically since taking on the role of UK and International Trustee.

What appeals to the Prince is the varied nature of the Scheme. He can visit projects all over the country and see young people learning a wide range of new skills, children who will be the next generation of working adults and who will have learned self-discipline and valuable communication skills. In recent years Prince Edward has become Chairman of the Special Projects Group which raises funds to support the Scheme in inner cities and as far afield as Africa and the Caribbean. Since 1989 the Scheme has been committed to Europe and funds have been raised to encourage young people to do their part of their Award project in another country. In 1990 a Wild Country Panel was set up in Bavaria, for example, to see if there was a demand for such a project there. This has not only proved popular with the Bavarians but also encouraged 1,000 young people to travel to Bavaria in 1991 for their expedition project. Young people within the EC travel to each other's countries on the Scheme thus broadening their horizons physically as well as mentally.

Many people raise their own funds to finance their overseas travel. For example twelve spirited young people raffled themselves as 'Slaves for the Day'. They became 'slaves' to the twelve winners, spending a day doing their gardens, washing their cars and cleaning their houses. The money they raised enabled them to travel to other parts of Europe. Some collect litter, and on one occasion a team of climbers organised a 'Climb Everest in a Day' stunt, abseiling up and down a 40-foot high wall 725 times – the height of Everest. Prince Edward is also Chairman of the Pegasus Project, an initiative in which three major airlines give four free tickets to enable young people to travel anywhere in the world for their Award expedition. The Secretary of the Pegasus Project, Robert Hughes, also happens to be the Financial Officer for British Airways, which is a help.

There is now a link between the Probation Service, the Youth Service and The Duke of Edinburgh's Award who all feel that young offenders benefit from participation and begin to take a pride in their community. Judge Colin Colston QC says that the Scheme offers:

> *valuable opportunities for offenders under the age of twenty-five to gain in self-confidence whilst at the same time putting something positive into the society in which they live. The four sections of the Award require commitment over a period of time and an improvement in the individual's performance. Experience has shown that potential employers tend to give considerable weight to applications by those who have participated in the Award.*

In view of its obvious value the Home Office have been persuaded to fund certain Award projects involving probationers.

Since 1986, apart from chairing regular committee meetings for the Duke of Edinburgh's Award Special Projects Group, Prince Edward has been actively involved in fund-raising events and has toured schools and projects throughout Britain. As International Trustee he has also visited projects in Portugal, Australia, Malta, the Caribbean, Canada and Hong Kong, making at least two overseas visits in this capacity each year. Throughout 1991 the Prince undertook a wide number of engagements to mark the Award Scheme's thirty-fifth anniversary and is already looking towards their ruby jubilee in 1996.

To mark the thirty-fifth anniversary, and at the same time raise awareness of the 1992 Olympic Games, Award Scheme participants carried the Olympic torch on a 1,500 mile journey around Britain. On 9 September, in front of Buckingham Palace, Prince Edward lit the original 1948 Olympic torch which was then carried by the first runner, Mark Davis. Sponsored by Mars, the run also raised funds to support British athletes, so that – in typical Award Scheme style – many organisations benefited from a single event. The lighted torch was carried by many different methods: on horseback, bicycle, canoe, by boat and, of course, on foot. It was seen all over Britain – Nantwich, Bingley, Cardiff, Derby, Altrincham, Edinburgh, Kelso – at one stage being flown from RAF Alconbury, going through drizzle in Sanquhar, and eventually arriving back in London at Canary Wharf. Its journey's end coincided with the news that over 86,000 people had joined the Scheme in 1991.

Throughout 1991 Prince Edward was present at many Award Scheme events, including a reception at Buckingham Palace and a dinner at the Dorchester Hotel for Duke of Edinburgh's Award Friends, a dinner for people taking part in the Award Scheme at the Guildhall, Windsor, and an annual garden party for them at Buckingham Palace. He also promoted the Scheme at the Longleat Balloon Fiesta at Longleat House, Wiltshire, where he had intended to go up in a hot-air balloon but was prevented by bad weather; instead he took a short tethered flight. He attended an Award Scheme garden party at Peterhouse Deer Park, Cambridge, and in June organised a fund-raising ball for Gold Award Holders on board the *QEII* berthed at Southampton. The event raised £138,000 for the Award Scheme. In September, as Patron of the Award Special Projects Group, he attended a youth rally at Bicton College of Agriculture as part of Devon's Year of Youth, and later that month spent a whole day in South Wales. There he attended an Award's Anniversary Service in Llandaff Cathedral, Cardiff, as well as a reception and lunch at Twyn-Yr-Hydd, Margam Country Park, West Glamorgan. He also visited Three Cliffs Bay to see Award participants take part in various activities and in the evening joined more Award participants for a barbecue at North Hills Farm on the Gower coast. It was a day of torrential rain and the Prince got soaked to the skin while watching participants display their skills at cliff rescue, surf livesaving and canoeing. On a brighter day in September he went to Uttoexter Racecourse in Staffordshire for the running of the Duke of Edinburgh's Award Trophy. During the year he also paid visits to Award projects in Stowmarket, Newmarket, Thetford, Derby, Birmingham, Strathclyde, Ayr, Canada and Hong Kong.

One of the highlights of Edward's year was organising a seventieth birthday party for his father in the grounds of Windsor Castle during the last weekend of July in a attempt to raise £1 million for various charities including the Duke of Edinburgh's Award. Some 6,000 people bought tickets for the party and entertainment and a banquet was arranged for 1,500. Inspired by the Award Scheme, Prince Edward had 'gold', 'silver' and 'bronze' tables, with tickets at £1,000, £500, and £250 respectively. During the party the Prince completed an obstacle course seated in a wheelchair to demonstrate that disabled people are just as capable of competing as the able-bodied. Now that the Duke of Edinburgh is in his seventies he is gradually handing over more of his responsibilities to his youngest son, whose youthful image is far more appropriate for the 1990s, certainly where projects involving young people are concerned. In 1990, for example, the Prince succeeded his father as President of the Commonwealth Games Federation and flew to Auckland to open the Commonwealth Games.

Like other members of his family, Prince Edward has geared his official working life to fit in as far as possible with his own interests. This means that many of the charities and organisations with which he is associated are connected with the arts and his own favourite sports. In 1990 he accepted invitations to become Patron of the London Mozart Players and the Scottish Badminton Union, for example. In 1991 he was kept particularly busy with both organisations, due to the bicentenary of Mozart's death and the hosting of the World Badminton Championships in Kelso Hall, Glasgow. He attended a concert by the London Mozart Players on 27 January to mark the beginning of the bicentenary year at St James's Palace, another at the Fairfields Halls, Croydon, in June, and on the actual date of the composer's death attended a banquet and a performance of Mozart's *Requiem* in St Paul's Cathedral. For the latter engagement the Prince was accompanied, somewhat unusually, by the Princess of Wales. Five days later he attended the launch of the London Mozart Players' promotional video 'Winning A Wider Audience' and a celebration reception and concert.

Each organisation with which he is associated (see Appendix II) makes many demands on the Prince's time. although his patronages increase each year, he has deliberately kept them to a manageable level so that he is not a mere figurehead but can take an active part. Only glamorous charity galas and high-profile events tend to be reported in the newspapers; the day-to-day duties which Edward fulfils remain unknown to the public at large. On 10 November 1991, for instance, Edward was guest of honour at the Boomerang Ball at Grosvenor House to raise money for the National Youth Theatre. Ticket cost £125 and were snapped up by the likes of Bill Wyman, Elton John and Ringo Starr, who dined on cream of vegetable soup with basil, Scotch smoked salmon fillet filled with spinach and baked in puff pastry, followed by pineapple and chocolate bavarois with Malibu sauce. Members of the National Youth Theatre ran a fun fair and sideshows, gameshow host Henry Kelly was Master of Ceremonies at an auction, and the Australian Grand Prix was recreated in miniature. With Australia as the theme of the ball, Dame Edna Everage was there to hurl insults and gladdies, for once upstaged by the Bruce Oldfield and Versace outfits worn by the audience. Because the Prince was present there was media interest, but it would be easy to get the impression that it was his only engagement of the month. In fact, besides committee meetings for the Duke of Edinburgh's Award Special Projects Group and production meetings for a new television project, his diary also included:

1 November   Final day of engagements in Hong Kong at the end of a seven-day overseas visit as International Trustee of the Duke of Edinburgh's Award and President of the Commonwealth Games Federation.

7 November	Morning: Visited Eltham College, London SE9, to open a new performing arts centre. Evening: Attended a gala performance of *Romeo and Juliet* by the Northern Ballet Theatre at the Royalty Theatre, London.
8 November	Morning: Visited the West Midlands to undertake engagements in connection with the Duke of Edinburgh's Award. Officially opened the new Cameron-Price factory at Stirchley, Birmingham, followed by lunch. Afternoon: Visited Rackhams Store in Birmingham. Visited TNT Express at Atherstone, Warwickshire. Evening: Attended a dinner in support of the Award Scheme at the National Motorcycle Museum, Bickenhill.
9 November	Attended the Royal British Legion Festival of Remembrance in the Royal Albert Hall.
10 November	Attended the National Youth Theatre of Great Britain's 1991 Annual Ball at the Grosvenor House, London W1.
12 November	As Chairman of the Duke of Edinburgh's Award Special Projects Group attended the Magnificent Seven Dinner, An Evening with Cole Porter, at the Hyatt Carlton Tower, London SW1.
15 November	As Chairman of the Duke of Edinburgh's Award Special Projects Group attended the Focus Multibroadcast National Schools Video Awards Gala Lunch and National Final in the Park Lane Hotel, London.

16 November	Morning: Attended the Hamilton Youth Fair at Bell College, Strathclyde. Attended a lunch given by the Convenor of Strathclyde Region in the Regional Offices, Hamilton. Afternoon: Visited the Duke of Edinburgh's Award 'Action in Ayr' gathering in the Magnum Centre, Irvine. Visited Sutherland House, Ayr, the Branch Headquarters and Social Centre of the Scottish Society for the Mentally Handicapped. Attended a reception for Friends of the Duke of Edinburgh's Award 'Action in Ayr' in Culzean Castle. Evening: Attended a reception and dinner in support of the Award in the Turnberry Hotel, Ayr.
20 November	Attended an evening reception for Members of the Diplomatic Corps.
22 November	Morning: Undertook a number of engagements in Manchester. Attended a lunch in support of the Booth Hall Children's Accident and Emergency Unit and the Macmillan Fund for Cancer Relief at the Piccadilly Hotel. Afternoon: Visited Booth Hall Children's Hospital, Blackley. Evening: Attended the Royal Exchange Theatre Company's production of *Medea*. Attended a supper at the Royal Exchange.

23 November   As Patron of the Scottish Badminton
Union attended the semi-finals of the
Carlton Vauxhall Scottish Open Bad-
minton Championships at the Kelvin
Hall International Sports Arena,
Glasgow.

Although November was by no means his busiest month, it was
still galling the Prince that the general public assumed he had
done nothing more than attend one charity ball. An opinion
poll carried out for the *Mail on Sunday* at the beginning of 1992
revealed that of the 1,127 people questioned only 3 per cent
considered that Prince Edward worked 'very hard' and 15 per
cent believed he worked 'fairly hard'. These opinions were
based entirely on media coverage. In the previous twelve
months he had, however, undertaken a total of 251 official
engagements.

At the beginning of 1991 the Royal Family found themselves
the target of criticism. Three weeks after the Gulf War began,
The Sunday Times criticised members of the Royal Family for
continuing to play sport and go to the theatre. Younger members of the family in particular were accused of insensitivity.
The Palace Press Office reacted by sending newspaper editors a
long list of engagements the Royal Family were undertaking in
connection with the Gulf but it was too late to dispel the myth.
'Prince Edward could be regarded as the only young royal with
something to contribute to the war since he runs his own
theatrical company,' said *The Times*, 'but so far he has not
offered its services to entertain the troops.' Theatre Division,
however, was not the Prince's company, he was merely an
employee. Nor was it a theatrical company with a repertoire of
plays or a permanent company of actors. By the time the Gulf
War broke out they had just one play on at the Garrick Theatre
and to suggest that this could be taken off and transported to
the Gulf was as ridiculous as it was impractical. Instead the
Prince visited British forces and RAF stations and boosted the
morale of wives and girlfriends left behind. These activities
may have been low-profile but they were of more practical use.
Prince Charles visited troops in the Gulf before the outbreak of
war, but it would have been impossible to guarantee the safety

of any member of the Royal Family in the region once the actual fighting had begun. Mercifully a ceasefire was called on 28 February, but Prince Edward was to suffer from the unfounded suggestion that he had not pulled his weight.

Prince Edward also suffers because many of his duties involve theatrical events which on the surface appear less worthy than visits to hospitals or factories. However, whilst one visit to a children's hospital might display royal compassion, the Prince's presence at a charity gala can raise hard cash which will help keep the hospital open. One organiser told me that if they hold a charity show they might raise £50,000 for their cause, but if a member of the Royal Family attends it can be increased to £250,000, with the added bonus of much greater media coverage. Such practical matters should be taken into consideration by the public.

Because of the Prince's love and knowledge of the theatre his patronage can be genuinely beneficial. In February 1987 Prince Edward became Patron of the National Youth Theatre of Great Britain and he is keen to encourage young people to become involved with the performing arts in general. While at university, he became Patron of the Cambridge Youth Theatre and the Cambridge Symphony Orchestra, and on a national level he is President of the National Youth Music Theatre. In 1988 he also became Patron of the National Youth Orchestra of Scotland.

The National Youth Theatre was founded in 1956 by Michael Croft, the same year as the Duke of Edinburgh's Award Scheme began. A former actor and a Master at Alleyn's School, Dulwich, Croft's original intention was to perform only the works of Shakespeare and his first production was *Henry V* at Toynbee Hall. In 1965, however, the NYT put on their first contemporary play at the Royal Court Theatre – David Halliwell's *Little Malcolm and his Struggle Against the Eunuchs*. Then in 1971 they took over the Shaw Theatre which they use for summer productions. They now produce a wide range of high-quality drama related to the needs of schools and the interests of young people. The NYT also offers opportunities for young amateur actors and actresses to work alongside professionals, such as Derek Jacobi and Helen Mirren, and gives new writers a chance to have their work performed. In 1981 the NYT lost their Arts

179

Council grant and they are now funded by commercial sponsorship. Prince Edward as Patron has the ability to attract such
funding; without him the Youth Theatre might find it much
more difficult to survive. Because of the reputation the NYT
has built up, the British Council now backs their overseas tours.
In April 1990, for example, Prince Edward travelled to Valen-
cia where the company was performing Lorca's *Blood Wedding*,
just as he had travelled with them to Moscow a year earlier. The
whole organisation has now developed on a regional basis and
there are over 400 Youth Theatres throughout Britain.

Prince Edward's NYT duties involve far more than attending
the occasional show. He oversaw the establishment of their
headquarters in North London and officially opened their new
rehearsal rooms in the Holloway Road in March 1988. The
following year he attended their Grosvenor House Ball, entertaining guests with a witty speech and raising £50,000 for the
NYT in the process; and he even took part in their 1987
production of *Trafford Tanzi*. Each year he supports the artistic
organisations with which he is associated by attending pre-
mieres and benefit performances.

Echoing Sir Noël Coward, it would seem that for Prince
Edward 'work is much more fun than fun' and he has the
satisfaction of knowing that each event he has attended has
benefited the relevant organisation to the tune of many thousands of pounds. Like his sister, the Princess Royal, Edward
adds a spirit of enjoyment to what would otherwise become
drudgery. When he meets the cast after a show, as when he
went to see Dustin Hoffman as Shylock in *The Merchant of
Venice*, there is always much laughter but it should not be
mistaken for flippancy. The Prince never loses sight of why he is
there.

Through organisations like the Duke of Edinburgh's Award
and the National Youth Theatre, Prince Edward is able to keep
in close contact with ordinary young people. Again, like his
sister, he sees the benefits that such organisations can offer the
youth of Britain. On 5 March 1992 the Princess Royal, as
President of the Patrons of Crime Concern, launched Splash,
an organisation involving police, schools and businesses to
provide activities for 10- to 16-year-olds during their school
summer holidays. In a hard-hitting speech she warned that

With Princess Anne and the Duchess of York during The Grand Knockout Tournament in 1987. (Jayne Fincher, Photographers International)

Production Assistant, Edward Windsor, arriving at The Palace Theatre to start work for Andrew Lloyd Webber's 'Really Useful Theatre Company'.
(Tim Graham, London)

many youngsters see theft and violence as a normal way of life and that a survey revealed a 'shockingly high' level of contact with crime. Youth crime rises by 25 per cent in the summer when teenagers have nothing to do and nowhere to go. Prince Edward knows that the Award Scheme and the Youth Theatre are concrete examples of organisations which can help to solve many of these problems by giving young people a sense of purpose, and this is a message that he and the Princess Royal will continue to put across. Richard Coyles, Deputy Chairman of the Police Federation, comments, 'It is important that a member of the Royal Family not only recognises the problem but takes an active part in trying to do something about it.'

Princess Anne may be vastly more experienced at public engagements than her youngest brother, but in some ways Prince Edward has a certain edge over her in that he has experienced life in the outside world. Working for the Really Useful Theatre Company in London and walking through the streets of Soho, he saw for himself the evidence of homelessness and drug and alcohol-related problems. When he complained in a speech about litter in the West End it was because he had personally been forced to walk through it every day. The setting for a royal visit is artificially smartened up, but the Prince saw the stark reality of ordinary life. It was as a direct result of this that he agreed to join the committee of Charity Projects, an organisation formed not only to help people in need but also to create greater public awareness of the scale of the problems. Through Charity Projects, Prince Edward launched Feet First, in which he appealed to the people of London to walk to work and give the money they would normally have spent on fares to the homeless. The Prince launched the scheme in March 1990 and £60,000 was raised in that one day, with Edward himself walking the 2 miles from his office at the Palace Theatre back to Buckingham Palace. So successful was it that a year later the Princess Royal used a similar idea to help her pet charity, Save the Children, requesting that people skip lunch and donate the money they would otherwise have 'eaten'. If people felt hungry during the day she hoped that would also give them a greater awareness of the starving millions in Third World countries.

Showing concern for today's younger generation is typical of Prince Edward's modern approach to his role. Much of royal life is influenced by the past and tradition, but under his father's progressive influence Edward has always looked to the future. As Chairman of the Pegasus Project he was invited to open the World Airline Entertainment Conference in 1991. Ed Riseman, one of the organisers, told me that Prince Edward was 'extremely computer-literate', displaying in-depth knowledge of even the most up-to-date equipment. His understanding was based on a genuine interest in computers and was not simply gleaned from a briefing by advisers. Prince Philip is credited with the introduction of computers at Buckingham Palace to improve the efficiency of administrative operations. From supplies to the Royal Mews to the favourite dishes of visiting guests, everything is now stored on disk. Even the Queen has a personal computer, a gift from Ronald Reagan during his term of office as President of the United States, with which it is said she works out the breeding programme of her horses. Edward is obviously also very aware that the Royal Family have to keep pace with the world to survive.

Prince Edward's public life is organised by his Private Secretary Lieutenant Colonel Sean O'Dwyer and an Assistant Private Secretary Sarah Warburton, in close consultation with the Prince. Although invitations arrive every day Edward and his staff have regular planning meetings to decide which should be accepted. Anniversaries are always taken into consideration for, as with the bicentenary of Mozart's death in December 1991, these dates are immovable. If a number of invitations come from one particular location Sean O'Dwyer will try and arrange them all on a single day. On 18 May 1991, for example, Prince Edward went to Cambridge. In that one day he visited Addenbrookes Hospital to meet staff and patients; went to the Perse School to meet staff and pupils; as a Patron of the Cambridge Youth Theatre attended a meeting of trustees at the theatre; visited the Cambridge Regional College and Cambridge Mencap's Edmund House; and finally as Chairman of the Duke of Edinburgh's Award Special Projects Group attended a garden party in Peterhouse Deer Park. In this way six different engagements were carried out in one visit.

On 29 February 1992 the Prince travelled to Lincolnshire and attended a reception for industrialists; opened a section of the sea defences between Mablethorpe and Skegness before viewing further construction work; visited the Richmond Caravan Park to view Award Scheme activities; attended the East of England Conference for the Voluntary Youth Sector; had tea with Officers of the National Voluntary Youth Organisations and the Principal Youth Service Officers of Lincolnshire County Council; and in the evening returned to the Richmond Caravan Park for a reception and entertainment for all those involved in the afternoon's events. That evening the Prince and Lieutenant Colonel O'Dwyer returned to Buckingham Palace to prepare for the next day's flight to Brunei where Edward visited the Royal Geographical Society's Rainforest Project.

Like all members of his family Prince Edward appears to have great stamina and the ability to survive on little sleep. In one month he can travel many thousands of miles throughout Britain. The hours are long, and the demands great. One day he can be opening a college of education's driver assessment centre, the next visiting a Boys' Brigade international camp. Each requires a certain amount of background research in order to talk knowledgeably to the people he meets. Each day the Prince and his Private Secretary will go through that particular day's itinerary, a copy of which is reproduced in miniature on a small card for the Prince to keep in his pocket. Included will be the names and positions of each person he will meet during the day. Each morning there will be correspondence to deal with, more invitations, requests for the Prince to write a foreword to a book (occasionally a publisher will even suggest a whole book), requests from would-be actors wanting to find work in the theatre, or a photographer wanting to take new pictures. Much of the correspondence can be categorised and passed to other departments. Some questions might, for example, be best dealt with by the Press Office, others can be forwarded to the National Youth Theatre.

Once an invitation has been accepted, each detail of the Prince's visit will be planned and timed, from the length of the journey to the number of steps it will take the Prince to reach a certain building. Lieutenant Colonel O'Dwyer will look at menus for official lunches and dinners, find out what bathroom facilities have been set aside for the Prince, what will happen in the event of bad weather, in what order people should be introduced to him, and whether the Prince will find himself unintentionally involved in any political or commercial scheme. One two-hour visit can involve as much as twelve weeks' planning, from discussions with the local police about security to organising where the press will be situated and how much access they will have to the Prince. On an overseas visit a recce will be carried out beforehand. If a walkabout is part of the Prince's programme, every building along the route has to be checked, and on the day itself police marksmen will be in position.

Travel arrangements are made for the Prince by Lieutenant Colonel O'Dwyer through the Crown Equerry Lieutenant Colonel Seymour Gilbert-Denham. At Buckingham Palace all the royal cars are kept at the back of the Mews behind the stables. There are twenty cars available, all especially adapted with bullet-proof glass. The windows are larger than usual and the seats are slightly raised, so that the occupants can be easily seen. If the Prince is travelling by helicopter or train, a car has to go on in advance to be there for his arrival.

The Royal Train no longer exists as such, but special carriages containing a bedroom, bathroom, sitting room and telephones (with 28 lines) are attached to ordinary rolling stock. These royal carriages have been made completely bomb proof; they are capable of withstanding a terrorist missile attack, and have an oxygen supply of their own which can be used independently in the event of a gas attack. The trains belong to British Rail and Prince Edward has to pay the expenses out of his Civil List allowance. Equally, if the Prince uses a helicopter of the Queen's Flight, which consists of three red Andovers and two Westland Wessex helicopters operating from RAF Benson, he has to pay for the privilege.

Sometimes Edward encounters unexpected expenses. On 25 February 1992, for example, he had intended to fly to West Sussex to undertake engagements in Chichester but was prevented from doing so by fog. Because he had booked a helicopter, which had already been taken to the Buckingham Palace launch pad, it still had to be paid for. Before the Prince can use the Queen's flight he has to obtain written permission from Her Majesty. Only the Duke of Edinburgh need not officially apply. For longer overseas flights the Prince will travel in a British Airways passenger jet, often on an ordinary scheduled flight with just a section of the first class passenger compartment reserved for his use. On a foreign visit the Prince may use a non-British airline if his flight is paid for by the host country. Those who travel with members of the Royal Family remark on how much easier it is going on a tour with Prince Edward. Unlike a Princess, he does not require numerous trunks of glamorous designer clothes, hat boxes or dressers. He does not require white gloves to be kept in pristine condition or need priceless tiaras and jewels for evening wear. He does not even need to be presented with a bouquet, and has certainly never demanded a hairdresser. Usually, when overseas, Prince Edward will be visiting by invitation and his hosts will pay for his travel and accommodation. At home his expenses are covered by his Civil List allowance.

Under the Civil List Act the Queen, her husband and children receive an allowance, except the Prince and Princess of Wales whose income derives from the Duchy of Cornwall. The Queen Mother and Princess Margaret are also included in the Act as a wife and daughter of a monarch, but the Duke of Kent, the Duke of Gloucester and Princess Alexandra are not. The Queen pays her cousins out of the Privy Purse which is revenue from the Duchy of Lancaster. Contrary to popular belief, the Civil List is not a personal income for the Royal Family, nor is it taxpayers' money. It comes from the revenue of the Crown Estates. In the year ending 31 March 1991 the gross income from Crown lands totalled £106 million, of which less than £9.8 million was returned to the Royal Family to cover the cost of more than 5,000 official engagements. A total of £61 million was paid to the Treasury as surplus revenue. It only takes very basic arithmetic to see that more goes into the Treasury than the Royal Family take out, even when the expenses of Buckingham Place, Windsor Castle and *Britannia* are taken into consideration.

Prince Edward's allowance until the year 2000, when the Civil List will be reviewed, is £100,000. Roughly 70 per cent of this money goes on staff wages, national insurance contributions and administration. In 1990 it was estimated that the salary of Prince Edward's Private Secretary alone amounted to £35,000 a year, without the other members of his staff. The remainder goes towards the cost of official entertaining, heating, lighting, stationery and travel. Not a penny is for the Prince's private use; hence his attempts to establish a career and income of his own. When Theatre Division collapsed in July 1991 his friends revealed that Edward felt quite genuinely unemployed. He had a vast number of royal duties to keep him occupied, but it was not the same as being a wage-earner.

Of necessity the Prince has to fund most of his official wardrobe himself, whereas his sisters-in-law feel more entitled to a clothing allowance. Edward will never be a leader of fashion – few Princes are – and tends to dress conservatively in public. Although men's suits do date through changing widths of lapels, width of trouser and turn-up, fashions last long enough for one outfit to give considerable wear; and suits can be made to look different with a variety of shirts, ties and pocket handkerchiefs. A brightly patterned sweater would quickly be recognised if Prince Edward wore it more than once, but one pinstriped suit looks very much like another. A suit also looks sufficiently formal and a jacket pocket can hold all sorts of essential items, from tissues to the day's itinerary. Furthermore, a suit solves a logistical problem. If Edward wore a coat it would always have to be taken from him on arrival at various functions, but a suit offers sufficient warmth and the jacket never has to be removed.

Today Edward's suits have become as much a royal uniform as the Queen Mother's matching coat/dress and upturned brim hat. Even in July 1991, when Edward joined the Royal Yacht for the start of the family holiday, he looked immaculate in a dark double-breasted suit with a dark blue tie and matching pocket handkerchief. Prince Edward's suits are mostly made for him by Hawes and Curtis Ltd, who have made clothes for Prince Philip, Prince Charles and Prince Andrew. Their tailors also make evening jackets and dresswear and will have Turnbull and Asser shirts made to co-ordinate with the suits. Edward has also bought ready-made suits from the Burton Group. Some of his shoes are made by John Lobb Ltd of St James's and he has been described by fashion experts as 'the young fogey of the Royal Family' for choosing 'traditional brogues'.

In 1991 the Prince was criticised for wearing an off-the-peg grey double-breasted suit, of which the trousers appeared to be too short and did not match his brown shoes. Occasionally it appears that the Prince has more suits than shoes and cannot always find a suitable pair. He certainly selects dateless footwear. Some pairs are from Wildsmith Company in London's Jermyn Street who say their shoes are made to last at least ten years.

Prince Edward's wardrobe includes some unusual outfits. Occasionally he will wear the Windsor Coat, an evening tailcoat of dark blue cloth with red collar and cuffs. Worn with plain black trousers and a white waistcoat, it is decorated with gilt buttons bearing the garter star surmounted by a crown. There are six buttons at the front (three on each side), two at the back (on the waistband), two on each cuff and two at the end of each tail. This jacket, sometimes called the 'Windsor Uniform', was introduced by George II in 1779 and has only been worn as evening dress in this century. The Prince will more often wear a dinner jacket with black tie for formal dinners, and tail coat with white tie and decorations for state banquets.

Another garment unique to the Royal family which Prince Edward wears in Scotland is a kilt in the Balmoral tartan. The grey and red Balmoral tartan was designed by Prince Albert in the 1850s. It is personal to the Sovereign and is worn by both male and female members of the family. It has also been used extensively in furnishing fabrics and carpets at Balmoral Castle. Prince Edward's kilts are made by the firm of Kinloch Anderson Ltd in Edinburgh which has been making kilts since 1868. They take approximately a month to make, and as they have the Prince's measurements on record no fitting is necessary. Prince Edward has never revealed whether or not he wears anything under his kilt, although the young Prince Andrew once complained about having to wear shorts under his, saying 'Papa doesn't!'

An inherited problem of Prince Edward's is his father's pattern of baldness which has affected him much earlier than either of his brothers. Prince Andrew shows no obvious signs of losing his hair yet, and although Prince Charles has a gradually increasing bald spot, the hair loss has been nowhere near as rapid as Prince Edward's. At first he appeared to be self-conscious about it and was seen wearing a variety of hats. At the May Ball at Jesus College in 1985 he wore a trilby; during rehearsals for the *Knockout* tournament in 1987 he wore a baseball cap; at a gathering on the Balmoral estate to mark the thirtieth anniversary of the Duke of Edinburgh's Award he wore a white cowboy stetson; and later at a firework display in Ballater to mark the end of a charity walkathon he wore a paper party hat. From a black fedora to a Russian fur, there was a period when he seemed to wear a hat or cap at every possible opportunity. Nowadays it would appear that he has come to terms with the situation and when he appeared in a television documentary in January 1992 the very first shot of him was an unflattering picture of the back of his head. As the Prince was involved in the editing he would surely have cut this out or changed the camera angle if it had caused him embarrassment.

Prince Edward's hair loss is genetic, but medical experts agree that stress can play a major part in the speed at which it progresses. It was noticeable that Prince Edward's hair receded dramatically in 1987 after the worry of leaving the Royal Marines and the subsequent heart searching. Doctors also say that men who go bald tend to grow more hair on their bodies, as if Mother Nature were trying to compensate. When, in July 1991, the *Sun* newspaper published a photograph they had discovered of Prince Andrew naked it was abundantly clear that he has a hairless chest. In contrast, both Prince Charles and Prince Edward, who are losing the hair on their heads, have very hairy chests. Had Edward been born to any other family he could have had a hair transplant, scalp reduction surgery, hair weaving or a toupée, but because he is constantly under the spotlight it would now be so obvious and the subject of so much comment or ridicule that he can do nothing but grin and bear it. He has his hair cut every two to three weeks by Mr Ivan of Trumpers in Curzon Street, who visits Edward at the Palace, but can do little but keep it short and neatly shaped. Edward has Prince Philip to blame for this, for the men on the Queen's side of the family tend to keep their hair much longer.

When Prince Edward's wax figure was unveiled at Madame Tussaud's in 1988 the hair was the first point he noticed. 'Mmm. He's got more hair than me,' the Prince joked. It was the first time his likeness had been placed in the collection and the sculptor had tactfully not included a bald spot. Prince Edward was the first member of the Royal Family to donate his own clothes to dress the figure, supplying a double-breasted dinner jacket, white dress shirt and bow-tie, to compliment the rest of the family group who are all in evening dress. In each instance exact copes of their own clothes had been specially created. Prince Edward is also the only member of the British Royal Family who has actually visited the Madame Tussaud's studio to sit for the sculptor, and the only one who has ever posed with their wax double for photographers. When asked if it was a good likeness he laughed, 'I don't know, I've never seen myself at this time in the morning!'

Prince Edward has always tried to lead as normal as life as possible within the confines of his position; hence his willing-ness to visit Madame Tussaud's studio personally to be mea-sured and photographed. He could have demanded that they visit him at the Palace like other members of his family; he could have requested that they make the clothes for the figure them-selves; but he was prepared to co-operate fully like a non-royal person being honoured. He is the first member of the Royal Family to witness a man being cleared of murder at the Old Bailey, having spent time watching proceedings in Number One court. His brothers and sisters may know the law, but he wanted to see it actually put into practice. On engagements he has mastered the art of mixing formality with friendliness. At an event in Battersea Park to publicise the Award Scheme he accepted an invitation to try archery and later played the drums; at the 1988 Berkeley Square Ball he was seen playing darts and at the Players Ball in aid of the National Youth Theatre a year later he had a go at the hoopla stall. Nobody would have dared to expect the Queen to take a bow and arrow or show dexterity with a drum kit, but Edward's youth and approachability made it acceptable. Prince Edward is also inter-ested in the sport of greyhound racing, seeing it as a way of raising money for charity, and in 1989 entered a dog called Druids Johno at a meeting in Canterbury. The Prince donated his winnings to the Royal Marines Deal Benevolent Fund. The dog went on to win numerous major races but was finally beaten in the 1990 Greyhound Derby and was retired due to injury that autumn. It was an unusual way for a member of the Royal Family to raise money for charity, but it was yet one more link with normality and typical of Edward to choose a less élitist sport than those involving horses.

Much of Prince Edward's official work may have passed unnoticed by the general public, but speak to any of the organisations of which he is patron and they have nothing but admiration for his tireless devotion and boundless enthusiasm, nor are they in any doubt about the practical benefits his support brings. Prince Edward's growing stature within the Royal Family was acknowledged in March 1989, on his twenty-fifth birthday, when the Queen appointed him a Commander of the Royal Victorian Order in recognition of his work. The Order was instituted by Queen Victoria as a mark of royal esteem and a reward for personal service to the Sovereign. It is not given lightly, or automatically, and it indicated that Prince Edward had truly proved himself as a working member of the House of Windsor. On state occasions the Prince wears the insignia on a neck ribbon and in the form of a medal on his chest, and his full honorary title now includes the letters CVO after his name.

Another sign of Edward's increased maturity came on 6 February 1992, the fortieth anniversary of Queen Elizabeth II's accession to the throne. While the Queen herself opted to spend the day in quiet contemplation in Norfolk, with only one official engagement, Prince Edward was chosen as her official representative. It was not the Prince of Wales as heir to the throne, or the much-lauded Princess Royal, neither of whom had engagements that day, but the Queen's youngest son. The choice was not insignificant. As Edward left the special commemorative service at Reading Minster to attend a reception at the Old Town Hall he was cheered by hundreds of well-wishers and showered with flowers by the waiting crowds. At that moment it was clear that Prince Edward was no longer an understudy. Having proved his worth he is now accepted in his own right as a leading player in the royal roadshow.

ENTR'ACTE

We know what we are
But not what we may be.

WILLIAM SHAKESPEARE,

Hamlet (Act IV, Scene V)

As spectators gathered at Hampton Court for the 1992 Real Tennis National Mixed Doubles Invitation Championship the name of one of the players puzzled them. The women's world champion, Penny Lumley, was to be partnered by a mystery competitor, Edward Warburton. Not even his fellow players had heard the name before, but when a tall rosy-cheeked young man walked on to the court everyone knew his face. In adopting his Assistant Private Secretary's surname Edward wanted to prove that he was there as a serious exponent of the game, not as a member of the Royal Family.

As soon as his identity was revealed it was automatically assumed that Edward would be the weak link in the partnership, simply because of the fact that he is royal. As it was, the duo came a very creditable third in the national competition and Edward was hailed as 'a new star' of real tennis. 'He produced some incredible strokes,' his world champion partner revealed, 'especially on his forehand which is very low and severe – copybook stuff – and he's got such fast reflexes that he retrieved some seemingly impossible shots.' Sadly, while it was

taken for granted that all the other players were experts because they had been selected to take part in a national championship, Edward had to prove that he was just as good. Only if
he could have remained as the anonymous Edward Warburton
would he have been able to play at the same level, and with
exactly the same expectations, as the other players.

Prince Edward's tragedy is that he was born royal. For much
of his life he has been forced to take on a role that is in many
ways foreign to his nature. He tried to play the part of the
average schoolboy, but could never really be like his school-
mates because he was unable to discuss his homelife and always
had a bodyguard. In New Zealand he played the teacher, not
altogether successfully. At Cambridge his student days were
remembered more for his stage performances than his academic record, and he opted out of a long-running part in the
Royal Marines. Each role required a different costume, but
there was always the same underlying conflict. For the Queen it
is different. She has never experienced any other life. She did
not go to school or university and even during her wartime
work with the ATS she was chauffeur-driven to the safety of
Windsor Castle each evening. At a far younger age than Edward is now she had already succeeded to the throne and taken
on the heavy mantle of sovereignty, destined never to experience any semblance of normality. She cannot go shopping, walk
down a street alone, or even escape for a day on the beach. She
cannot see her own married children in their homes without
making an appointment. Never having known freedom, she
has accepted the role wholeheartedly. Being royal is a way of
life.

Almost cruelly, Edward has been pushed out into the real
world but is still forced to keep one foot within the Palace.
Whatever the situation, be it playing a game of real tennis or
taking part in an amateur Shakespeare play, he is never allowed
to forget that he is a Prince. His aunt, Princess Margaret, once
likened her life to being trapped in a gilded cage. Yet for
someone who is completely trapped there comes a gradual
acceptance and in many ways a permanent sense of security.
For Edward, however, the door of the cage has been unlocked.
He has been able to taste freedom, but his wings have been
clipped. Yes, he has been free to follow a career of his own

choosing but the pressures on him to succeed are infinitely greater than any other employee simply because of who he is. In his choice of marriage partner he has apparently been free, yet the woman he marries will always have to fit in with *his* lifestyle, give way to certain royal traditions, face a lack of privacy and ultimately put her own life at risk, for anyone who marries into this extraordinary family could at any time become the target of a fanatic's bullet or a terrorist bomb. It is not a choice that every woman wants to make and it has certainly narrowed the field for Edward. For everything in his life, it would seem, there is a price to pay.

It has taken Edward time to find himself. Sometimes he has over-acted in his role as Prince. As a result he has at various times been considered priggish, precocious or just plain arrogant. If ever he has played down his status he has faced criticism for not pulling his weight within the Royal Family. It is a no win situation. He continually has to be on his guard, but then he is accused of being aloof or reserved. If he attempts to be too familiar, it provokes complaints that the dignity of the monarchy is being destroyed. If he remains impassive, he is cold and unfeeling. If he shows emotion, he is 'the weeping wimp of Windsor'. One of his aides at a recent function said, almost apologetically, 'He does so want to be liked.' It was as if this were some terrible admission, as if it were wrong for a Prince to care what people thought. The implication, perhaps, is that Prince Edward needs to develop a thick skin like his father. Many who have come into contact with him either socially or professionally would consider it a great pity if he did. A caring, sensitive nature would be sadly suppressed. In his own words, 'Members of the Royal Family are, in reality, ordinary human beings.' Prick them and they do indeed bleed. During a visit to a school in Wales the Duke of Kent suddenly disappeared. An extensive search found him looking for the gentlemen's toilet. 'I'd never thought about royalty having to go to the lavatory,' said one of the teachers, and when a broadcast about a year in the Queen's life showed Her Majesty eating a piece of christening cake, one of the *Daily Mail* TV reviewers, Marcus Berkmann, remarked that he suddenly realised it was the first time he had ever seen our monarch eat and added, 'I suppose Queens do have to eat.' Princess Alexandra once said, 'I am a human being first, a member of the Royal Family second,' but all too often this very obvious fact is forgotten.

Unless you are born into or happen to marry into the Windsor family it is virtually impossible to appreciate the full implications of being royal. What is termed Prince Edward's 'private life' actually requires as much administration and planning as his public life. If he decides to spend a weekend helping out on the farm at Gatcombe Park in the summer, or if he wants to visit a friend one weekend, he cannot simply go. He does not need to undertake as much advance preparation as the Queen of course, but the mantle of royalty can never be completely cast aside. Even in private Prince Edward has to have round-the-clock security protection. Communications have to be established for even the shortest visit so that the Prince can always be contacted should any emergency arise. Not only might it be something dramatic within his own family but if, for example, a Head of State or overseas Prime Minister were assassinated, Prince Edward would be thought disrespectful if he were later seen enjoying himself.

The day before President Kennedy was assassinated in 1963 Princess Grace of Monaco went to a county fair where she was photographed taking aim at imitation ducks in a shooting gallery. Because of the time difference between Monaco and America the photographs were published in the States after the assassination, and the former American film star was accused of insensitivity and callousness for holding a gun in such circumstances. Few would believe that the pictures had been taken before the tragedy and Princess Grace went to great lengths to set the record straight. This is exactly the type of situation Prince Edward has to avoid. As every detail of his life is monitored by the media, his Private Secretary has to keep the Buckingham Palace Press Office constantly up to date with the Prince's whereabouts so that they are always ready with an answer and, whenever possible, one step ahead of every newspaper editor. If a tabloid journal came up with a fabricated story about the Prince being a guest at a wild party in Gloucestershire, the Press Office would need to be able to say with certainty that the Prince was in Scotland at the time. Equally, if a scandal arises at an event where the Prince genuinely happens to be present, they have to be ready with 'no comment' until they can assess the full facts. Almost like Big Brother in George Orwell's *Nineteen Eighty-Four*, someone knows where Prince Edward is and what he is doing every second of his life.

If the Prince wants to have lunch with his mother it involves making an appointment for invariably she will be at an official function herself or at the very least en route to an afternoon event. With lives that are planned months in advance, spontaneity is rare. If Edward wants to speak to his father about a private matter his own valet will first speak to the Duke's valet to see if there is a moment free. Prince Edward cannot just walk in to his father, for he might be in the middle of a meeting. Equally, the Queen could be having a dress fitting, a portrait sitting or a private audience with an ambassador. This means continually having to consult diaries even for informal family get-togethers. This is why their summer holiday at Balmoral is so important to the Royal Family, because it offers a rare opportunity for relaxation, be it picnicking in the hills, riding through the heather or fishing in the River Dee. Yet even on holiday they feel unable to sit and do absolutely nothing. Each day of the vacation has to be filled with activity or it would seem like time wasted.

In his own leisure time Prince Edward prefers individual pursuits. Each morning, when in London, he will swim alone in the Palace indoor pool or play squash. He plays golf, rides a great deal and enjoys walking with the family dogs. These are mainly solitary activities and Edward's love of animals stems from the fact that neither horses nor dogs have any conception of 'royalty'. They show genuine loyalty and affection, unswayed by titles. This is possibly another reason why he communicates so well with children and enjoys being able to entertain his young nieces and nephews with magic tricks. Being able to pilot planes and gliders offers Edward another type of freedom, and whether water-skiing or abseiling he deliberately selects activities which present a personal challenge. When visiting New Zealand in February 1990 he joined Duke of Edinburgh's Award gold medal participants in shooting the rapids – or white water rafting, as they call it – on Lake Rotoiti in a South Island national park. Wearing a wetsuit he was also part of a twelve-man crew shooting the Granity Falls, the most powerful

rapids on the Upper Buller River. For two hours the exhila-
rated Prince was just another youth having fun.

During his nine months in Wanganui the Prince met New
Zealand round-the-world yachtsman Peter Blake who coached
him in yacht racing, and they later took part together in the
New York Yacht Club Challenge. Edward then skippered a
smaller craft at Cowes, partnered by John Perry, and came
third in one of the races. Speeding through water in a boat
Edward once again experienced freedom, and at Balmoral he
will often take a rowing boat out on a Scottish loch to relish the
feeling of being alone. Like his cousin, Viscount Linley, Edward
also enjoys driving. In a celebrity Land Rover race during the
1984 Gatcombe Park Horse Trials he almost beat former
Formula One racing champion, Jackie Stewart, but was just
pipped at the post. Unlike his cousin, however, Edward has no
endorsements, despite being seen in Scotland doing estimated
speeds of 90 miles per hour.

With his brothers and sister-in-law Prince Edward enjoys
skiing, but usually avoids their much-publicised visits to Klosters, preferring to escape from the media mêlée. The Prince
once did a deal with press photographer Steve Wood, the son of
celebrated news photographer Henry James Wood. Edward
allowed Mr Wood to take photographs of him for a few days on
condition that he then handed over the film and left him in
peace. The photographer handed over his nine rolls of film and
returned to London. The Prince brought the film home, duly
returned it to the photographer, and the pictures were subsequently published.

Besides skiing, another popular royal pastime is shooting,
and Prince Philip encouraged Edward to use a gun from an
early age. At Gordonstoun Edward was captain of the school
clay pigeon shooting team, and nowadays often takes part in
charity tournaments. In 1988 he was a member of Jackie
Stewart's team at the renowned Gleneagles Hotel, Scotland, in
aid of cancer research. Each year he hosts a shooting weekend
for friends at Sandringham; arriving on Thursday evening
they leave after Sunday lunch. Because it is a small gathering
Edward and his guests stay at Wood Farm on the Sandringham
estate rather than in the 'Big House'. Originally belonging to a
Dr Ansell, the stone house with its red roof was bought for

Prince Charles to enjoy some privacy while he was a student at Cambridge, but Prince Edward now stays there more frequently. The weekend is informal and his guests all join in preparing meals and doing the washing-up. It is a rare glimpse of normality.

One personal challenge Prince Edward set himself was that of learning the game of real tennis. Initially it was the development of a skill to gain his Award Scheme gold medal, but it has now become a major part of his life. He could have chosen lawn tennis which many members of his family play, but he opted instead for the much more difficult game which now only he amongst present-day royalty can play. The game originated in the fourteenth century as *jeu de paume* in which French monks batted smooth stones around the monastery walls for relaxation. It crossed the channel in its present form during the reign of Henry VIII and was called 'royal tennis', the word 'real' being a corruption of 'royal'. Having mastered the game, Prince Edward's first public match was in the summer of 1989 at the royal Palace of Falkland, some 30 miles north of Edinburgh in the Lomond Hills, where the oldest surviving real tennis court in the world celebrated its 450th anniversary. Prince Edward played in an exhibition doubles match, partnered by Sally Jones. A real tennis court is larger than that for lawn tennis and has high walls around it. The courts have in fact changed little since medieval times, with their buttresses, open galleries and sloping porches known as 'penthouses'. At the Falkland Palace there are four small apertures set high in the back wall known as 'lunes'. To hit a ball through one of the lunes means an immediate win. The players use heavy rackets, which look out of proportion, to cut or slice the heavy felt-covered balls over a curved net. The ball can be played off the walls, penthouses and floor.

Edward was originally taught real tennis at Cambridge by Brian Church, but is now coached by the ex-world champion Chris Ronaldson. At Falkland Palace when he produced a winning shot Prince Edward appeared to apologise to his opponents, but as he returned to his partner Sally Jones his fist was quite definitely clenched in triumph. 'That was one of my best shots,' he told her, 'so I don't know why I'm apologising!' Despite the 90° temperatures that day, Edward looked cool and relaxed in tennis whites with traditional long trousers. 'No, it's not vodka!' he quipped when members of the press saw him sipping a large glass of water. Spectators enjoyed the unusual sight of a member of the Royal Family completely at ease, clowning around when he made a mistake yet still playing with determination. He admits, though, that one of the reasons why he loves real tennis so much is that it is 'one of the few games left where playing the game is more important than actually winning.' Today he plays up to three times a week at one of the two clubs of which he is a member, Holyport near Windsor and Hampton Court. He admits also that if time allowed he would play even more and when not being coached by Chris Ronaldson his opponent is often his Private Secretary Sean O'Dwyer.

One of the advantages of being royal is that Prince Edward can include sporting activities in his working life. In October 1988, for example, he attended the Great Court Run at Trinity College, Cambridge, firing the starting pistol for Olympic runners Sebastian Coe and Steve Cram to recreate the legendary 'Chariots of Fire' race in which students tried to complete a circuit of the Great Court before the clock had finished striking twelve. Both Cram and Coe beat the 46-second deadline, with Coe marginally in front. The event raised £50,000 for the Great Ormond Street Hospital Wishing Well Appeal and Prince Edward presented a glass trophy to Sebastian Coe to celebrate his victory before flying to Oxford where he started off a sponsored cycle run. On 23 January 1990 Edward flew to Auckland to open the Commonwealth Games. After reading out a message from the Queen in front of the 35,000 spectators, the Prince waved and cheered as the teams paraded around the stadium and later visited every event, overstaying his scheduled time in the Badminton Court to watch a match between England and India. In 1991 he was guest of honour at the Tennis and Rackets Association Annual Dinner, and was present at the opening ceremony of the Rugby World Cup at Twickenham where he watched the England v. New Zealand match. The only way he can survive royal life is to weave his personal interests into his duties. He might not have chosen to be born a Prince, but few could blame him for grasping at the pleasures that are available. His life is too restricted for him not to make the most of opportunities when they arise.

Despite the obvious restrictions, Prince Edward is under no illusions about the advantage of his royal birth. He has the sort of lifelong security that most people can only dream of, and whilst he would prefer to have a career of his own to provide complete fulfilment, he could still survive quite easily without one, as Princes have in the past. His willingness to work should be applauded; it means that he never loses sight of reality and keeps in touch with everyday life, but his life will always be a privileged one. Being a Prince might at times feel like a golden millstone around his neck, but it has also been a life-saving rock. Possibly as plain Edward Windsor, born on a council estate in Bethnal Green, he might have been an unremarkable young man struggling to earn a living; as Prince Edward, born in a Palace in central London, the world has been his oyster. The shell has been hard to crack and he might not always have made the best choices in his life, but at least the choices have been his. Not everyone is that fortunate.

On the other hand, his royal birth has undoubtedly had the effect of stifling Edward's professional potential. If he had not been the monarch's son he would have been much more likely to succeed in the career of his choosing. Now if he succeeds he receives little credit for his endeavours because he is seen to have an unfair advantage. It is always an uphill struggle. Having fought to be 'ordinary' for so long, the Prince is finally learning to conduct his public and private careers in tandem. Rather than battle against his status, it is preferable to use it positively. After Theatre Division collapsed in the summer of 1991 he began looking for an opening in the field of television. As a Prince he has an immediate inroad, for no television company in the world is going to turn down the opportunity to use a member of the Royal Family. (When the BBC broadcast a documentary portrait of the Queen's life in 1992 it received the highest viewing figures of any documentary programme since records were first kept.) Edward's problem was finding the right project. His name might open doors but he couldn't afford to be seen entering the wrong one. As if fate had taken a hand, in the autumn of 1991 the perfect project fell into Prince Edward's lap.

BBC producer Peter Hiscocks and a team of researchers had been unravelling the mystery of the 'Saturday Night Soldiers'. These were 150 men, all gardeners, gamekeepers and estate workers at Sandringham, who in the First World War formed themselves into the Sandringham Company of the 5th Battalion Norfolk Regiment to fight for king and country. These volunteers, dubbed the 'Saturday Night Soldiers' and all known to the Royal Family, marched off proudly on 5 August 1914, the day after the outbreak of war, but apparently not one returned. The official explanation was that they had been killed in the Battle of Gallipoli exactly a year later and had died bravely in hand-to-hand fighting. This was in fact a cover-up by the establishment to shield George V from the truth. The men had in reality been callously executed by the Turks. Hopelessly outnumbered the men had surrendered, but instead of being held as prisoners of war they were all shot through the head. Incredibly, one soldier, Arthur Webber, survived the shooting and was eventually able to return to England, keeping the awful secret to himself until his old age when he eventually told his grandsons. The discovery of his story was the culmination of some three years research and final confirmation that Peter Hiscocks' beliefs were correct. He had already found out that the bodies of the Sandringham estate workers had been discovered by the regiment's chaplain, Charles Pierpoint Edwards, hidden in a ravine near the beach in Gallipoli. With the mystery resolved, Peter Hiscocks wrote to the Queen. 'Her Majesty was very moved by the story,' he told journalist John McEntee. 'Her grandfather was never told the truth of what happened to his loyal workers, many of them personal friends. The establishment did not want to upset him.'

The Queen agreed that a television documentary could be made about the Sandringham Company and gave Peter Hiscocks access to the Royal Archives. She saw it as an opportunity finally to solve a 76-year-old mystery. Scarcely a family in the Sandringham area had not been affected in some way by the men's mysterious disappearance and many were still unaware of their fathers', grandfathers' and great-grandfathers' tragic fate. Over the years many theories had been put forward, the most bizarre being that the whole company had been captured by aliens from another planet. Through the Queen's interest

Prince Edward became involved in the project and was the natural choice to narrate the documentary. He was involved in developing the script and gave suggestions for the filming before finally appearing in front of the cameras with Sandringham House as a backdrop to tell the story of 'workers from my great-grandfather's estate . . . perhaps now their fate has been discovered these men can at last rest in peace.' Entitled *All the King's Men*, the documentary was broadcast on 17 December 1991 to wide acclaim. 'Has Prince Edward finally found his calling?' asked the *Daily Mail*. 'As a television presenter of a moving story from World War I he seems to the manner born.' Once again reviewers noted his natural voice, free from the plummy Windsor accent that instantly set Prince Philip and Prince Charles apart. Although Prince Edward can do an excellent impersonation of his eldest brother's voice, his own is free of royal intonation. Time and again it has been called 'ordinary'. He can wish for no greater compliment.

Unlike the ridicule he received for the *Grand Knockout Tournament*, *All the King's Men* finally gave Prince Edward credibility within the field of television, and he was suddenly respected and taken seriously. Instantly he was in demand for similar television projects and as he relaxed over Christmas and New Year at Sandringham, enjoying *al fresco* meals in the mild December weather, picnicking with his relatives in a timber cabin in front of a roaring log fire, he was already formulating new ideas.

As 1992 dawned Prince Edward began discussions for a new television project, and as the years go by we can expect to see him taking a more active part on both sides of the camera. Interested in the technology and the actual making of programmes, he is keen to branch into the production side. His main love, however, will always be the theatre, and in 1992 Edward took what many believed to be the first step towards becoming an independent producer. After a successful production of the Lionel Bart musical *Oliver*, the National Youth Music Theatre mounted *Billy*, the musical version of Keith Waterhouse's novel *Billy Liar*, in August 1992. Prince Edward was closely involved in this production, giving advice and support. Having worked for Andrew Lloyd Webber, the

Prince's experience of mounting a full-scale musical is invaluable.

However, despite the obvious comparisons, Prince Edward has never intended to rival his former employer with whom he remains on very friendly terms. Many of his close friends feel that Edward is now confident enough to go it alone in commercial theatre production, but his royal duties will always prevent him from becoming a full-time impresario. Certainly he has the stamina and enthusiasm to devote equal energy to both. Only time will tell whether he can succeed.

As far as his royal career is concerned, Prince Edward's future is assured and his official diary remains full. In 1992 he undertook a full review of the international side of the Duke of Edinburgh's Award Scheme, putting forward his own recommendations for improvements, which he will ensure are implemented. Although the Scheme bears his father's name, it is Edward who is now in control and as the years go by he appears to be taking on an increasing number of Prince Philip's duties. While Prince Charles will inherit the Queen's role, the Duke of Edinburgh's workload will become Prince Edward's. Just two years after becoming President of the Commonwealth Games Federation the Prince flew to Barcelona in July 1992 for a meeting and was clearly as adept and forthright in the role as the Duke of Edinburgh had been.

In the flesh Prince Edward is far taller and stronger than he appears in photographs; his bright blue eyes can flash with cold steel like Princess Margaret's if angered but also show a depth of compassion and warmth especially when confronted by children or the elderly. In public his quietly spoken manner and dry sense of humour often belie his strength of character, but Edward has fiery Hanoverian blood in his veins. One only has to look at his recent ancestry to see the characteristics he has inherited. Like his 'Gan Gan' (great-grandmother Queen Mary), he has a hidden sense of fun that only the Royal Family see at its best. Rigidly correct in public, with a shyness that was sometimes mistaken for severity, Queen Mary had a straightforward earthiness when out of the limelight. She smoked Woodbines in private and could be heard using surprisingly unroyal phrases. 'Well Mr Baldwin, this is a pretty kettle of fish,' she said to the Prime Minister about the abdication crisis, and

once when feeling seasick on board the Royal Yacht her sentiments were reported back to the King by one of the crew: 'Her
Majesty says never again, buggered if she will!'

The strengths of Prince Edward's maternal grandmother,
Queen Elizabeth the Queen Mother, have been well documented but the character of his other grandmother is almost
unknown. Prince Philip's mother, Princess Alice, was as remarkable and courageous as the Queen Mother, but in contrast
preferred to remain in the background. When Prince Edward
was a young child, Princess Alice lived at Buckingham Palace
where she had a second-floor suite next to what was then the
schoolroom overlooking the Mall. Prince Edward and Prince
Andrew saw her daily and remember sitting out in the garden
with her while she told them Bible stories.

Although outwardly frail, Princess Alice (a grand-daughter
of Queen Victoria and the sister of Earl Mountbatten of
Burma) had an unquenchable inner strength. Prince Edward
was unaware of it, but his grandmother was born deaf. With no
specialists or hearing aids at this time she seemed destined
never to be able to speak but with great determination she
learned to lip-read so well as a child that her deafness was
unnoticeable. By the age of fifteen she was also fluent in French
and German. In 1903 she had married Prince Andrew of
Greece and was a nurse during the First World War, frequently
risking her own life. Personal tragedy seemed to dog her.
During a revolution she and Prince Andrew were exiled from
Greece in 1921, travelling to England with Prince Philip in a
padded orange box for safety. In 1937 her daughter Cecile was
flying to London for a family wedding when the plane crashed
in flames. There were no survivors. Princess Alice was devas-
tated but diverted her energies into setting up a small religious
community and dressed in the habit of a nun for the rest of her
life. This was how Prince Edward saw her every day, after she
had taken up residence at the Palace in old age. If any of the
Queen's children were ill, with chicken pox or mumps for
example, the Queen could not risk being infected herself and
so Princess Alice helped nurse them. She did not mind being
isolated. When his grandmother died in 1969 Edward was five
years old. It was his first experience of death, but her calm inner

strength and dignity had already influenced the young boy. He has since tried to emulate her qualities.

From the Queen, Edward has inherited his sense of duty; from Prince Philip an independent and rebellious nature that will not allow him to be swallowed by convention or dragged under by the tide. Both have encouraged him to follow his own beliefs and he knows that whatever happens in the future he will have their support. At the same time they are acutely aware of their son's resolute character. Less volatile than Princess Anne, not as outwardly ebullient as Prince Andrew, Prince Edward is more immovable in his convictions. When he knew that he had made a mistake in joining the Royal Marines he was not prepared to stay there just to save face. Despite setbacks in his theatrical career he has never lost heart and still forges ahead with determination. Even hardened cynics have come to admire his strength of character.

Like his brother Prince Charles, Edward has a sensitivity and forbearance which are never far from the surface. When hostage Terry Waite was finally released from his long and painful captivity in Beirut the Queen lent him a cottage on the Balmoral estate, where he could begin the process of readjustment in peace and quiet. Of his own volition Prince Edward visited Mr Waite with words of sympathy and support – a simple but much-appreciated gesture. By the spring of 1992 Terry Waite began to face the world again and one of his public appearances was with Prince Edward to watch England's victory in the rugby Grand Slam at Twickenham on 7 March. When Edward himself wants peace he has been known to join Prince Charles on Handa Island, one of Scotland's most beautiful bird sanctuaries, quietly tramping over the island to get back to nature. Only the presence of five detectives highlights the fact that these are no ordinary brothers.

Whether consciously or unconsciously Prince Edward can never ignore the continuity or tradition running through his life. In the 1969 *Royal Family* film one scene showed him on a long stool in front of an impressive fireplace in the Saloon at Sandringham House. Twenty-three years later, when the next major fly-on-the-wall documentary about the Queen's life, *Elizabeth R*, was shown on 6 February 1992, there was a shot of Edward sitting on the same stool, in exactly the same position as when he was just five years old. Scarcely anything in the room had changed other than the fact that one or two pieces of furniture had been reupholstered during the intervening decades. Such is the royal way of life. Although on the surface certain aspects may appear to move with the times, no amount of force on Edward's part will disturb his roots. He will grow and develop, but will always be inextricably bound to the past. He may enjoy his forays into the outside world but ahead lies one more tradition that will only serve to emphasise his heritage.

On marriage Prince Edward will receive a Dukedom. It could be that of Albany or Clarence, although experts think he will be created Duke of Sussex. Sussex first became a peerage title when King Stephen bestowed it as an Earldom on William d'Aubigny in 1141 and it has been used sporadically until 1943. Queen Victoria created her third and favourite son Prince Arthur, Earl of Sussex and Duke of Connaught and Strathearn on 24 May 1874, titles which have been extinct since the death of Prince Arthur's grandson, Alastair. As Prince Edward is believed to be Queen Elizabeth II's favourite son, this may well be a suitable title to bestow.

Edward himself, it is said, would prefer to be honoured as the Duke of Cambridge, another now vacant title. The Cambridges were known as members of the 'Old Royal Family', a term used to describe the descendants of George III as opposed to those of Queen Victoria. Lady Mary Cambridge, later the Duchess of Beaufort, was a cousin of Queen Mary's and a great favourite with all the Royal Family. The last holder was the Marchioness of Cambridge, widow of the 2nd Marquess (previously Prince George of Teck). Her death in recent years has left the Cambridge title available for Prince Edward. Whatever title the Queen chooses to bestow on her youngest son, for a man intent on keeping one foot in the non-royal world, it could prove to be more of a burden than an honour. As the monarch has bestowed additional titles on her other children, there can be no escape for 'Eddie'.

No one can pretend that the road ahead will be easy for Prince Edward. He has already suffered more than his fair share of pitfalls, but at least he now has the resources of experience and maturity to draw on. The underlying cause of his problems is being born with a character title, but with no script or direction to follow. It has been left to him to improvise and establish his own role in life, and any mistakes have been watched by a large audience. Today the Prince is emerging from a difficult debut to take centre stage with a performance that is far more self-assured. As the lights go down on his twenties and he enters a new decade another story will unfold. When he looks across the footlights towards the darkened auditorium of the future, this Prince wants the world to know, 'You ain't seen nothin' yet.'

APPENDIX I

PRINCE EDWARD FACTFILE

FULL TITLE
His Royal Highness The Prince Edward, CVO.

BORN
8.20 pm. Tuesday, 10 March 1964, at Buckingham Palace.

CHRISTENED
2 May 1964, at Windsor Castle by the Dean of Windsor, Robert Woods.

NAMES
Edward Antony Richard Louis

GODPARENTS
Prince Richard of Gloucester
Earl of Snowdon
Duchess of Kent

Princess George of Hanover
Prince Louis of Hesse

EDUCATION
October 1968–December 1969
   Private lessons in Chelsea with Miss Adele Grigg.
January 1969–July 1971
   Tutored by Lavinia Keppel, Buckingham Palace schoolroom.
September 1971–July 1972
   Gibbs School, Kensington.
September 1972–July 1977
   Heatherdown Preparatory School, Ascot, Berkshire.
September 1977–July 1982
   Gordonstoun, Elgin, Morayshire, Scotland.
September 1982–June 1983
   Spent two terms as a house tutor/junior master at the Collegiate School, Wanganui, New Zealand.
October 1983–June 1986
   Studied archaeology and anthropology at Jesus College, Cambridge, changing to history at the start of his second year.

QUALIFICATIONS
9 'O' levels
3 'A' levels:
   English Literature (Grade C)
   History (Grade D)
   Politics and Economics (Grade D)
1 'S' level:
   History (Grade 2)
BA Hons Degree:
   History (2:2)

CAREER
May 1982
   Undertook a potential officers' training course with the Royal Marines.

September 1982

Joined the Royal Marines as a Second Lieutenant at the Commando Training Centre, Lympstone, Devon.

October 1983–June 1986

While studying at Jesus College, Cambridge, undertook a number of officer training courses under the Royal Marines University Cadet Entry Scheme. In December 1985 spent two weeks with forty Commando Royal Marines in Belize to gain experience of their operational role. Also spent time with 539 Assault Squadron and the Brigade Air Squadron.

September 1986

Joined the Royal Marines full-time after leaving Cambridge.

January 1987

Resigned his commission from the Royal Marines.

February 1988

Became a full-time Production Assistant with Andrew Lloyd Webber's Really Useful Theatre Company, based at the Palace Theatre, Shaftesbury Avenue, London, where he worked on the administration for *Cats*, *Starlight Express*, *Phantom of the Opera* and *Aspects of Love* in London and New York.

July 1990

Left the Really Useful Theatre Company to help set up Theatre Division. Worked as Technical Administrator on *The Rehearsal* at the Garrick Theatre and *Same Old Moon* at the Globe Theatre, London.

July 1991

Theatre Division announced its collapse after failing to score a major success.

September 1991

After playing the role of Siward, Earl of Northumberland, in Shakespeare's *Macbeth* for the Haddo House Players, the Prince involved himself with various television projects which included working as narrator for the BBC documentary *All the King's Men*, broadcast on 17 December 1991. Throughout 1991 the Prince increased his royal duties, undertaking 256 official engagements during the year.

HOBBIES/INTERESTS

Flying (gained his private pilot's licence on 9 August 1982), real tennis, squash, badminton, clay pigeon shooting, sailing, yachting, canoeing, riding, abseiling, rugby, golf, swimming, water-skiing, windsurfing, skiing, greyhound racing, theatre, cinema, photography, conjuring, gliding (made his first solo glider flight in 1980), driving (passed his driving test on 27 July 1981), and classical music.

PUBLICATIONS

Full Marks for Trying, published in 1983 under the pseudonym Fenton Ryder.

Wrote the Foreword to *Knockout: The Grand Charity Tournament*, published in 1987 by Collins.

PRINCIPAL STAGE PERFORMANCES

Brindsley Miller in *Black Comedy*, Gordonstoun, 1981

Lord Fancourt Babberley in *Charley's Aunt*, Wanganui, 1983

Deputy-Govenor Danforth in *The Crucible*, Cambridge, 1983

Jester and various characters in *Captain Curious and his Incredible Quest*, Cambridge, 1984

Various characters in *Catch Me Foot!*, Cambridge 1985

Biondello in *The Taming of the Shrew*, Aberdeen, 1986

Prince Florizel in *The Winter's Tale*, Aberdeen, 1987

Sandringham Slammer in *Trafford Tanzi*, National Youth Theatre, 1987

Narrator in *Peter and the Wolf*, London, 1987

Lord Darlington in *Lady Windermere's Fan*, Aberdeen, 1990

Siward in *Macbeth*, Aberdeen, 1991

APPENDIX II

**PRINCE EDWARD'S PATRONAGES AND
OFFICIAL APPOINTMENTS**

1 March 1982	Honorary Life Member of the **Automobile Association.**
1 July 1990	Member of the **Berkeley 21 Club.**
1 June 1986	Patron of the **Cambridge Symphony Orchestra.**
1 January 1985	Patron of the **Cambridge Youth Theatre.**
1 June 1991 to 31 December 1996	Patron of the **City of Birmingham Symphony Orchestra and Chorus.**
1 February 1990	President of the **Commonwealth Games Federation.**
1 September 1989	Honorary Member of the **County of Berkshire Real Tennis Club.**

1 August 1990	Honorary Member of the **Dorchester Club.**
1 June 1987 to 31 December 1993	International Trustee of the **Duke of Edinburgh's Award International Association.**
1 January 1988 to 31 December 1994	UK Trustee of the **Duke of Edinburgh's Award.**
1 January 1988	Honorary Member of the **European International E22 Class Association.**
1 May 1989	Honorary President of the **Falkland Palace Royal Tennis Court.**
1 January 1988	Honorary Member of the **Friends of Southwark Globe.**
1 March 1990 to 31 December 1995	Patron of the **Friends of the Wanganui Opera House.**
1 June 1987	Honorary Life Member of the **Green Room Club.**
1 January 1987	Patron of the **Haddo House Hall Arts Trust.**
1 May 1990 to 31 December 1995	Patron of the **London Mozart Players.**
1 July 1987	President of the **National Youth Music Theatre.**
1 September 1987	Patron of the **National Youth Orchestra of Scotland.**
1 February 1987	Patron of the **National Youth Theatre of Great Britain.**
1 February 1990 to 31 December 1995	Patron of the **Ocean Youth Club.**
4 July 1991 to 31 December 1996	Visitor to **Queen Victoria School,** Auckland.

7 May 1991	Honorary Member of the **Racquet and Tennis Club,** New York.
1 June 1991 to 31 December 1996	Patron of the **Royal Exchange Theatre Company.**
1 May 1990 to 31 December 1995	Patron of the **Scottish Badminton Union.**
1 January 1986	Patron of the **Royal Tournament.**
1 August 1989	Patron of the **Union 212 Theatre Company.**
1 November 1984	Honorary Member of the **United Oxford and Cambridge University Club.**
1 July 1983	Honorary Member of the **Wanganui Collegiate School Old Boys Association** (UK branch).
1 January 1989	Honorary Member of **White's Club.**

HONOURS

In March 1989 the Queen appointed Prince Edward a **Commander of the Royal Victorian Order (CVO).**

Prince Edward also has the **Silver Jubilee Medal** and the **New Zealand 1990 Commemoration Medal**.

APPENDIX III

OVERSEAS VISITS

1969   Accompanied the Queen in the Royal Yacht *Britannia* on a semi-official visit to **Norway** in August.

1976   Accompanied the Prince of Wales to **Montreal, Canada** to watch Princess Anne compete in the Olympic Games in July.

1977   Went on a school trip to the **Italian Alps**.

1978   Accompanied the Duke of Edinburgh on a private visit to **Germany** and **Lichtenstein** in April.
In July and August accompanied the Queen and Duke of Edinburgh to **Canada** for the Edmonton Commonwealth Games.

1982–83	Spent two terms at Collegiate College, **Wanganui, New Zealand**. During his time in New Zealand, made private visits to **Australia**, the **South Pole, Rarotanga, Aitutaki, Fiji, Niue, Tonga, Western Samoa**.
1983	In December represented the Queen in **New Zealand** at the State Funeral of former Prime Minister and Governor-General the Rt Hon Sir Keith Holyoake.
1985	In December spent two weeks in **Belize** with forty Commando Royal Marines.
1987	Undertook official engagements in **Canada**. Visited **Portugal** for the Duke of Edinburgh's Award Scheme.
1988	Undertook official engagements in **Canada**. Visited **Australia** for the Duke of Edinburgh's Award Scheme.
1989	Visited **Malta** for the Duke of Edinburgh's Award Scheme. Visited **Moscow** with the National Youth Theatre. Travelled to **Harare, Zimbabwe**, for a private canoeing safari on the Zambezi river.
1990	Undertook official engagements in **Canada**. Visited the **Caribbean** for the Duke of Edinburgh's Award Scheme. Visited **Valencia, Spain**, as Patron of the National Youth Theatre. Visited **Warsaw, Poland**, with the Cambridge Youth Theatre. Opened the Commonwealth Games in **Auckland, New Zealand**. Visited **Newcastle, Australia**, to see damage caused by earthquake, visited victims still in hospital and attended a fund-raising concert in **Sydney**.

1988–90 While employed by the Really Useful Theatre Company the Prince visited **Los Angeles, New York, Paris, Tokyo, Toronto** and **Vienna** in connection with his work.

1991 As International Trustee of the Duke of Edinburgh's Award Scheme, carried out engagements in **Canada**, in **Montreal, Calgary** and **Vancouver**, then visited **Victoria** as President of the Commonwealth Games Federation.
Later attended the Duke of Edinburgh's Award International Forum in **Hong Kong**.
Spent three days in **Norway** for the eighteenth birthday celebrations of Crown Prince Haakan Magnus.

1992 Visited the Royal Geographical Society's Rainforest Project in **Brunei**.
Attended the Commonwealth Games Federation meeting and the 1992 Olympic Games in **Barcelona**.
As Trustee of the Duke of Edinburgh's Award International Foundation, visited **Bermuda, Jamaica, St Lucia, Barbados, Trinidad** and **Tobago** and undertook official engagements in **Newfoundland** and **Labrador, Canada** and attended the Grenfall Centenary celebrations. Prince Edward has also travelled overseas on school trips, private skiing holidays and visits to see family and friends in **Europe**.

APPENDIX IV

ORDER OF SUCCESSION

Prince Edward is currently seventh in line to the throne. As males take precedence he supersedes his sister, the Princess Royal, but will himself be pushed further down the line by any subsequent children of the Prince of Wales and the Duke of York. The first twenty-five in order of succession are as follows:

HRH The Prince of Wales
HRH Prince William of Wales
HRH Prince Henry of Wales
HRH The Duke of York
HRH Princess Beatrice of York
HRH Princess Eugenie of York
HRH The Prince Edward
HRH The Princess Royal
Mr Peter Phillips
Miss Zara Phillips
HRH The Princess Margaret, Countess of Snowdon
Viscount Linley
Lady Sarah Armstrong-Jones

HRH The Duke of Gloucester
Earl of Ulster
Lady Davina Windsor
Lady Rose Windsor
HRH The Duke of Kent
(The Earl of St Andrews would be next in line but for his marriage to a Roman Catholic. His rights are, however, transmitted to his son who follows)
Lord Downpatrick
Lord Nicholas Windsor
Lady Helen Windsor
(HRH Prince Michael of Kent would be next in line but for his marriage to a Roman Catholic. His rights are transmitted to his two children who follow)
Lord Frederick Windsor
Lady Gabriella Windsor
HRH Princess Alexandra, the Hon Lady Ogilvy
James Ogilvy

BIBLIOGRAPHY

ALLISON, Ronald & Riddell, Sarah: *The Royal Encyclopedia* (Macmillan, 1991).

ARONSON, Theo: *Royal Family – Years of Transition* (John Murray, 1983).

BROWN, Craig & Cunliffe, Lesley: *The Book of Royal Lists* (Sphere, 1983).

COURTNEY, Nicholas: *Sporting Royals Past and Present* (Hutchinson/Stanley Paul, 1983).

DUNCAN, Andrew: *The Reality of Monarchy* (Heinemann, 1970).

EDGAR, Donald: *The Queen's Children* (Hamlyn, 1979).

FINCHER, Jayne & Garner, Valerie: *My Young Friends* (Weidenfeld & Nicolson, 1989).

FISHER, Heather & Graham: *Monarchy and the Royal Family* (Robert Hale, 1980).

FISHER, Graham & Heather: *Prince Andrew* (W.H. Allen, 1981).

FLAMINI, Roland: *Sovereign: Elizabeth II and The Windsor Dynasty* (Bantam, 1991).

FOSTER, Nigel: *The Making of a Marine Commando* (c. 1987/88).

GRAHAM, Tim: *On the Royal Road* (Weidenfeld & Nicolson, 1984).

HALL, Trevor: *The Royal Family Yearbook* (Colour Library, 1983).

HAMILTON, Alan: *The Royal Handbook* (Mitchell Beazley, 1985).

HOEY, Brian: *Monarchy* (BBC Books, 1987).

HOLDEN, Anthony: *Charles* (Weidenfeld & Nicolson, 1988).

JAMES, Paul: *Anne: The Working Princess* (Piatkus, 1987).

JAMES, Paul: *Diana: One of the Family?* (Sidgwick & Jackson, 1988).

JAMES, Paul: *Margaret: A Woman of Conflict* (Sidgwick & Jackson, 1990).

JAMES, Paul: *Princess Alexandra* (Weidenfeld & Nicolson, 1992).

JAMES, Paul: *The Royal Almanac* (Ravette, 1986).

JAMES, Paul & Russell, Peter: *At Her Majesty's Service* (Collins, 1986).

JAY, Anthony: *Elizabeth R* (BBC Books, 1992).

KEAY, Douglas: *Royal Pursuit: The Palace, The Press and The People* (Severn House, 1983).

LACEY, Robert: *Majesty: Elizabeth II and the House of Windsor* (Hutchinson, 1977).

LITTLE, Bryan: *The Colleges of Cambridge* (Adams & Dart, 1973).

LONGFORD, Elizabeth: Elizabeth R (Weidenfeld & Nicolson, 1985).

LOUDA, Jiri & Maclagan, Michael: *Lines of Succession* (Orbis, 1981).

MILLER, Compton: *Who's Really Who* (Sphere, 1987).

MONTGOMERY-MASSINGBERD, Hugh: *Atlas of Royal Britain* (Windward, 1984).

NASH, Roy: *Buckingham Palace* (Macdonald, 1980).

ROSE, Kenneth: *Kings, Queens and Courtiers* (Weidenfeld & Nicolson, 1985).

STRONG, Sir Roy: *Cecil Beaton: The Royal Portraits* (Thames & Hudson, 1988).

VARNEY, Michael & Marquis, Michael: *Bodyguard to Charles* (Robert Hale, 1989).

WEIR, Alison: *Britain's Royal Families – The Complete Genealogy* (The Bodley Head, 1989).
ZIEGLER, Philip: *Crown and People* (Collins, 1978).

INDEX

Index

Index

Perse School, 182
Peter and the Wolf, 117
Peter the Great, 132
Pettifer, Julian, 75
Phantom of the Opera, 1, 117, 123-4, 135
Phillips, Mark, 3, 36, 162
Phillips, Peter, 10, 17, 43, 47
Phillips, Zara, 10
Plato, 45
Poland, 134, 140
Police Convalescence and Rehabilitation Trust, 113
Pollard, Sue, 106
Portugal, 112
Press Council, 20, 22
Price Waterhouse, 104
Prince Edward Island, 112
Prince Philip Trust Fund, 168
Prince of Wales Theatre, 128
Privy Council, 2, 78
Privy Purse, 185
Probation Service, 172

Queen's Flight, 184
Qunard, Peter, 137

Rabett, Katie, 143
Rackhams Store, 176
Radio Times, 103
Ramsey, Dr Michael, Archbishop of Canterbury, 37
Reagan, Ronald, 182
Real Tennis National Mixed Doubles Invitation Championship, 191-2
Really Useful Theatre Company, 2, 5, 116, 118-22, 123-7, 128, 134-6, 155, 181
Reeve, Christopher, 106
Regent Street Christmas lights, 114
The Rehearsal, 138-9
Rhys Jones, Griff, 107
Rice, Anneka, 107
Rice, Tim, 116, 126
Richard I, King, 146
Richard II, King, 146
Richard, Cliff, 107
Richards, Viv, 107
Richmond, Kirsty, 47
Riseman, Ed, 182
Roberts, Rhian-Anwen, 155
Ronaldson, Chris, 77, 197, 198
Rook, Jean, 72
Royal Air Force, 65
Royal Alexandra Children's Hospital, 165
Royal Ascot, 158, 168
Royal British Legion, 176
Royal Court Theatre, 179
Royal Exchange Theatre, 177
Royal Family (television film), 22-4, 28, 32, 204-5
Royal Geographical Society, 183
Royal Marines, 5, 7, 8, 38-9, 58, 65, 77, 83-98, 143-4, 188, 192, 204
Royal Marines Deal Benevolent Fund, 189
Royal Marines University Cadets Scheme, 59, 65
Royal Marriages Act (1772), 156
Royal New Zealand Air Force, 63

Royal Opera House, Covent Garden, 81
Royal Protection Squad, 119
Royal Tournament, 97, 104, 114, 155
Royal Train, 184
Royal Victorian Order, 190
Royal Yacht Squadron Ball, 153
Rugby World Cup, 198
'Ryder, Fenton', 65

Sainsbury's, 133
St Andrews, George, Earl of, 33, 156
St James's Palace, 171
St Paul's Cathedral, 41, 51, 162, 175
Salem, 44, 45
Same Old Moon, 139-40, 141
Sanderson, Tessa, 106
Sandringham, 154-5, 196-7, 200, 204-5
Sandringham Company, 200-1
'Saturday Night Soldiers', 200-1
Saturday Superstore, 101
Save the Children Fund, 80, 103, 168, 181
Savile, Jimmy, 128
Scandic Crown Hotel, 135-6, 138
Schools Design Prize, 114
Schools Music Association, 121
Science Museum, 114
Scott, Robert Falcon, 64
Scottish Badminton Union, 174, 178
Scottish Society for the Mentally Handicapped, 177
Sea Spirit, 46
Seymour, Jane, 107
Seymour, Katie, 31
Shackleton, Sir Ernest, 64
Shaffer, Peter, 50
Shakespeare, William, 115, 179
Shaw Theatre, 179
Shea, Michael, 55
Sheldon, Sir Wilfred, 11
Shulman, Milton, 24
Simpson, Anne, 136
Smith, Mel, 107
Smith, Mike, 109
Snowdon, Lord (Antony Armstrong-Jones), 3, 15, 116
Sonja, Queen of Norway, 156-7
South Pole, 64
Soviet Union, 129-34
Spencer, Countess, 70
Spitting Image, 74, 103
Splash, 180-1
Staffordshire police, 104
Stark, Koo, 143
Starlight Express, 123-4, 134, 138
Starr, Ringo, 175
Stars Organisation for Spastics, 121
Stephen, King, 205
Stephenson, Pamela, 107
Stewart, Jackie, 107, 196
Streep, Meryl, 134
Strong, Sir Roy, 95
Summer Proms, 114
Sun, 22, 91, 120, 145, 188
Sunday Express, 7, 93-4
Sunday Mirror, 151

227